The Political Languages of Emancipation
in the British Caribbean and the U.S. South

The Political Languages of Emancipation in the British Caribbean and the U. S. South

DEMETRIUS L. EUDELL

The University of North Carolina Press
Chapel Hill & London

Manufactured in the United States of America
Set in Minion type by Tseng Information Systems, Inc.

♾ The paper in this book meets the guidelines
for permanence and durability of the Committee on
Production Guidelines for Book Longevity of the
Council on Library Resources.

Library of Congress Cataloging-in-Publication Data
Eudell, Demetrius Lynn.
The political languages of emancipation in the British
Caribbean and the U.S. South / Demetrius L. Eudell.
p. cm.
Includes bibliographical references and index.
ISBN 0-8078-2680-4 (cloth : alk. paper)
ISBN 0-8078-5345-3 (pbk. : alk. paper)
1. Slaves — Emancipation — West Indies, British.
2. Slaves — Emancipation — Southern States.   I. Title.
HT1093.E93   2002
326′.8′0972909171241 — dc21   2001053067

06 05 04 03 02 5 4 3 2 1

To my two mothers,
Jannie Eudell and Sylvia Wynter

Contents

Acknowledgments

The process of writing a book cannot be accomplished without enormous intellectual and emotional support. First of all, I would like to thank my dissertation committee at Stanford University, George Fredrickson, Karen Sawislak, and Sylvia Wynter, for seeing me through the process without much complication.

I would also like to thank the Mellon Foundation, which provided me with excellent support for graduate studies, as well as the Department of History at Stanford for its financial assistance. A Fulbright Scholarship allowed me to conduct research in Jamaica at the University of the West Indies during the 1993–94 academic year. While I was there, Verene Shepherd and Swithin Wilmot in the Department of History displayed collegiality beyond the call of duty for which I would like to express my deepest gratitude; I also thank Victor Chang, then head of the Department of Literatures in English, and Carolyn Allen, a lecturer in the department, both of whom made Kingston my home away from home. Thanks for the dinners and the trips to Hellshire Beach, without which I would not have survived an often grueling process. In this respect, the Golden Girls at Barrington Drive also deserve mention for their hospitality.

A summer grant in 1995 from the Center for European Studies at Stanford assisted me with travel to Kew, England. A generous Thurgood Marshall Dissertation Fellowship at Dartmouth College also helped fund travel to England, as well as generally providing me with two years of excellent support (1995–97) for the writing of the thesis. I would in particular like to thank Ed Berger, then director of graduate studies, and Keith Walker, then chair of the Program in African and African American Studies, for their support during my stay in Hanover.

No work can be completed without the assistance of the staffs at archives and research institutes. I would like to thank the wonderful staff at the Public Record Office in Kew, England, for its never-ending courtesy, efficiency, and professionalism. It was genuinely a pleasure to conduct research at the PRO. The staffs at the National Archives in Washington, D.C., and the Freedmen and Southern Society Project at the University of Maryland, College Park, were also helpful. The reference and interlibrary loan staff and the staff at the microtext room at Dartmouth College assisted me with numerous queries.

The staff at the University of North Carolina Press has been simply tremendous. The editorial guidance of Elaine Maisner, with whom I have worked over the past year, has been entirely pleasurable. The anonymous readers' reports strengthened the argument of the book, and I thank the scholars for their very careful and informed reading of the work.

Since I began teaching at Ohio State University (OSU), I have piled up additional debts. I would like to thank the Department of African American and African Studies as well as the College of Humanities for allowing a reduction in my teaching load so I could dedicate more time to completing the manuscript. I was given excellent research assistants and would like to thank Christopher Johnson, Ryan Nissam-Sabat, and Derrick White for their aid in tracking down articles and books. Gary Van Cott deserves special mention for his tireless devotion to this project, as well as colleagues who have supported me during my stay at OSU: Leslie Alexander, Magbailey Fyle, Beverly Gordon, Alamin Mazrui, Beverly Moss, Lupenga Mpande, Linda James Myers, Ike Newsum, Viola Newton, Maurice Shipley, and Martha Wharton. The administrative staff in the department and in the Extension Center and the Frank Hale Cultural Center made my stay at OSU enjoyable.

Many friends and relatives have sustained me throughout this process. Katherine Dawes graciously provided me with lodging for a summer while I was conducting research in Washington, D.C. My colleagues at Institute N. H. I. have seen me through graduate school, exams, research trips, writing my thesis, and now publication. Jason Ambroise, Patricia Fox, Jason Glenn, Taj James, Carmen Kynard, and Sharla Manley have become like family to me. Though we do not communicate as often as I would like, our friendship is nonetheless very important to me. My dear friend Keith Walker has endured many conversations about this book as well as totally unrelated issues. Georgette Norman must also be thanked for sharing her numerous political and intellectual insights regarding the nature of social change and the transformation of consciousness.

This book is dedicated to my mother, Jannie Eudell, who prepared me in life and has sustained me through it all. My first intellectual influence, she has provided me with innumerable insights into life and work. The most significant influence on my formal intellectual development, Sylvia Wynter, has also generously given of herself over the past ten years. The debt to my two mothers can never be repaid. I only hope this small token can make them proud.

The Political Languages of Emancipation
in the British Caribbean and the U.S. South

The passing of a great human institution before its work is done, like the untimely passing of a single soul, but leaves a legacy of striving for other men. The legacy of the Freedmen's Bureau is the heavy heritage of this generation. To-day, when new and vaster problems are destined to strain every fibre of the national mind and soul, would it not be well to count this legacy honestly and carefully? For this much all men know: despite compromise, war, and struggle, the Negro is not free. In the backwoods of the Gulf States, for miles and miles, he may not leave the plantation of his birth; in well-nigh the whole rural South the black farmers are peons, bound by law and custom to an economic slavery, from which the only escape is death or the penitentiary. In the most cultured sections and cities of the South the Negroes are a segregated caste, with restricted rights and privileges. Before the courts, both in law and custom, they stand on a different and peculiar basis. Taxation without representation is the rule of their political life. And the result of all this is, and in nature must have been, lawlessness and crime. That is the large legacy of the Freedmen's Bureau, the work it did not do because it could not.

— W. E. B. Du Bois, *The Souls of Black Folk*

Introduction

In tracing the origins (where? who? when?) of a particular mental habit, expression or gesture, one must be aware of continuities, but also of disappearances and discontinuities. Tradition, which is a society's way of reproducing itself mentally, must be analyzed, as must the historical lag produced by the slow adaptation of mental structures to change, and by the different speeds at which different areas of history evolve. The history of mentalities is in fact a particularly good school in which to learn the inadequacies of a linear conception of history. Inertia is a crucially important historical force, and it belongs less to matter than to human minds, which often evolve more slowly. While they use the machines they have invented, men keep the mentality of earlier days. . . . Mentalities change slower than anything else: and their history is a lesson in the slow march of history.
— Jacques Le Goff, "Mentalities: A History of Ambiguities,"
   in Le Goff and Nora, *Constructing the Past*

[I]n tracing history in terms of contemporary self-understanding — which is what the history of ideology really amounts to — one is not playing a barren game of pitting one cause against another cause, or one factor against another factor; one is exploring the contemporary perception of possibilities and impossibilities, and *the limitations of that perception.*
— J. G. A. Pocock, "1776: The Revolution against Parliament,"
   in *Virtue, Commerce, and History*

It does not follow that a paradigmatic revolution — the equivalent in political speech of one of [Thomas] Kuhn's "scientific revolutions" will entail the occurrence of a political revolution; a power structure may survive by successfully transforming its idiom. . . . [Therefore] history might be defined as a history of change in the employment of paradigms, the exploration of paradigms and the employment of paradigms for the exploration of paradigms.
— J. G. A. Pocock, "Languages and Their Implications,"
   in *Politics, Language, and Time*

It was once noted that, although "the literature on slavery has reached impressive proportions, very little has been written so far on the comparative history of emancipations" so that while "[c]omparative slavery has become a flourishing enterprise, . . . the postemancipation responses and adjustments of those who had formerly been masters and slaves remain relatively undeveloped as subjects for cross-cultural historical study."[1] In the time since these assertions were made more than two decades ago, the historiographic context has certainly changed, with comparisons of postslavery societies being increasingly produced.[2] Nevertheless, the ongoing debate on reparations for the descendants of Black slaves makes it clear that the claim that the present conditions of Blacks can be directly traced to a history of enslavement has more political currency—and therefore is made more frequently—than the claim that such conditions can be ascribed to the formation of postslavery societies in the Americas.[3]

By comparing the intellectual foundations and the general ideological context in which the emancipation of Black slaves unfolded in the British Caribbean during the 1830s and in the U.S. South during the 1860s and 1870s, the present work should add to this historiography. Although the formative influence of slavery cannot be denied, it can also be argued that events during the postslavery era, beginning with the way in which emancipation was conceptualized and then later implemented, bear some direct relation, conceptual as well as institutional, to the contemporary conditions with which the descendants of slaves remain confronted. Thus, as it has been suggested in the case of Brazil, shifting the comparative focus from slavery to the postslavery context will enable such connections to be revealed: "[P]resent-day concerns about the black man's experience in the Americas might be studied profitably not only in terms of the history of race relations, or of slavery, but also in view of the conditions under which societies abolished slavery and ushered the Negro into an era of freedom."[4]

In order to produce meaningful generalizations about slave systems, it has been proposed that the comparative study of these societies "should be concerned less with concurrent time spans and metropolitan institutional differences than with equivalent stages of economic and social growth," given that the organization of the society, especially with regard to the sugar estate, "followed a common pattern from Brazil, through Barbados, St. Dominique, Jamaica, Cuba, Louisiana or any other place of the Caribbean region."[5] The argument here extends this assertion to the postslavery situation, addressing issues across time periods and, to a certain extent, across regional, political, agricultural, and sociocultural differences, although both areas analyzed here initially formed part of the British Empire.

In this work, special reference has been given to the postslavery conditions of Jamaica and South Carolina — in particular, the roles played by the special magistrates in the former and the agents of the Bureau of Refugees, Freedmen, and Abandoned Lands in the latter — in facilitating the "transition to freedom." It is readily admitted that some of the ground covered in the present discussion has already been tilled in previous scholarship. As it has been eloquently noted, "There are no new truths. There are only new perspectives for seeing what you already know."[6] Yet, given that the effects of the historic process of slavery and its abolition linger in the contemporary societies under examination, the situation merits continual examination.

In this respect, this study should offer some empirical and interpretive contributions. With regard to the former, although scholars have acknowledged the parallel function served by the Freedmen's Bureau and the special magistrates,[7] little systematic study has followed on this proposal.[8] Using the Jamaican governors' despatches to the Colonial Office in which the reports of the special magistrates were enclosed, as well as the reports of agents of the Freedmen's Bureau, as the empirical basis for the argument, the present investigation illustrates why a detailed examination of these two postslavery institutions can provide insight into the way in which the emancipation process evolved.

Moreover, the methodological approach employed in this inquiry provides a new intellectual departure. Given the importance of the control of labor to the system of slavery and later its centrality in the postslavery context, it is logical that the historiography of emancipation has been dominated by an emphasis on the work of the slaves or on social behaviors in the context of work. Such a perspective is enabled by an understanding of slavery as being predominantly a "system of labor" — an interpretation, as Moses Finley has demonstrated, of only recent invention (that is, since the eighteenth century).[9] Indeed, the exploitation of the labor of those of African descent in the Americas constituted a central element of the system of slavery. However, it was not the only element. In fact, Blacks had to be thought of as less than fully human in order for their labor to be exploited, just as the indigenous peoples of the Americas had to be represented as irrational beings (and also less than completely human) in order for their lands to be expropriated.[10] The logic of this assertion implies that the end of slavery does not have to be defined *only* as the transition from slave labor to wage labor. It can also be described in terms that understand slavery as a system of social relations — indeed, as a cultural system.

Orlando Patterson's formulation of slavery as a form of "social death" underscores this approach, although slavery can be understood as being more than a system of violent, physical domination. It has been one mode (caste, racial, and religious hierarchy being others) of stabilizing human orders, what has been identified as the "institutionalization of marginalization."[11] Human societies have always seemed to organize themselves on the basis of insiders and outsiders, included and excluded, self and other, hierarchies without which, it has usually been believed, the social order would collapse. Yet this system of classification could not occur without some kind of intellectual legitimation. Therefore, an examination of the terms within which a society understands its social reality can reveal why a set of behaviors appear rational, even if (or especially when) deleterious effects result for some members of the society: "It is necessary then to look at the conceptions a society has of its activities, the sort of concepts it can deploy, its language, in order to understand what can count as a rational action or a rational way of living one's life."[12] Such an approach is used to examine the postslavery situations in the British Caribbean and the U.S. South.

The strategy employed here is certainly not meant to deny the important (indeed, indispensable) economic dimensions to the question of the abolition of slavery and, thus, should not be viewed in oppositional terms to this and other approaches. Rather, this work should be considered as a complement to the existing scholarship on the emancipation process in the Americas. The present argument maintains the premise that the social and the symbolic cannot be separated: "All social activity has a symbolic dimension that gives it meaning, just as all symbolic activity has a social dimension that gives it point."[13] Otherwise stated, the institution of slavery had both a productive and a signifying mechanism. No one understood the psychic dimension of slavery and postslavery cultural hierarchy better than the slaves and ex-slaves themselves. And it was precisely on the basis of such an understanding that some former slaves' actions, such as the response to the issue of the apprenticeship of children, appeared illogical to the former slaveholders as well as to some of their allies. At the same time, the former slaves remained concerned about economic issues, as they continually insisted that the political freedom granted as a consequence of the abolition of slavery needed to have an economic foundation, which usually meant facilitating access to land. For the former slaves, it was not an either-or question.

Given that humans understand their social context through language, this work examines the transition from the order of slavery to the postslavery period through the conceptual lens of "political languages." Using languages as heuristic devices implies "idioms, rhetorics, specialized vocabularies and grammars, modes of discourses or ways of talking about politics which have been created and diffused, but far more importantly, employed" in specific circumstances. This methodology has been increasingly applied to understand the development of ideas in "their concrete contexts" and is deployed here in order to interpret the thoughts and actions of the ex-slaves, ex-slaveholders, and government officials. Utilizing this approach, the historian becomes "in considerable measure an archaeologist" — that is, someone "engaged in uncovering the presence of various language contexts in which discourse has from time to time been conducted." From this perspective it can be asserted that the "historian-archaeologist" writes "a history of rhetoric rather than grammar, of the affective and effective content of speech rather than its structure," or, in other words, of *parole* rather than *langue;* of context more than text.[14]

According to its proponents, this approach eschews the older model of intellectual history that emphasized sources and influences of ideas as well as the more contemporary "deconstructionists' anti-humanist claim that no text is, in any meaningful sense, the work of a conscious agent." Following this line of reasoning, the argument here insists that the participants in the emancipation process "clearly intended to say some things and not others." Without denying the "prison house of language," that is, the employment of certain political languages inherited from specific intellectual traditions, the present discussion concerns itself more with "the context of the alternatives available within the contemporary frameworks of ideas and institutions"; that is, "the contemporary perception of possibilities and impossibilities, and *the limitations of that perception.*"[15]

In this vein, J. G. A. Pocock's elaboration of the concept of "political languages" is employed as the basis for the theoretical architecture of this investigation. Pocock argued that languages emerge as products of history, while at the same time they can become historical agents that help to "produce changes in linguistic consciousness and so in the history of language use itself." The debate on the abolition of slavery provides an excellent example of a transformation in the linguistic and political consciousness of a society, or a shift in paradigms, to appropriate Thomas Kuhn's use of the term. Because language is never neutral, for "it invokes values, it summarizes information, it suppresses the inconvenient," the task of the historian becomes "to identify the 'language' or 'vocabulary' with and within which the author operated, and to show how it functioned paradigmatically to prescribe what he might say and how he might say it." In other words, the historian can describe the languages of politics as well as the politics of language.[16]

Using this methodology, I treat political thought "strictly as a historical phenomenon and — since history is about things happening — even as historical events," that is, "as things happening in a context which defines the kinds of events they were." Given that humans "think by communicating language systems," Pocock noted, "these systems help constitute both their conceptual worlds and the authority-structures, or social worlds, related to these." In a progression on Marx's inversion of Hegel (that is, the idealist-materialist dispute), which asserted that human consciousness was primarily a function of material conditions, this formulation moves beyond a rigid either-or dualism, by insisting that the social-historical context cannot be separated from its conceptual foundation, as each constitutes the condition of possibility of the other. Therefore, an individual's thinking can be viewed not only as a "social event, an act of communication and of response within a paradigm-system," but also as "a historical event, a moment in a process of transformation of that system and of the interacting worlds which both system and act help to constitute and are constituted by."[17]

The use of a "political languages" framework does have some resonance with the often-maligned term "ideology." In a now classic statement, Marx and Engels defined this concept as the rhetorical strategy whereby "the ideas of the ruling class are . . . the ruling ideas," and in order to maintain dominance, they must "represent [their] interests as the common interest of all the members of society." In order to do so, ruling classes must rigorously give their "ideas the form of universality, and represent them as the only rational, universally valid ones." Yet a transformation can occur "as soon as it is no longer necessary to represent a particular interest as general or the 'general interest' as ruling."[18] Under slavery, the interests of the slaveholders were often represented as if they were the general interests of the society, comprising slaveowners, free nonslaveowners, and slaves. Of course, the great transformation occurred when the abolitionist movement detached slavery from this representation as the embodiment of the general interest.

In order to avoid the pejorative connotations associated with the concept of ideology, the "political languages" approach adopts the redefinition of this seminal idea proposed by Paul Ricoeur. Rather than understanding ideology as the concealment of the material interests of ruling groups, and therefore a distortion of the social reality, Ricoeur has reinterpreted this phenomenon using Clifford Geertz's insight that related "all the distorting functions of ideology to a more basic function, that of mediating and integrating human action at its public level." The central issue remained the relation between domination and legitimation: "[C]ould we not say that the main function of a system of ideology is to reinforce the belief in the legitimacy of the given systems of authority in such a way that it meets the claim to legitimacy?" According to this definition, ideologies should not be simplistically identified as being based on either true or false consciousness, as all ideologies have direct social effects in the behaviors of its adherents: "[A]ction in its most elementary forms is already mediated and articulated by symbolic systems."[19] Thus, if, as Aristotle contended, humans are political animals, then the languages employed to understand the social context (languages being both the objects and the instruments of consciousness) should be studied in order to understand why a society organizes itself in a specific manner. In other words, what Pocock perceptively termed "paradigms of value and authority" should now become the objects of inquiry.[20]

Such paradigms or political languages can have material force only if they are expressed in institutions. Thus, to study the diffusion and institutionalization of political languages, it becomes necessary to examine "the material and social structures through which they have been disseminated."[21] In this context, the creation of the special magistracy and the Freedmen's Bureau represented the expressions of the new postslavery political languages. As such, they were discontinuous with certain aspects of the previous order of slavery; however, at the same time, these agents and their organizations (even if nonconsciously) reinforced ideas and structures that perpetuated the order of racial hierarchy that placed Blacks at the bottom of the social system.

The latter dynamic forced the ex-slaves to challenge and reinterpret the dominant political languages, in a process identified as "the antinomian use of language: of the use by the ruled of the language of the rulers in such a way as to empty it of its meanings and reverse its effects." Pocock insisted that "[a]ppropriation and expropriation are important aspects of what we have to study; I say this because I am constantly accused of denying their importance by those for whom I can never make them important enough."[22] Without a doubt, the former slaves in Jamaica and South Carolina appropriated and expropriated the dominant political languages of liberty and freedom and thus emptied them of their official meanings. As well, they adapted the concepts often espoused by their allies such as self-improvement and self-elevation to their own purposes.

Indeed, in tandem with his redefinition of ideology, Ricoeur also reconceptualized the idea of utopia. Rather than equating the concept with escapism, he returns to its etymological origins, "no-place"; utopia represents an exterior glance on the social reality (although one informed by it). From the perspective of utopia, the givenness of the system of authority, and thus the organization of the society, is called into question. A utopian viewpoint unmasks "the pretense proper to every system of legitimacy." It becomes the way to rethink the order of things, the "fantasy of an alternative society." This mode of thought "proceeds from the possible to the real, from fantasy to reality," and thus makes social transformation imaginable. If ideology (here political languages) functions to integrate cultural systems, perspectives of utopia, like those of the former slaves, attempt to subvert them.[23]

As a consequence, it becomes important "that the study of political languages takes its point of departure from the languages of ruling groups, which articulate their concerns and are biassed in their favor." Yet the discussion should not end there as these meanings are always being challenged and contested, which makes it "also important that the more institutionalised a language and the more public it becomes, the more it becomes available for the purposes of a diversity of utterants articulating a diversity of concerns."[24] Political languages are constantly "being disengaged from the texts and contexts in which they appear" and reappearing "in modified forms and with diversified results, in other texts and contexts." Hence, rather than viewing the slaves' and ex-slaves' responses to their social and political situations through the lens of resistance, it is being asserted that they acted as both transmitters of the dominant political languages as well as creators of new forms of these ideas.[25]

The status of Abraham Lincoln provides a classic example of the dynamic of transmitter-creator demonstrated by the ex-slaves. It appears incontrovertible that Lincoln endorsed a gradualist approach to the abolition of slavery. In fact, it seems as if he became the great emancipator despite himself. Lincoln, who continually supported the colonization of Black Americans outside of the United States, made it clear that abolition remained subordinate to larger political objectives: "My paramount object in this struggle is to save the Union, and is not either to save or destroy slavery. If I could save the Union without freeing any slave, I would do it; and if I could save it by freeing all the slaves, I would do it; and if I could do it by freeing some and leaving others alone, I would also do that."[26] The contemporary reinterpretation of the Emancipation Proclamation (1863) often emphasizes that this decree had an extremely cautious tone. In actuality, this declaration, which liberated slaves only in rebellious territories, was weaker than the Second

Confiscation Act (1862), which provided for the freedom of slaves who belonged to disloyal masters, regardless of residence.[27]

None of this would have really mattered to the former slaves for they reinterpreted the Emancipation Proclamation to their advantage. This strategy provides an example of how political languages can be disengaged from their original contexts and modified with diversified results. It remains one of the great ironies of history that Lincoln, who made clear his belief in White supremacy, has also become a symbol of Black liberation. It seems that the former slaves have used him as much as he thought he used them to save the Union. Rather than being naive, the ex-slaves were being strategic as they continually insisted the president of the United States, a self-described democratic nation, should live up to the political universals expressed in the governing laws of the land.

Although other examples could have been selected for this study, Jamaica and South Carolina, societies whose slave laws were modeled on those of the Barbados Slave Act of 1661,[28] have been chosen as synedoches for the evolution of the emancipation process in their respective political contexts. This choice has been made not only because in many ways the transition after slavery in the British Caribbean and the United States began in these locations but also due to the significant place each maintains in the development of slavery and postslavery politics. Although atypical in some respects, the situation in Jamaica was unquestionably important for the Colonial Office in the formulation of imperial policies, a development that had begun during the era of slavery and continued into the postslavery period. The House of Commons Committee that examined the question of abolition used evidence taken primarily from the Jamaican experience in its investigation, and when the question of the early termination of the apprenticeship system arose, Jamaica again took center stage in the public and parliamentary debates. In the minds of many English citizens, including the antislavery activists who focused their attention on the island, Jamaica was synonymous with the West Indies.[29] Thus, an emphasis on Jamaica is not meant to suggest uniformity in experience across the British Caribbean, although on one level this argument can be made, such as with respect to claims of the former slaves. Rather than uniformity, issues of continuity and persistence of political structures become important. In particular, this line of analysis is germane to the 1865 Morant Bay rebellion, which reflected a general trend of riots and labor strikes that resulted from dissatisfaction with the emancipation process in the British slave colonies.

The actions of the South Carolina plantocracy gave the state a political prominence resembling that of Jamaica. Just as the Jamaica Assembly remained the most powerful and outspoken of the legislative colonies, a similar claim could be made for the state of South Carolina. From the intransigence of its political leaders at the Constitutional Convention, who insisted on the protection of the institution of slavery, to the 1830s nullification controversy, to the postslavery Ku Klux Klan trials, South Carolina maintains a significant place in the history of slavery and of racial hierarchy in the United States. The American Freedmen's Inquiry Commission whose preliminary and final reports helped to lay the foundation for the emancipation process acknowledged the unique position of the state: "This is one of the States in which the system of negro slavery seems to have reached its furthest development, with the least modification from contact with external civilization. There it appears to have run out nearer to its logical consequences than in any other we have visited."[30]

Moreover, as was the case in the Caribbean, Blacks constituted a numerical (as distinct from a political) majority. While this characteristic had little political relevance before the Civil War, after the abolition of slavery, when Blacks would be gradually enfranchised, this phenomenon would give South Carolina a particular history (with Mississippi), whereby Blacks would for a brief moment play an important role in the governing of the state's legislative affairs. Furthermore, in a certain respect, like Jamaica, South Carolina served as a compass indicating the direction in which the emancipation process would proceed, for the reorganization of the postslavery United States began on the state's Sea Islands in what has now become understood in the classic phrase as a "rehearsal for reconstruction." Related to this "rehearsal" was the question of landownership, also raised in Jamaica, which emerged in part as a result of the issuance of Sherman's Special Field Order No. 15, giving birth to the idea of "40 acres and a mule."[31]

Limited access to land for the former slaves represented one issue among others that arose in both political contexts during the immediate postemancipation period. Other problems such as the entrenchment of a non-Black planter power structure, an unresponsive judicial system, and an unfair policy of taxation provide additional parallels. It is precisely on the basis of such common elements that the argument here centers on political languages. To this effect, the present examination does not attempt to provide a comprehensive social, political, or economic history of emancipation, although it has borrowed from the insights of these approaches. Comparative histories of slavery and emancipation that focus on the products cultivated (tobacco, cotton, rice, and sugar), imperial background (Spanish, Portuguese, French,

English, and Dutch), formal political organization (legislative versus crown colony government in the British Caribbean), religious differences (Catholic versus Protestant), divergent legal traditions (Reception of Roman law versus lack of Reception of Roman law),[32] or the resistance of the slaves and ex-slaves have correctly paid attention to the variety of social conditions and the responses to these in the slave societies of the Americas. The analysis here remains fully aware of significant differences and thus is not intended to minimize how widely the system of slavery could vary from region to region. Yet the conceptual framework used to legitimize slavery itself and, in the post-slavery period, the subsequent system of racial hierarchy causes many of the differences to dissolve, especially when the fact that slavery and its abolition formed a part of a single world system is taken into account. In other words, it should be consistently reinforced that, despite the differences, the political languages employed to subjugate Blacks under the institution of slavery as well as during the postslavery era did not necessarily vary widely in the Americas.

In addition to the present introduction, the argument organizes itself around five chapters and a conclusion. Chapter 1, which serves as a prologue, provides the intellectual background that in a large part determines the development of the terms of emancipation in the postslavery context. It shows the Judeo-Christian intellectual background, noting the important intellectual shifts that take place. Indeed, abolition was part of a significant change and constituted an indispensable element in what was essentially a cultural revolution.

The second chapter outlines the way in which the ex-slaveholders in both contexts, as soon as slavery ended, attempted to circumscribe the freedom of the ex-slaves. With the Abolition Acts in the British Caribbean and the Black Codes in the United States, the planters used the very legal measures that were, in principle, designed to secure the freedom of Blacks to undermine this freedom. Invoking the political language of local autonomy in the former and states' rights in the latter, the ex-slaveholders attempted to replicate the structure of social, cultural, and labor relations that had existed under slavery. A call for immigration as well as a specious use of the franchise in both contexts also defined the extent to which the planters would go in order to reconstruct a slave society after abolition. The use of these political languages reveals paradoxically that the planters could no longer behave in a certain manner toward Blacks as they were now forced to act according to the logic of an ostensibly new social order. Moreover, given the record of recalcitrance on the part of the former slaveholders, the question does arise as to why, after slavery, so much trust was placed in the ex-slaveholders and their actions but so little in the ex-slaves, for whom emancipation was ostensibly implemented.

In order to demonstrate that a cultural agenda of "reconstruction" and the more explicitly articulated social and political program operated *pari passu,* the next chapter examines the role of the special magistrates and the Freedmen's Bureau officials in the emancipation process. Striving for a re-construction of the Black ex-slaves by inculcating discipline for wage labor, a nuclear-family life-style, and the tenets of a Christian education, these offi-cials functioned as secular missionaries or, as the humanitarians during the Port Royal, South Carolina, experience often referred to themselves, as "evan-gels of civilization." The Beaufort representative of the American Missionary Association affirmed this mission "to *unlearn* them [the ex-slaves] and learn them *from,* the vices, habits and associations of their former lives." Another evangel, originally from New York, phrased the task most cogently in de-scribing her job: "I preach and teach and civilize and reconstruct generally." Moreover, in order to accomplish this goal, as Eliphalet Whittlesey, the first assistant commissioner for the North Carolina Freedmen's Bureau, made clear in a circular letter, new and more subtle methods must be employed. Against the physical coercion employed during the era of slavery, Whittlesey insisted that the "school-house, the spelling-book, and the Bible will be found better preservers of peace and good order than the revolver and the bowie-knife."[33]

Central to the process of cultural reconstruction carried out by those who have been described as "the mid-wives of a new order" was the political lan-guage of "free labor" that had earlier been employed during the antislavery crusade. Eric Foner has aptly described the relationship between the former slaves, former slaveowners, and the bureau agents, an insight that can also be extended to the special magistrates. Rather than being the pawns of planters or the bleeding-heart advocates of the ex-slaves, these officials were agents of the free-labor ideology itself, and thus they would support the position that reinforced this political language: "To the extent that this meant putting freed-men back to work on plantations, the Bureau's interest coincided with those of the planters. To the extent that the Bureau demanded for the freedmen the rights to which northern laborers were accustomed, it meant an alliance with the Blacks. The issue was how the freedmen should be induced to work."[34] The issue, one could add, was also that the former slaves needed to be in-duced to work only by virtue of a specific conception of the social order and what constituted the general good that was becoming increasingly dominant at the time.

Within such an understanding, for many of these "evangels" labor acquired the qualities of a religion, as can be seen from its being equated with freedom. It became something of a gospel, with all the fervency implied. In 1865 the commissioner of the Freedmen's Bureau, Oliver O. Howard, expressed to a Black gathering that "he would promise them nothing but their freedom, and freedom means work." To ensure a disciplined, while ostensibly free, labor force a few months before abolition was to take effect, the governor of Jamaica, the marquis of Sligo, conveyed the identical sentiments in a "letter of advice" read to the Black slaves across the island. In a statement as unequivocal as any to be found affirming the belief in labor as the criterion of social and cultural value, Sligo stressed that "every one is obliged to work. Some work with their hands, others with their heads; but no one can live and *be considered respectable* without some employment."[35] In other words, the social relations associated with the issue of work can be viewed not only in terms of labor control and exploitation but also as a means to organize the general society, and these relations most centrally reinforce what it means to "be considered respectable" — that is, to be considered fully human.

The fourth chapter addresses the contradiction inherent in coercing the former slaves into a system ostensibly based on free labor, that is, the idea of race, or what Josiah Nott, coauthor of *Types of Mankind*, referred to as "the vexed question of original unity."[36] The comments of Sligo and Howard reflected the extent to which emancipation policies were often framed from a perspective other than that of the Black ex-slaves. This dynamic occurred as a result of a specific ideology of race to which the political language of abolition was inextricably linked. Before the end of slavery, racial conceptions of both monogenesis (belief in the singularity of human origins, such as with the chain-of-being schema) and polygenesis (belief in the plurality of human origins) structured Anglo-American slave societies, with both legitimating the legal subordination of the Black population group.[37] In the wake of the debate on Black enslavement and the social movement that ended slavery, however, a new understanding of race was born, but one that maintained some preabolition assumptions. Within the terms of this discourse Blacks were beginning to be seen as less evolved, often posited in cultural terms, such as with the special magistrates and the bureau agents, but in some later instances the political languages were expressed in more explicitly biological-genetic terms. What is generally referred to as "racism" seems to have emerged as the resolution of the question of the terms on which a postslavery society would be integrated, given the new conception of freedom that came with the increasingly industrial organization of reality of metropolitan Britain and the U.S. North.[38] Well before the Civil War ended slavery, Alexis de Tocqueville perceived this phenomenon that "the prejudice which repels the Negroes seems to increase in proportion as they are emancipated, and inequality is sanctioned by the manners whilst it is effaced from the laws of the country." As a result, "the prejudice of race appears to be stronger in the States which have abolished slavery, than in those where it still exists; and no where is it so intolerant as in those States where servitude has never been known."[39] There is therefore no correlation between racial animosity and slaveholding, as ideas of Black inferiority seem to have emerged as powerfully in nonslaveholding contexts in the United States.

The case of John Bowen Colthurst, a staunch antislavery advocate who served as a special magistrate in Barbados and St. Vincent for more than three years, provides an excellent example. Colthurst insisted that abolishing slavery represented "a source of unalloyed joy and gratitude to God," for the institution was a "direct infraction of the laws of God" and thus had "to be cleansed and purified by laws based upon, his [God's] revealed word." Yet, and logically so, he saw no contradiction in contending that "[i]t is true, nevertheless, that [Johann] Spurzheim or [Franz Joseph] Gall, on dissecting Sambo's head, might declare that his skull did not exhibit the first order of intellectuality; but that the organs of amativeness, cheerfulness, and perhaps combativeness, were fully developed."[40] Although most of the magistrates' musings did not refer so explicitly to the scientific debate on the question of race, as it has been noted with the missionaries "a subtle but nevertheless discernible shift" in racial attitudes occurred during the period of apprenticeship.[41]

In the U.S. context, this dynamic also appeared in the political languages of the antislavery Republican Party, as many Northerners "approached Reconstruction with their racial prejudice largely intact."[42] When attacked by the Democrats for being "pro-Negro," spokesmen in the party, especially in the West, responded that Republicans constituted the "real White man's party," denying any intention of granting Blacks legal or social equality. As the editor of a Chicago newspaper suggested, it did not follow necessarily "that we should fellowship with the negroes because our policy shakes off their shackles." It can therefore be argued that "a strong overtone of racism" was "inherent in the antislavery outlook of many Republicans."[43] Thus, as was the case with its British Caribbean counterpart, an antislavery stance did not obviate notions of Black inferiority. In fact, these were logical suppositions given the way in which emancipation had been conceptualized. As a result, having not completely transformed "the vexed question of original unity," that is, the belief in the lesser humanness of Blacks, the subordination of the now free Black and ex-slave population group was translated into a postslavery context.

A paradigmatic revolution (as occurred with abolition) does not necessarily translate into a political revolution; thus, "a power structure may survive by successfully transforming its idiom."[44] Abolitionists and emancipators in the United States and the British Empire could not undo the problem of racial hierarchy, for in a paradoxical manner the political languages espoused by these groups, occasionally beyond their conscious intentions, helped give rise to another form of it.

The postslavery form of racial subordination was solidified with the brutal repression of the 1865 rebellion in Morant Bay, Jamaica, and the reunion of the North and the South in the 1870s, and these events are analyzed in the fifth chapter. To consider Governor Eyre's response to the Morant Bay uprising as reasonable, one did not have to agree with Prime Minister Benjamin Disraeli's racial absolutism, "All is race, there is no other truth"; or even with Thomas Carlyle's conception of Blacks in the Caribbean not needing much exertion to secure their basic needs.[45] Disraeli's *Tancred* and Carlyle's famous essay, "Occasional Discourse of the Nigger Question," nevertheless provided the kind of intellectual framework based on a specific conception of the historical past that made such brutality seem just and legitimate. However, to have agreed with Governor Eyre and his supporters, one could not have considered the centuries of labor for which the Caribbean ex-slaves, unlike their former masters, were never compensated, or the social and economic conditions that made Morant Bay the logical result. In other terms, the ex-slave understanding of emancipation had to be negated. From the shifting of the tax burden onto working peasants, to the decrease in real wages beginning in the 1840s, to the loss of savings due to bank failures, to the general planter policies that attempted to reinstitute slavery (such as the reintroduction of the whip in 1859 and the treadmill in 1864 as forms of punishment), and, most centrally, to the suppression of ex-slaves' voting privileges and commercial enterprises, an atmosphere of distrust and conflict had been created, thus making the Morant Bay insurrection the logical consequence.[46]

It has been pointed out that the reunion of the North and South in 1877 with the Hayes-Tilden Compromise represented no watershed in U.S. history: "In effect, Hayes's friends at the Wormley Conference were giving up something they no longer really possessed in exchange for something that had already been secured by other means. While on the other hand the Southerners were solemnly accepting something that had been secured by other means in exchange for adherence to a course to which, by that time, they were already committed. It was, on the whole, one of the strangest bargains in the annals of horse swapping." The significance of Redemption, in other words, remained largely symbolic, especially given that by 1876 only South Carolina, Florida, and Louisiana had not been "redeemed," with the other Republican administrations having lasted on average three and a half years. When one takes into account the "more than three centuries of the white and the black man's history in the South," the role of the Radical lasted for only a brief moment. Redemption, on the other hand, had more enduring intellectual consequences: "[I]t was not the Radicals nor the Confederates but the Redeemers who laid the lasting foundations in matters of race, politics, economics, and law for the modern South."[47]

The conclusion highlights the main implications of the principal findings of the investigation. It extends the discussion of the paradoxical nature of the emancipation process in Jamaica and South Carolina, with implications for their larger imperial and national contexts. The abolition of slavery had extraordinary repercussions; indeed, as demonstrated in chapter 1, it remained a central element in the development of the "great transformation." But why would it leave unanswered fundamental questions, so that it would impel, in each case, a century after their respective abolitions, another social movement that attempted to address these same issues?

Chapter One

The Song That Antislavery Sung
Abolition and the Great Transformation

We ask, in short, that we shall be free: in labour, free; in trade, free; in action, free; in thought, free; in speech, free; in religion, free—perfectly free.
—Reverend Andrew Reed, evangelical dissenter, 1830s

[I]n using the same *word* we do not all mean the same *thing*. With some the word liberty may mean for each man to do as he pleases with himself, and the product of his labor; while with others the same word may mean for some men to do as they please with other men, and the product of other men's labor. Here are two, not only different, but incompatible things, called by the same name—liberty.
—Abraham Lincoln, address at Sanity Fair, 1864

Any discussion of the political languages employed in the emancipation process in the Anglo-Americas should first contextualize the meaning of slavery and freedom. More than any other term, the word "freedom" has permeated the political discourse of the Anglo-Atlantic world. As Eric Foner noted in his recent book on the subject, there are no ideas "more fundamental to Americans' sense of themselves as individuals and as a nation" than those of freedom and liberty.[1] And, one could add to this formulation, no idea pervades the historical imagination of the United States more than its self-representation as the "cradle of liberty." It has often been suggested that this political language, inherited from the mother country, has a legacy dating back to the thirteenth-century Magna Carta. This self-understanding was most clearly illustrated by the renowned jurist Sir William Blackstone when he commented on the 1772 Somersett case: "And this spirit of liberty is so deeply implanted in our constitution, and rooted even in our very soil, that a slave or a negro, the moment he lands in England, falls under the protection of the laws, and with regard to all natural rights becomes *eo instanti* a freeman."[2]

Blackstone's representation of the idea of individual liberty as a natural phenomenon ("rooted even in our very soil") erased the cultural process that instituted such a belief. Isaiah Berlin has noted that rather than being an age-old doctrine, such an idea is comparatively modern, having emerged only in recent historical time: "There seems to be scarcely any consciousness of individual liberty as a political idea in the ancient world. Condorcet has already remarked that the notion of individual rights is absent from the legal conceptions of the Romans and Greek; this seems to hold equally of the Jewish, Chinese, and all other ancient civilizations that have since come to light. The domination of this ideal has been the exception rather than the rule, even in the recent history of the West."[3] Such an assertion necessarily implies that the opposition of slavery and freedom should not be considered as being universally valid in all cultural contexts.

Studies of slavery on the continent of Africa have illustrated the culture-specific nature of the slavery-freedom opposition, even after the encounter with European colonialism has been taken into account. Although one should be cautious about speaking in simplistic generalizations, in Africa those who were slaves usually had fallen outside the protection of a lineage group. This situation could occur for many reasons—for example, being sold as spoils of war, for the breach of social mores (such as committing homicide or adultery), or in order to repay debts (resulting from either voluntary or involuntary means). Orphans and abandoned children considered "supernaturally dangerous" (such as twins in some cultures) could also be enslaved. In times of great famine, members of some groups would be exchanged for provisions, while other groups would employ kidnapping to acquire outsiders. Indeed, the development of slavery on the African continent reveals that the antithesis of slavery has not always been the idea of freedom: "In most African societies, 'freedom' lay not in withdrawal into a meaningless and dangerous autonomy but in an attachment to a kin group, to a patron, to power—an attachment that occurred within a well-defined hierarchical framework. . . . Here, the antithesis of 'slavery' is not 'freedom' qua autonomy but rather 'belonging.'"[4]

When the institution of slavery was opposed to a discourse of freedom, which existed in the slave societies of Greece and Rome, the social reality of the slave nonetheless differed from the experience of the Americas. In these societies, slaves could marry, own property, even own other slaves. They were not categorically prohibited from obtaining an education; in fact, in Rome some became doctors, and many served as bureaucrats and functionaries. Roman slaves could often acquire and inherit wealth; indeed, some were wealthier than nonslave Romans. Moreover, there seemed to have been an element of social mobility in the Roman example, for slaves were not excluded from becoming citizens as they were in Greek society. In tandem with the African case, slavery in the Greek and Roman societies illustrates that the modern (Western) understanding of slavery as a chattel or property without any rights, used primarily as a source of labor, has meaning primarily within specific historical and cultural circumstances.[5] Despite the fact that some slaves probably endured harsh labor, slavery was not a mode of production in Greece and Rome, nor in Africa was such the case.[6] In this respect, the culture-specific nature of slavery in the Americas becomes more pronounced as fundamental differences existed between the practice of slavery in the New World and elsewhere. In the Americas, slavery formed the basis of the labor system, and thus even the later development of what would be called "free labor" was generated from the matrix of slavery. Moreover, no other society made slavery isomorphic with a racial population group, whereby Blacks served as the negation to all that was normatively constituted as being human. David Walker phrased the situation most aptly when he stated that despite the existence of slavery in other societies, only the Americans compounded the misery of Blacks "by telling them that they were not of the human family."[7]

Although the legacy of the ancient world, especially the influence of ideas emanating from the Roman Empire, cannot be denied,[8] this cultural field of meaning in the Americas had its origins, to some extent, in certain medieval conceptions of the world, contrary to the Hartzian thesis that the United States "uniquely lacked a feudal tradition." This contention adopted Tocqueville's interpretation of the U.S. political culture that Americans were "born equal."[9] Although it would take a somewhat different form in the Anglo-Atlantic world (such as the shift from Catholicism to Protestantism, reformed Protestantism in the colonies), the idea of freedom that emerged in Latin Christian Europe during the Middle Ages would over time have a significant influence on the development of this concept in England and the United States in the late eighteenth and nineteenth centuries. The idea of liberty espoused during the prenational period of the United States remained inseparable from the assertion of Christian liberty centuries before the rearticulation of this idea. According to Saint Augustine (*De Civitate Dei*), true liberty from original sin could exist only under certain conditions, that is, within the Christian community. The *civitas* (city) became coterminous with Christianity, and, by extension, to be fully human one also had to be Christian. When the Puritans wanted to create "Cities on the Hill" or the colonists thought of themselves as creating "perfect states," these claims constituted the reassertion of the idea of the *civitas* as the "perfect community," one not only politically autonomous but also "sufficient in providing for life's necessities."[10] In this instance, a secularization process has occurred where religious ideas have been translated into a political (and less explicitly religious) context. However, one could also argue that a revolution, in both the political and the etymological sense, has occurred because Christian ideas such as the "kingdom of God" and "city of God" were themselves originally political ideas of the Greeks and Romans that were translated into a more explicitly religious, Judeo-Christian paradigm in the Middle Ages.

As is well recognized, the vocabulary of Christianity is punctuated with metaphors of slavery and freedom. Beyond geography and time, salvation was to provide the only pathway to true human emancipation, realized with eternal life after physical death occurred. As a result, for the medieval order "only the universal, the unchanging and consequently the timeless, was truly rational."[11] True freedom therefore entailed being the bondservant of Christ, as opposed to living under the bondage of sins such as lust and corruption. The implication remained that liberty should not be mistaken for the license to do as one felt; in fact, self-denial became a central tenet of the faith. One voluntarily gave obedience to a set of ethical standards that were believed to have been divinely inspired. This attribute illustrated that the conception of

Christian freedom from its inception was regulated with explicit boundaries of what represented appropriate behaviors.

By the end of the eighteenth century, significant changes had certainly taken place in the Anglo-Atlantic interpretation of Christian liberty. Most centrally, these societies would be increasingly organized by secular conceptions of the Enlightenment. Yet, although secular ideas like rationalism had been developing for over a century, these would continue to be mediated through a Christian point of reference. In the official context, nonetheless, the understanding of liberty began to take on explicitly political connotations, as it was now said to be guided by reason and rationality. One had to overcome passion and irrationality, just as lustful desire (emanating from mankind's depraved and fallen condition) had to be suppressed within the logic of medieval Christian liberty. In both cases, freedom was embodied in a set of behavioral norms, not in the license to do whatever one wanted; otherwise, in the former one became an infidel, and in the latter, an irrational savage. Precisely within such an intellectual frame one finds Hobbes's contention that without an absolute monarch there is no order, no freedom. As was the case with its medieval Christian counterpart, the rationalist notion of freedom also entailed obligation — in effect, subordination to higher authorities.

The 1776 revolution against the British Parliament exemplified the dynamic that eighteenth-century conceptions of freedom were circumscribed by notions of obligation and subordination. In this vein, the subsequent adoption of the U.S. Constitution should not necessarily be interpreted as the canonization of individual liberty, Gordon Wood's penetrating analysis notwithstanding.[12] During this era and into the beginning of the next century, there continued to be a profound "distrust of the socially unbounded individual." The liberties of the colonists were predicated on the idea of reciprocal obligation to the parliamentary monarchy of the mother country. It was as English citizens, rather than on the basis of natural rights, that the colonists insisted their liberties were being violated: "This collection of historic rights, privileges, and exemptions, both corporate and individual, were throughout most of the 18th century held to be an inheritance that Americans enjoyed not so much as men, but as British (English) subjects."[13] As a consequence, the transformation of 1776 has been characterized as "a truly British revolution; one which even involves a revolt against being British."[14]

Central to this revolutionary conception of freedom was the republican political language of virtue, the belief that self-fulfillment could be realized only in the capacity of being a citizen, whose independence and personal autonomy had been secured by property in the form of freehold land. The

"Anglo-American variant" of this mode of thought appeared during the 1776 revolution against Parliament in the claim that decolonization would allow the colonies to escape the corruption and tyranny overtaking the mother country, and therefore cease to compromise their virtue. For colonists outside the political elite, these ideas took a more explicitly religious tenor. A Puritan ethos of self-respect was also represented as being capable of meeting the requirement of virtue, and because religion was understood to be the primary medium for the espousal of morality and virtue, Protestant clergy "saw in the break with England and in the morally regenerative effects of republicanism a heaven-sent opportunity to cleanse America of sin once and for all." Continuing a Judeo-Christian tradition, this millenarian conception fused the sacred and the secular by "identifying the Kingdom of God with the prospects of the American republic," creating "the most important element feeding into the Americans' gradually evolving idea of progress."[15]

Terms such as "autonomy," "freedom," "virtue," "dependence," "progress," and "liberty," all of which referred to the culture-specific conception of what constituted the general good in the Anglo-Atlantic context, provided a source of contention throughout the nineteenth century. It was, in effect, precisely within such a field of understanding that the struggle for the abolition of slavery was vigorously fought. For many of the abolitionists, slavery represented a hindrance to progress, personal liberty, and the development of morality and virtue among the slaves as well as among the slaveholders.[16] However, as Lincoln's address at Sanity Fair indicates, the liberty of slaveholders like John C. Calhoun called for the enslavement of others: "That they [equality and liberty] are united to a certain extent, — and that equality of citizens, in the eyes of the law, is essential to liberty in a popular government, is conceded. But to go further, and make equality of *condition* essential to liberty, would be to destroy both liberty and progress. The reason is, that inequality of condition, while it is a necessary consequence of liberty, is, at the same time, indispensable to progress."[17]

Although from a historical point of view, the proslavery position may seem to have been discredited by the abolitionist position, Calhoun's assertion nevertheless demonstrated an insight with respect to political practices of the U.S. government and society even outside the purview of slavery. The removal of Indians from their homelands in the 1820s and 1830s (continuing a three-century-old process of displacement) would be justified in precisely the terms that Calhoun espoused in regard to the role of slavery. Although an acrimonious congressional and societal debate occurred between those arguing for improvement of the Indians and those favoring displacement (with both assuming the inferiority of the Indian, the only difference being one of degree), it eventually became policy to remove them. In the words of one congressman, the country could not "check the course of human happiness — obstruct the march of science — stay the works of art, and stop the arm of industry, because they will efface in their progress the wigwam of the red hunter, and put out forever the council fire of his tribe."[18]

Calhoun's understanding could occur for a couple of reasons. As historians have shown, the slaveholders did operate within a world view different from industrial capitalism, although they remained implicated in this system.[19] Yet, more important, the defense of slavery as a positive good represented an ideology that was under siege, being promoted by a dominant group whose legitimating synthesis of the world was being disenchanted. As a result, such groups can often provide insight into the future hierarchies of the social order that will displace them. South Carolina governor James Henry Hammond and George Fitzhugh represented the archetype of the proslavery ideology in their critique of the industrialization movement in the Northern states and, indeed, globally. Fitzhugh insisted that war resulted from society organized around free competition: "Self-interest makes the employer and free laborer enemies." In fact, when Northern industrialists pushed for the recruitment of immigrants, it was simply because they wanted "cheap, obedient, [and] tractable labor."[20] Essentially, the free-labor system for the workers became another form of slavery or, at least, of social and political domination. Such was the critique of Hammond. "You will say that man cannot hold *property in man*. The answer is that he can and *actually does* all the world over, in a variety of forms, and *has always done so*."[21]

While some abolitionists could perceive the new hierarchies emerging with the free-market, free-labor system, many could not. Thus, how can one account for the insight of the abolitionists with respect to the hierarchies structuring the system of slavery with the blindness to those implicit in the new social order of industrial capitalism? Such has been the source of a debate among historians, initiated, in some respects, by the 1964 republication of Eric Williams's *Capitalism and Slavery,* originally issued in 1944. In this work, Williams developed an argument that linked the abolition of slavery in the British Caribbean to the rise of industrial capitalism.[22] Without questioning the sincerity of some of the evangelical abolitionists, Williams insisted that it took more than a change in the individual moral consciousness of the antislavery advocates to bring slavery to an end. The intention of such an analysis was to displace the purely moral and humanitarian interpretation of abolition that Williams saw represented in British imperial historiography.[23]

While contending that antislavery activists like Thomas Clarkson personi-
fied "all the best in the humanitarians of the age," Williams nonetheless detected a contradiction in the political claims of the abolitionists, for often "in
their attitude to domestic problems they were reactionary." As examples Williams noted that some antislavery advocates did not display genuine concern
for the social and economic conditions endured by members of the working
classes: "The Methodists offered the English worker Bibles instead of bread
and Wesleyan capitalists exhibited open contempt for the working class."[24]

Moreover, Williams insightfully pointed out that the enactment of abolition transpired at a particular moment in history: "[The humanitarians]
could never have succeeded a hundred years before when every important
capitalist interest was on the side of the colonial system." Such a revelation
necessarily implies that historians need to explain why, after the enslavement
of Africans "had become the foundation stone of the Atlantic economy" and
after the British Parliament reissued a pamphlet in 1788 justifying the African slave trade and Black slavery, a complete reversal occurred within an extremely short historical time frame: "Indeed the British about face on the
issue of coerced labor could be almost described as instantaneous in historic
terms. By the early nineteenth century they had become so convinced of its
immorality and economic inefficiency that they were running an expensive
one-nation campaign to suppress the international slave trade." It was such
a reality that Williams found inadequately explained by a purely moral and
humanitarian interpretation of British slave abolition.[25]

Although his critics have used terms such as "sweeping," "cynical," "reductionist," and "paranoid" to describe *Capitalism and Slavery*,[26] the implications
of the Williams thesis remain vast and, in large part, unexamined. Diverging
from the dominant practice of writing history, Williams never pretended to
separate historical questions from the present social context, and, indeed, he
insisted upon the relevance of an analysis of the "age of revolution" for understanding our contemporary political crises: "The crisis which began in 1776
and continued through the French Revolution and the Napoleonic wars until
the Reform Bill of 1832, was in many respects a world crisis similar to the crisis
of today, differing only in the more comprehensive range, depth and intensity of the present. It would be strange if the study of the previous upheaval
did not at least leave us with certain ideas and principles for the examination
of what is going on around us today."[27] Such an emphasis may also explain
why the critics of Williams have tended to focus on the declension aspect
of his thesis and not another central, if not more important, dimension of
his argument: that the capital accumulated from the West Indies financed the

industrial revolution in England and, in essence, became part of the process that created the wealth that made possible England's rise to global dominance in the nineteenth century. Contrary to the way in which the Williams thesis has been simplified to one dimension, two central concepts were implicit in the paradigm of "capitalism and slavery": capitalism led to the destruction of slavery, and slavery laid the basis for capitalism.

Before the publication of *Capitalism and Slavery,* other Black intellectuals insisted (and many since have insisted) upon this dual understanding of "capitalism and slavery." While addressing the United States and the former French colony of Haiti, respectively, W. E. B. Du Bois's *Black Reconstruction* and C. L. R. James's *The Black Jacobins* illustrated the centrality of slavery in the formation of what became the modern Western world system. Moreover, these scholars emphasized that the abolition of slavery in the Americas had to be understood in the context of the transformative political and economic forces of the time, especially with regard to the shift in power from the holders of landed wealth to the capital-owning class, the bourgeoisie.[28] Despite the insistence of Williams and other Black scholars, mainstream historical representations of the past have remained speciously silent on the idea that the profits derived from slavery laid the basis for industrial capitalism and the resultant accumulated wealth of Western Europe. It has probably not been by accident that the descendants of slaves have had to reconceptualize the dominant historical framework and emphasize the historical relation of slavery (and its aftermath) to the contemporary global racial and political context. Thus, it has often been marginalized and contested works such as Walter Rodney's *How Europe Underdeveloped Africa* that have pushed the implications of the thesis of *Capitalism and Slavery.*[29]

So why has the question posed by the Caribbean school not preoccupied mainstream historians to the extent that the issue of declension has?[30] Is it that the issue of declension has been perceived to have a stronger conceptual basis for critique? Or is it due to a specific political and intellectual orientation that the other significant aspect of the Williams thesis has to be dismissed? Probably some of both remained at work. Ironically, even the issue of declension has yet to be resolved completely. Assessing the debate on the role of capitalism in bringing the slave system to an end, Selwyn Carrington noted that Caribbean historians have affirmed important aspects of Williams's original formulation against his critics, who often were not specialists in the history of the region.[31] Furthermore, the insistence that the declension issue constituted the sine qua non of the validity of the Williams thesis can be called into question. It has been asserted that the soundness of the Williams thesis did not depend primarily on this issue; rather, it has been the interpreters of *Capitalism and Slavery* who "assume that his position hinges on the belief that the plantation was in decline." The critics of Williams have presupposed that the only way for the plantation colonies to have become a hindrance to metropolitan objectives would be if they were experiencing economic decline. It is ironic because such an argument remains indistinguishable from the economic determinism of which Williams has been so zealously accused. The central issue remained that the plantation system became irrelevant in advancing the interests of industrial capitalism (which can be defined in intellectual as well as economic terms); thus, a shift occurred in "the thinking elements of Britain's governing elite away from principles of the mercantile system towards the laissez-faire principles of Adam Smith."[32]

Although it may not have been explicitly stated as such, the Williams thesis can be related to a forum in the *American Historical Review* concerning the relation between the humanitarian impulse and the abolition of slavery. The participants attempted to account for the "limitations" of the humanitarian ideology of the antislavery advocates in nonreductionist terms, because Williams, it was argued, defined the impulse for abolition purely in terms of economic motivations. An analysis of this discussion can bring to light the utility of a political-languages approach for understanding the emancipation process in the Anglo-Americas. According to primary instigator Thomas Haskell, "[t]he way out of the current historiographic impasse is to find a way to establish the connection without reducing humane values and acts to epiphenomena in the process." The prevalent formulation of this relation, according to him, has been the "social control" or "class hegemony" thesis, whose emphasis on the ascendancy of a new entrepreneurial class, the bourgeoisie, implied that "class interest is the medium—and presumably the *only* important medium—through which substructural changes influence developments in the superstructure." Haskell disagreed with this explanatory model, maintaining that "a shift in the conventions of moral responsibility" occurred not as a result of the rise of a new class but rather by "the expansion of the market, the intensification of market discipline, and the penetration of that discipline into spheres of life previously untouched by it." Thus, "whatever influence the rise of capitalism may have had generally on ideas and values through the medium of class interest, it has a more telling influence on the origins of humanitarianism through changes wrought in *perception* and *cognitive style*."[33] It does seem as if Haskell has avoided the trap of economic determinism only at the level of the individual, not at the level of the society as he views the social emanating from the market.

For Haskell, David Brion Davis's *The Problem of Slavery in the Age of Revolution* represented the most sophisticated articulation of the social control–class hegemony thesis. In an attempt to avoid a reductionist analysis that viewed the relationship between the attack on slavery and the needs of capitalists as based purely on economic or class interests, Davis employed the concept of self-deception to explain the motivations of the abolitionists. With a primary interest in "antislavery and the social system as a whole," he used the concept of self-deception because, although the abolitionists attacked the brutalities of slavery and of the slave trade, they did not, as Williams had already pointed out, condemn all social oppression. "As a social force," Davis argued, "antislavery was a highly selective response to labor exploitation." This understanding was especially true with regard to the abolitionist claims made by the Quakers, which "provided an outlet for demonstrating a Christian concern for human suffering and injustice," while at the same time it gave "a certain moral insulation to economic activities less visibly dependent on human suffering and injustice." When one considers the vocalization of the problems associated with industrialization, Davis noted, "no abolitionist could plead ignorance of the charge that moral outrage was being directed against oppression overseas while similar or worse oppression was complacently tolerated at home." Abolitionists generally responded to critiques of the wage-labor system by accentuating "the moral contrast between what they conceived of as the free and slave worlds." Their strict adherence to this distinction, he intimated, indirectly legitimated the exploitation of the working class: "[B]y picturing the slave plantation as totally dependent upon physical torture, abolitionist writers gave sanction to less barbarous modes of social discipline."[34]

Against Haskell's contention that "it is difficult to reconstruct the historical actor's unconscious intention or to distinguish between consequences that are unconsciously intended and consequences that are unintended and even random," Davis replied that "the concept of self-deception is so central to any quest of self-understanding or social analysis that it cannot be discredited by a kind of positivistic behaviorism." However, he stressed that one has to separate the origins of antislavery sentiment "from the *conditions* that favored the acceptance of antislavery ideology among various governing elites. This is a distinction that Haskell continually blurs." The latter phenomenon implies ideological hegemony, which "is not the product of conscious choice and seldom involves insincerity or deliberate deception." The issue becomes, in effect, "not conscious intentions, but the social functions of ideology."[35]

John Ashworth intervened in the debate supporting the position of Davis but with a qualification: "Davis has only himself to blame for talking about self-deception and thus opening himself to Haskell's criticism." He proposed that Davis should have used the idea of "false consciousness, the notion that the awareness of historical actors is incomplete, with the result that they misperceive the world around them." Understandably, Ashworth noted, historians have been reluctant to employ this concept, "perhaps because it smacks of condescension toward the past, perhaps because the word 'false' is insufficiently nuanced." Yet it seemed to Ashworth that "we cannot do without the concept. Otherwise we are limited to the understanding of events that contemporaries possessed. The most important factors to them will have to be the most important for us." Seen in this light, Haskell's objection to the employment of self-deception was justified: "The way out of this impasse lies, quite simply, in a recognition that society rather than the individual generates false consciousness." Using the now suspect (if not discredited) "let them eat cake" statement attributed to Marie Antoinette, Ashworth pointed out that "the nature of her involvement in society obscured from her the realization that peasants could not in fact afford cake"; thus, it is not the subject that deceives himself or herself but reality.[36]

This debate concerning the origins of the movement to abolish slavery and its relation to the rise of industrial capitalism reenacted its nineteenth-century predecessor, although in somewhat different terms. The most trenchant criticism of the proslavery advocates had always been to insist that those who favored abolition were not without economic motivations. Commenting on British slave abolition, Duff Green, editor of the *U.S. Telegraph,* asserted that "humanity and religion have very little more to do with it. . . . It is all cant avarice, sacrificing the interests of the West Indies to their own." According to Green, the only religion operating was "the Christianity of pounds, shillings, and pence."[37] Whereas the proslavery advocates contended that the abolitionists were hypocritical in their explanation of what was perceived as a contradiction, Davis employed the concept of self-deception, Ashworth that of "false consciousness," and Haskell stressed social conventions and the limits of moral responsibility. Nevertheless, it still seems that there may be another explanation for the ostensibly contradictory claims of the abolitionists.

To account for the seemingly contradictory behaviors of the antislavery advocates noted in the forum, it can be now asserted that the perceived limited altruism was a systemic consequence prescribed by the political languages utilized to understand their social context. Language is "not only a prescribed way of speaking, but also a prescribed subject matter for political speech."[38]

One could therefore argue that the abolitionist movement was not only, as Davis has suggested, "a highly selective response to labor exploitation" but also a *logically* selective response given the abolitionists' understanding of what constituted exploitation versus the natural order of things. The struggles (or exploitation) of the working classes that emerged in the wake of the post-slavery free-trade and free-labor system were as unseeable to the abolitionist-bourgeois perspective as had been the suffering of the slaves within the logic of the plantocracy of John Calhoun, James Henry Hammond, and George Fitzhugh. The question arises, Were both camps simply deceiving themselves?

In the place of terms such as "self-deception" and "false consciousness," it is being proposed here that one could employ the notion, alluded to in the introduction, of "contemporary self-understanding" to comprehend the relationship between self-interest and the motivation for social and political change. Contrary to Ashworth's suggestion that relying on the description by contemporaries of their own reality is limiting, a wider understanding of the intellectual context of the ideas of the historical actors could be a useful way out of the present "historiographic impasse." For what is the telling of history if it is not the "most important factors" to historical actors? One does not have to agree with the slaveholder's conception of Blacks to acknowledge that these ideas took on a force of their own that, in a significant manner, determined the nature of the social reality. A difference emerges because scholars are not necessarily limited to the reasons that were given in the past to explain the historical context. It does seem, nevertheless, that an essential part of the task should be explaining precisely why these factors appeared as the most important to the historical actors.

The emphasis on one mode of subordination over another does not necessarily imply "self-deception" or "false consciousness." Rather than deceiving themselves, antislavery advocates were, one could argue, *being* themselves. Slavery had always constituted the albatross of the landed and commercial preindustrial world, its Achilles' heel that was vulnerable to attack from its critics, because it could not admit that the cost of the system was the sacrifice of the lives of slaves. In the postslavery period, where, in the words of the Reverend Andrew Ward, we shall be "perfectly free," there was also a cost.[39] This sacrificial position, which as the condition of its existence could not be recognized, would be assumed throughout the Americas by a poor ex-slave Black population, to which the harsh conditions that working classes confronted in industrialized nations was conceptually and structurally related. When the abolitionists did not protest the poor conditions of Blacks after slavery (or of the "free" working classes before and after slavery), it was due to their behaving according to the prescriptions of their political languages, implicit in the culture-specific, laissez-faire understanding of the world.

Examples taken from the abolitionist movements in England and the United States may provide clarification. During the early stages of the industrialization process when many English working-class families found themselves struggling to survive, factory workers would try to organize combinations and strikes in order to increase their wages and generally to improve their working conditions. In 1799, however, the House of Commons passed a Combination Act that made these forms of negotiations illegal. William Wilberforce, an important figure in the English abolitionist movement, was one of the statesmen primarily responsible for seeing through the passage of this legislation.[40] One way of analyzing the situation is to accuse Wilberforce of "self-deception" or of "false consciousness." Another would be to argue that Wilberforce's self-understanding was logically derived from the self-regulating conception of freedom implicit in the abolitionists'—indeed, protobourgeois—political languages. Thus, his position should no longer appear contradictory as the nontransformative aspects of abolitionist thought cannot be detached from its revolutionary moorings.

This same dynamic emerged in the early stages of freedom in the United States. Laura Towne was one of many Northern missionaries who went to the South Carolina Sea Islands in the wake of the social upheaval caused by the Civil War. This experience eventually became her life's work, as she dedicated much of her time and her personal wealth to the education of the former slaves. Nevertheless, Towne remained adamant against the government giving the ex-slaves gifts of food because she felt such charity would demoralize Blacks: "Better let the people suffer a little and find their own level than try to prop them up at Government expense and by increasing the public debt."[41] From a certain humanitarian perspective, Towne's position may appear unsympathetic; yet, within the political language of "self-reliance," her assertion is comprehensible because it was prescribed by a paradigm that represented being successful in terms of individual self-exertion and not in terms of societal or institutional access (and, by extension, lacking success as due to a lack of exertion and not to societal or institutional barriers). Here, the antislavery sentiment continued to borrow from its historical antecedents, where the issue of dependence, which first arose in the wake of the separation from England, has been reasserted in the postslavery situation, doing so at the level of the individual. It could be argued that Towne was probably attempting to help secure the virtue of the former slaves.

The political languages of the special magistrates, the agents of the Freedmen's Bureau, and their respective central governments signaled that an intellectual shift occurred in tandem with the political changes that spawned abolition (and, in turn, that abolition helped to spawn). In effect, the political transformation could not have occurred without a conceptual transformation. Consequently, rather than equating laissez-faire capitalism with a specific interest group, it could be argued that it was the then emerging industrial bourgeois ideology that conflicted with plantocratic organization of society. Davis has noted the abolitionist movement helped to clear a path for British industrialists by providing "a bridge between industrial and preindustrial values [and] by combining the ideal of emancipation with an insistence on duty and subordination." Again, freedom was tied to obligation. This change, he further pointed out, resulted from a new understanding of human identity: "The emergence of an international antislavery opinion represented a momentous turning point in the evolution of man's moral perception, and thus in man's image of himself."[42]

This assertion can be generalized to describe the new "paradigm of value and authority" that constituted and, in turn, was itself constituted by the changes wrought with industrialization and the abolition of slavery. A radical rupture occurred in the nineteenth century "in the way people were accustomed to thinking of themselves," and this was nowhere more evident than in the political languages of abolitionists and emancipators. This new "model of human self-realization" appealed to "man's innate desire for self-improvement" for it was claimed that human nature was to better one's condition, as Adam Smith had argued in *The Wealth of Nations.* Yet Karl Polanyi demonstrated that this representation of being human as "economic man" (*Homo oeconomicus*) led to "the institutional separation of society into an economic and political sphere." Economic activity was no longer submerged in social relations but imputed with a distinct motive. The subsequent hostile attitudes toward the poor should therefore be understood as a central element of this philosophical world view.[43]

In effect, the special magistrates and the agents of the Freedmen's Bureau became part of the putting in place of this new world view, necessary for a new cultural order, an epochal shift identified by Polanyi as the "great transformation." These officials played a role in a historic process whereby one ground of explanation was swept away and another was established. Although important changes cannot be denied, from the perspective of the former slaves, it could often seem like the exchange of one logic, that of slavery, for another, that of a free-labor, free-market society, where they still found themselves struggling to realize their hopes and aspirations on their own terms.

Martin Delany, the Black nationalist leader who also served a stint as a Freedmen's Bureau agent at Hilton Head, found it troubling that White abolitionists did not help Blacks on the practical economic level by employing them. Many Black abolitionists saw it as a refutation of certain antislavery principles, with one stating that the only thing White abolitionists were willing to give Blacks was sympathy. A disappointed Delany insisted that this was "not the song that anti-slavery sung."[44] Yet, in many instances, such was precisely the song that antislavery sung. The perspective from which Delany saw the postslavery situation, his understanding of emancipation, would be one that impelled another intellectual transformation, one beyond the hierarchies that would be created in the wake of the abolition of slavery.

Chapter Two

A Steady and Certain Command of Labour

Political Languages in the Immediate Postemancipation Anglo-Americas

In course of time we may hope to see the black population, which was kept down by legal oppression and licentious morals, consequent on a state of slavery, advance in numbers under the institution of marriage, and in the enjoyment of property. Every increase of numbers, if accompanied by education and civilized habits, will lead to increase of industry, and be productive of wealth.

But, supposing everything to be done, which by bounties on emigration, locating captured negroes, and natural increase of population, can be expected, it will still remain a problem, whether it would be possible to maintain sugar cultivation to its former extent, for this is what is meant by the term "prosperity"; while, on the other hand, the term "ruin" is used to designate, not the poverty of the people, not the want of food or raiment, not even the absence of riches or luxury, but simply the decrease of sugar cultivation.
—Lord John Russell, 1839

When the apprenticeship period ended in the English Caribbean in August 1838, the former slaves in Jamaica conveyed their gratitude to the governor of the island and the queen of the British Empire. They did so in letters, for the most part dictated to missionaries, because one of the effects of slavery left most Blacks unable to write. One freedman who knew how to write could do so only in his native Arabic. Ninety-year-old Robert Peart of Manchester, who had been a slave for seventy years, felt compelled to express his appreciation for what was understood at the time to be full freedom. "For myself, my countrymen and my countrywomen who may be alive in Jamaica," Peart stated, he wanted to give "thanks to Almighty God, and next to the English nation, whose laws have relieved us from the bondage in which we have been held." He pleaded to God to grant long life to Queen Victoria and to bless her and Sir Lionel Smith, "our governor, father, and friend, whom we all love and will obey."[1]

The Baptist members of Brown's Town Chapel in the parish of St. Ann echoed Peart's sentiments. After affirming their "determination to obey the laws under which we are now placed," the congregation expressed the feeling that harmonious labor relations would appear in the future: "We are desirous of remaining on the properties to which we have been attached, and are willing to work for such wages as our employers are able, without injury to themselves, to give us." The concern here for the prosperity of the planters was not unique. A group of laborers from Manchester demonstrated a similar consideration for the interests of the ex-slaveholders: "We will be industrious to earn an honest livelihood, and do all we can to make employers prosperous and happy."[2] Hence, rather than being on the verge of unsettling the stability of the social order, as planters continually asserted, many freedpeople intended to behave, as the congregation at Four Paths in Clarendon indicated, as "loyal, obedient, peaceable, and industrious subjects" of their "gracious Queen."[3]

In October 1865 Rufus Saxton, the first assistant commissioner of the Freedmen's Bureau in South Carolina, found that the ex-slaves in his state also seemed to display a lack of resentment toward the society that formerly sanctioned their enslavement. Against petitions claiming that the ex-slaves were planning an insurrection, Saxton forcefully argued that "this is a dangerous misrepresentation, designed to injure a race whose only crime is that they have been freed by the act of the United States Government." He remarked that Blacks were "grateful and joyful at their emancipation and nothing is further from their thoughts than insurrection." According to Saxton, this attitude existed because "negroes are not a vengeful race—at the slightest show of kindness they seem to forget all their past grievance"; and thus he proposed rather than maligning Blacks, "[t]hey deserve credit for their peaceful and orderly conduct."[4]

A month after Saxton related his impressions to Commissioner Howard, a similar statement was also made at the Colored People's Convention of South Carolina. The convention formed part of a series of national and state meetings organized by Blacks to demand political rights, doing so by invoking the political languages espoused in the Declaration of Independence.[5] Held at the Zion Church in Charleston, the convention lasted for six days. On the third day it passed a resolution that clearly demonstrated the extent to which the ex-slaves, as distinct from their former owners, adhered to the original revolutionary and transformative principles of Christianity: "*Resolved,* That as the old institution of slavery has passed away, that we cherish in our hearts no hatred or malice toward those who have held our brethren as slaves, but we extend the right hand of fellowship to *all,* and make it our special aim to establish unity, peace and love amongst all men."[6] Regardless of what must have been the strategic nature of these assertions (for what other political languages could they or should they have employed?), the South Carolina meeting, as was the case of other state conventions, was marked by claims of willingness, on one level, to integrate into the dominant American society.

The demeanor of the former slaves in both Jamaica and South Carolina, which could easily be understood as being deferential to Whites, should not be interpreted as displaying a lack of political awareness. John Clark, the pastor of Brown's Town Chapel who transcribed his congregation's statement to the governor, remarked that conflicts began to occur immediately after the first of August, the day full emancipation took effect. When members of his church had prepared to go to work, Clark stated, "on scarcely a property were the managers prepared to enter into agreement with them." A few actually made offers; however, the laborers would not agree to the terms, leading Clark to conclude that, if offered reasonable conditions, the ex-slaves would continue to work for their former masters. Although it was clear that the freedpeople adhered to some of the social norms (promising to be "loyal and industrious subjects of the Queen"), the ex-slaves nevertheless understood their political interests and acted on the basis of rational and informed choices to secure these interests.[7]

The South Carolina context was also marked by the freedpeople bearing a clear recognition of their political interests. In the fall of 1865 Commissioner Howard pleaded with Blacks on Edisto Island to vacate lands that were to be restored to their former owners, laying aside any bitter feelings they may harbor. One freedman responded that it was not a simple case of forgiveness, especially given that the same political system continued to operate: "The man who tied me to a tree and gave me 39 lashes and who stripped and flogged my mother and my sister and who will not let me stay in his empty hut except I will do his planting and be satisfied with his price and who combines with others to keep land away from me well knowing I would not have anything to do with him if I had land of my own — that man, I cannot well forgive. Does it look as if he has forgiven me, seeing how he tries to keep me in a condition of helplessness?"[8] Having been assured homesteads, the Edisto Island ex-slaves could not easily forget the federal government's promise to them. Although in this instance they did not succeed in their aim, the firm stance of the freedpeople demonstrated an acceptance of the idea of land as the material and metaphysical foundation for autonomy[9] and indicated that they would mobilize to ensure their political and social interests.

The objective of the Black ex-slave populations to be integrated into society as free and independent persons was not to be an easy task, as slavery had provided much of the social and political structures of many New World societies. The colonial secretary Edward G. Stanley, instrumental in getting the Abolition Act passed in Parliament, acknowledged that abolition in the colonial possessions would necessarily involve extensive changes as "the qualification for seats in the Assembly, and for the enjoyment of many other civil franchises, often presuppose the existence of property in slaves."[10] In other words, the enslavement of Blacks was "the organizing principle for West Indian society" as the institution became the condition of possibility of freedom for some members of the society.[11] A statement made in reference to nineteenth-century politics in the United States can as well be applied to the situation in Jamaica: "No other issue in American history has so monopolized the political scene."[12] It has been argued that the institutional basis of slavery led some planters in the British Leeward Islands to preserve such an order, although it may not have necessarily served their economic interests: "The slave system had become more than an economic enterprise which could be abandoned when it became unprofitable. It had become the basis of organized society throughout the British West Indies, and therefore it was believed to be an indispensable element in maintaining the social structure and in preserving law and order in the community."[13] If the enslavement of Blacks served to maintain the stability of the social order, then attempts by Blacks to be integrated on nonhierarchical terms within the society logically created conflict, given the rooted nature of the belief that the subordination of Blacks served the general good of society. Without this general good being redefined, the interests of the ex-slaves would continue to clash with the interests of the planters, and often with those of both central governments, whose initiatives of abolition, if only partially so, attempted to forge such a redefinition.

As could be expected, the ensuing struggle of the postslavery societies occurred within terms that had been influenced by the way in which slave societies had been instituted.[14] With abolition effected, the planters espoused claims in which they attempted to reassert their authority, while the ex-slaves made counter and transcendent claims to secure freedom on their own terms. An analysis of these claims can reveal parallels with respect to how the postslavery societies conceived of themselves, acknowledging the ways in which the new order of things both diverged from as well as converged with the governing principles of the former way in which these societies were organized. Such an interpretation can be used to lay a foundation in order to understand how in both instances Blacks would be subjected to a new form of tyranny, enacted by the brutal repression in Jamaica in 1865 with the Morant Bay rebellion and in the United States with Redemption in 1877, an event that restored "the erring sisters of the South to their old place around the family altar."[15]

The political language that emerged most forcefully in the postslavery context based itself on the primacy of local autonomy in the British Caribbean and on the idea of states' rights in the United States. Elsa Goveia noted that "[t]here was a general concurrence in opinion in the West India islands that nothing was more improper than to interfere between master and slave."[16] Frederick Douglass described the belief in "the right of each State to control its own local affairs" as one that was "more deeply rooted in the minds of men of all sections of the [United States] than perhaps any one other political idea."[17] Although this political language had been employed in South Carolina from the Nullification controversy, this claim was most passionately reasserted in the wake of the Civil War, when the abolitionist movement would eventually displace the political legitimacy of the institution of slavery by redefining what constituted the general good. As one British abolitionist insisted, this process would even serve the slaveholders' interests: "[T]heir [the slaves] speedy emancipation affords the only rational prospect for preserving the public peace, and of securing the permanent interests of the planters themselves."[18] Perhaps ironically, the triumph of abolition did not mean that the interests of the ex-slaveowners would be neglected. In fact, the emancipation policies of the British Parliament and the U.S. federal government often recognized the legitimacy of the property in slaves; they simply did not support it to the extent that the planters desired. Consequently, it became increasingly evident that the emancipation process would be defined by aspects of both change and continuity, the latter resulting from the important historical force of inertia, whereby "mentalities change slower than anything else."[19]

With Jamaica's history of cultivating some of the most fervent proslavery advocates such as Edward Long and Bryan Edwards,[20] it was no surprise that the most articulate call for local autonomy in the British West Indies came from this Assembly. Part of this response can be accounted for in the difference in the formal political organization of the island. Unlike crown colonies such as Trinidad, Jamaica operated as a legislative colony not directly controlled from England. The insistence on local autonomy emerged whenever any idea for amelioration or abolition of slavery arose. During 1831 planters held parochial meetings all over the island, passing what Governor Belmore called "intemperate and violent resolutions." There was talk of resistance and secession; for instance, planters in the Vere parish requested of the king "that he absolve his colonial subjects of their allegiance and enable them to seek the protection of some other power, thereby to ensure ourselves, and guarantee the small remnant of property which we have now left us." Yet, when the Christmas rebellion occurred later in the year, rather than seeing their inflammatory language as having any influence on the situation, the planters blamed intervention of Baptist missionaries and the imperial government for the insurrection. According to members of the Assembly, "the primary and most powerful cause of the rebellion" was "the unceasing and unconstitutional interference of His Majesty's ministers with our local legislatures." The Assembly members did not, of course, make such a claim with respect to the £500,000 loan to indemnify the planters for their loss of property in slaves.[21]

To voice their staunch opposition to abolitionist measures, a committee of planters traveled to London in November 1832 "to represent to His Majesty's ministers the ruinous consequences" that would occur "should they obtain their goal of emancipation." They spoke of suffering under financial and political oppression due to the interruption of the commerce with the United States as well as from sugar production there and in Cuba, whose landowners "can still import slaves." Acknowledging the globally interactive nature of the trade, the planters contended that while the "advanced civilization of the age abolished the slave trade," the "philanthropists should not have been satisfied with the extinction of the British trade . . . removed from her own house," for it had not been "extinguished, but transferred to Colonial rivals." The British government, they claimed, having "declared itself the enemy of the slave trade," was now "unwilling or unable to complete the abolition it had begun."[22] Ironically, at this very moment, the imperial government was engaged in precisely such endeavors with its attempts to abolish the slave trade in Brazil and Cuba.

The committee felt no need to defend the institution of slavery in Jamaica, as the members understood well the centrality of slavery to the founding of the colony: "Her laws and customs, which relate to slavery," resulted from the unavoidable consequences under which the island was placed by the mother country, "which in granting to the English army some share of the lands they had conquered, made it a condition of the grant that the lands should be cultivated by slaves." According to the planters, since the policy change of the imperial government the island had reached a state of "almost irretrievable ruin." Insisting that slavery must continue forever, what the committee feared most was the sinking "into the poverty and barbarism, into which the Negroes will undoubtedly relapse, so soon as the control of their masters is removed."[23]

However, should Parliament persevere with its objective "that slavery is a stain on the Religion and humanity of England which must be removed," the planters ironically requested "from the honor and justice of the nation fair and full compensation for the demolition of our fortunes." Should compensation be refused, they would "humbly require that the Island of Jamaica be separated from the parent country," so that once "absolved from her allegiance to the British Crown, she *be free either to assume independence, or to unite herself to some state* by whom she will be cherished and protected and not insulted and plundered."[24] Although Jamaica did not go as far as South Carolina and secede from the British Empire, the identification of slavery with what increasingly became a sectional interest had become clear.

Although the planter committee had pointed out that the central government's original endorsement of slavery had speciously changed, in its representation of the situation, it exaggerated the differences between the two positions. While it was clearly undeniable that support for abolition in Parliament had been gradually increasing, especially since the passage of the Reform Bill in 1832,[25] the Colonial Office did not completely disregard the position of the slaveholders. The last clause of the Abolition Act testified to the consideration given to the planters' interests, granting compensation to "the persons hitherto entitled to the Services of such Slaves."[26] It has been remarked that emancipation in the British West Indies "reflected all that is quintessentially English: respect for order, legal processes, and the rights of property."[27] Although it might be an overstatement to imply that abolition in the British colonies transpired smoothly, given the influence of the 1824 and 1831 slave rebellions in Jamaica (the latter of which evoked the Haitian Revolution in the minds of some Whites)[28] and the suppression of strikes by the ex-slaves,[29] the sanctity of property remained unquestioned.

Evidence of the success, if only partial, of the political language of local autonomy, the abolition of slavery in the British West Indies "left the planter class with its holdings and political power intact."[30] Even an imperial historian has questioned "why such faith was reposed in colonial legislatures when it was their negligence or obduracy which had made the Abolition Act necessary."[31] However, in executing the Abolition Act, the Colonial Office clearly conceived of an important role for the local assemblies in administering its provisions, contending "much will remain to be done by the local legislatures, which, with reference to the peculiar circumstances of each Colony, and to the local knowledge possessed by them, is best entrusted to their care." As long as measures from these bodies were not "inconsistent or repugnant to the spirit of the enactments of the Imperial Parliament," no intervention would be necessary, for as Secretary Stanley proclaimed, "[i]t has been the anxious wish of His Majesty's Government to interfere no further in the adjustment of this great question than appeared absolutely necessary to insure the practical and uniform establishment of the great principle which they have in view."[32]

This conciliatory attitude toward the West India interest seems even more precarious when viewed in the context of the group's response to the 1823 Amelioration Acts and other related policies. When the abolition of the slave trade in 1808 did not lead to an improvement in the general character of slavery, abolitionists turned their attention to the social conditions of the slaves. In 1823, however, in order to stave off Sir Thomas Foxwell Buxton's proposal of bringing the issue of slavery before Parliament, George Canning, Tory leader in the House of Commons, introduced some resolutions to reform the system. Circumventing Parliament by having ministers of the government meet privately with the West India interest and agreeing to reform slavery, Canning effectively neutralized the abolitionists' attempt to force the issue on Parliament. These negotiations resulted in some institutional legal reforms — for example, in Barbados Whites could now be punished for the murder of a Black and free Coloreds could testify against Whites; in St. Vincent and Grenada the whip was removed from the field; and in some islands Sunday market day was changed, labor was forbidden on the Sabbath, and the exercise of corporal punishment was restricted. Amelioration became official colonial policy, and it was expected that the colonial assemblies would cooperate in implementing this new policy.[33]

Part of the reason the Colonial Office proceeded with such caution stemmed from the political power that the West India interest held in Parliament and the cabinet during this time. As a consequence, policies such as slave registration were instituted so as to avoid direct interference with such an influential body. Nevertheless, the planters insisted that the Amelioration Acts represented an infringement upon the colonies' traditional constitutional rights. As the final result, amelioration policies were not fully implemented in legislative colonies like Jamaica and Barbados, although in crown colony Trinidad they were folded into the 1824 Order in Council. Even though the local assemblies partially conceded to political pressure, in no colony did they completely meet even the modest expectations of the Colonial Office.[34] This behavior could have easily forecasted their response to abolition a decade later. Given that a precedent for recalcitrance on the issue of slavery had been set with the response to the Amelioration Acts, again the question could be raised as to why so much trust for the emancipation process would be placed in the hands of the local assemblies.

In the U.S. context, the Joint Committee on Reconstruction also raised the issue of the amount of power granted to those who had remained consistently hostile to the abolition of slavery. The question for Congress, the committee stated, remained "whether conquered enemies have the right, and shall be permitted at their own pleasure and on their own terms, to participate in making laws for their conquerors." The public honor was being turned over to recent enemies, who "without justification or excuse, rose in insurrection against the United States."[35] Yet before the end of the Civil War President Lincoln had stressed the notion that the South should not be perceived as an enemy, claiming that although he "would not hold one in slavery," he could not denounce those who did. The North, he suggested, bore as much responsibility for slavery as the South, and thus in a statement conveying the same intent of the Jamaican planter committee, he asserted: "When southern people tell us they are no more responsible for the origin of slavery than we; I acknowledge the fact."[36] The latitude subsequently accorded to the former slaveholders after emancipation becomes quite logical within this intellectual frame and political context.

Due to their interests being continually given more weight, the planters in the British West Indies and the United States took substantive liberties with instituting new laws to govern postslavery political and social relations. In both contexts, the laws outlined protections of the freedpeople; however, in maintaining the presumption of atavism and criminality—beliefs central to the structuring of slave societies—these laws attempted to reenact the relations of domination that existed under slavery. As an example, in Antigua, which with Bermuda bypassed the apprenticeship phase to immediate and unqualified freedom, the legislature passed a Contract Law in 1834 that bound the former slaves to the plantation and that gave the planters total control over their labor. The Colonial Office disallowed the act, which the island governor had approved. The second version that replaced the initially proposed act did not leave the freedpeople at the total mercy and whim of the employers, although the political system that kept them landless continued to circumscribe their bargaining power.[37] In other words, the same effect had been achieved.

Near the end of the apprenticeship period, the legislature in British Guiana also passed a series of laws to regulate more stringently the behavior of the former slaves. A vagrancy law mandated that persons able "to maintain themselves wholly or in part" but "willfully refusing or neglecting to work" could be punished "on the view of a single magistrate with thirty days confinement and hard labour." The local government also canceled the stipendiary magistracy. Additionally, servants could be punished for any misdemeanor with either a month of imprisonment and hard labor or a fine of five pounds, whereas employers could be subjected only to a voidance of contract or a maximum five-pound fine. These laws were eventually disallowed by the Colonial Office, but "their intent was clear enough."[38] These negotiations signified to the planters that in order to control the life and labor of the ex-slaves, the legal system, which had formerly codified the subordination of Blacks, would now have to be employed as a secondary strategy to achieve this objective.

The Jamaica Assembly, notorious for its advocacy of proslavery interests, was no less so with respect to executing laws to address the postslavery situation of Blacks. The Abolition Act, which all local legislatures had to pass as the condition of receiving compensation funds, contradicted, as Secretary Stanley pointed out, some of the intentions of the Imperial Act of Parliament. For instance, the thirty-ninth clause of the Jamaica Act declared that the special justices with the consent of the master or manager must appoint apprentices as constables "who shall be empowered to maintain peace and order on [the] plantation." Stanley suggested that "in order to bring it within the scope and intention of the British Act" it should be made clear that this constable would have to answer to the special magistrate. Another clause that required modification, the sixtieth, mandated that in cases of emergency "it shall be lawful for the owner or other persons in the management of such property . . . to require and compel the immediate and continued service of any or all of the apprenticed labourers." To prevent the obvious potential for abuse of the non-contracted time of the ex-slaves, Stanley recommended the urgent necessity be limited to extraordinary circumstances such as fires and tempests; otherwise, because of the way in which the law had been constructed, "it might operate unfavorably and unjustly toward the apprenticed labourer."[39]

Notwithstanding these objections, which clearly indicated that a strong imbalance existed between the consideration given to the planters' interests and that accorded to those of the ex-slaves, the Colonial Office approved the law, upon which Stanley declared that "adequate and satisfactory provision hath been made by law, in the Island of Jamaica, for giving effect to the said re-cited Act of Parliament." In adopting this course, however, Stanley remarked that confirmation did not mean that the ministers of Parliament had "overlooked the existence of various defects in the Act" but rather "they feel themselves justified in pronouncing them *not to be of such vital importance* as to render the Act either inadequate or unsatisfactory."[40]

Yet there was no consensus on this assertion. In what a House of Commons Committee on Apprenticeship described afterward as a "conciliatory and deferential tone," which "contemptuously disregarded" any propositions that benefited the apprentices, Stanley received the Jamaica Abolition Act in a "spirit of confidence and goodwill," which he trusted "will henceforth always be found to exist between the Colony and His Majesty's Government." At the same time, he admitted ironically that "the Legislature will not be compelled by the motives to which [he had] alluded to acquiesce in the suggestions" offered to remedy "the imperfections of the Act." These imperfections worsened in the subsequent acts to amend the initial Abolition Act (which expired at the end of 1835), and Parliament felt the need to reject these Acts-in-Aid, as they were called, because of the prevailing belief that "the colonial Acts respecting apprenticed labourers have superseded that Act of Parliament." For the House of Commons committee these "flagrant instances of bad faith" served "to abundantly testify that the confidence, so courteously expressed, in the integrity of the Jamaica legislators was most miserably misplaced."[41] This approach would continually serve as a source of tension throughout the emancipation process.

The political languages articulated in the Black Codes passed in 1865 and 1866 in Southern states resembled the strategy of maintaining local power in the British Caribbean with the acts passed after abolition. In a manner parallel to the Colonial Office's disallowance of extremely restrictive acts, some of the Black Codes would be nullified by the Civil Rights Act of 1866 and be countermanded by Freedmen's Bureau officials. However, one of the most stringent codes, that of Mississippi, was approved by Commissioner Howard.[42] These laws forecasted "the future attitude of former Confederates toward the place of the Negro in the South and in American life." Although variations existed in these laws due to differing local conditions, they contained some unifying elements. The similarity occurred because of the widespread belief, as Carl Schurz described in the report of his 1865 tour of the South, that one "cannot make the negro work without physical compulsion." Such a conviction, Schurz noted, was bound "to have a very serious influence upon the conduct of the people entertaining it."[43]

The Black Codes must therefore be examined for their effect on the post-slavery political climate. From the perspective of White Southerners, and especially the planters, these laws were designed to protect Blacks as well as to maintain order in a society emerging from a war, one that totally transformed the political and social order. That some attempted to reinstitute slavery with these laws in all but name cannot be denied. On closer analysis, however, the Black Codes embodied what has been described as the "mind of the South";[44] thus, the Janus-faced aspect becomes logical when understood as the expression of the Southern understanding of its social and political situation — one, ironically, that will no longer be relegated exclusively to the South, if it ever was.

Many of the Blacks Codes contained provisions that conferred civil rights on the ex-slaves. Blacks could now sue and be sued, make wills, and give testimony in cases where a person of color was involved, either as plaintiff or defendant. According to the terms of these codes, Blacks could also acquire property and be protected in their rights of property as well as in their individual rights of person. Florida, Georgia, South Carolina, and Virginia passed specific laws regulating the domestic relations of Blacks, while most states now encouraged marriage among the freedpeople, a claim on which the allies of the ex-slaves later insisted. One of Virginia's laws went so far as to assert that children born of these unions could now be legally defined as "legitimate." The Florida legislature even passed an act to establish schools when the number of Black children in a county warranted it, although this expenditure would be covered by assessing a one-dollar tax on Black males between the ages of twenty-one and fifty-five.[45]

The duality implicit in the Florida legislation typified the tenor of the Black Codes, as can be readily discerned from the rules regarding the contracts between employers and workers. Labor relations were a central element to these laws because, as the Florida law suggested, "it is essential to the welfare and prosperity of the entire population of the State that the agricultural interest be sustained and placed upon a permanent basis." Most of these acts required that the contracts be written, especially if the period covered extended more than thirty days. In South Carolina and Mississippi, where two of the harsher Black Codes existed, city officers and White witnesses had to attest to the validity of the contracts. Additionally, employers who enticed laborers away from contracted situations could be imprisoned for up to a year in Louisiana, or, at the discretion of a jury in the case of Florida, either whipped a maximum of thirty-nine stripes, made to stand in the pillory for three hours, or fined up to $1,000.[46]

This air of legality only served to maintain an imbalance between privileges of the ex-slaves and those of the ex-slaveholders, for it was highly unlikely that any planter would be subjected to the punishment elaborated in the Florida act. While many of the laws affirmed the laborer's right to leave the plantation for reasons such as the South Carolina code stated—"an insufficient supply of wholesome food [or] for an unauthorized battery upon his person or one of his family"—most of the labor terms were directed toward restricting the liberties of the ex-slave workers. Employers maintained enormous discretion, as, for example, in Louisiana, where they had the right "to make a reasonable deduction from the laborer's wages for injuries done to animals or agricultural implements." With additional penalties like the subtraction of double the amount of wages for time lost due to refusal to work according to contract (also in Louisiana), Blacks would have great difficulty in asserting any control under such a labor system.[47]

The apprenticing of children remained another important consideration in drawing up the Black Codes. Apprenticeship was deemed necessary, as the South Carolina code stipulated, for boys between the ages of two and twenty-one and girls between the ages of two and eighteen "who have neither father nor mother living in the district in which they are found, or whose parents are paupers, or unable to afford them maintenance; or whose parents are not teaching them habits of industry and honesty; or are persons of notoriously bad character, or are vagrants." In addition to clothing, feeding, and providing medical assistance for children, the employers had the duty of instructing them in a "useful trade or occupation" and, more important, in the words of the Georgia code, in the "habits of industry, honesty, and morality."[48]

Paradoxically, this objective of "honesty and morality" could sometimes be achieved by kidnapping the children of the freedpeople. Freedmen's Bureau assistant commissioners in Maryland, North Carolina, and the District of Columbia reported in the fall of 1866 numerous cases of illegal indentures of apprenticeship that had occurred since emancipation, and usually when parents were willing and able to care for their children. Although parents could choose to apprentice their children, in the United States and the British Caribbean they refused almost uniformly to do so.[49] While clearly an attempt to secure fixed labor, the apprenticeship of freed children after abolition cannot be separated from the larger cultural issue of maintaining an identity based on the possession of Blacks, as evidenced in the case of Albert Hamlin, who after abducting an apprenticed teenager was forced to leave his home and family in Abbeville, South Carolina.[50]

Reflecting the general society's concern with independence, derived from the cultural understanding of freedom, the issues of vagrancy and idleness seemed to have most concerned the framers of the Black Codes. The Texas "Act to define the office of vagrancy, and to provide for the punishments of vagrants" gave the classical interpretation of a vagrant: "an idle person, living without any means of support, and making no exertions to obtain a livelihood by any honest employment." Yet these terms constituted political languages that were not value-neutral; for they were not only descriptive but also prescriptive, as they would determine how the society behaved toward Blacks in the postslavery period. In actuality, the definition of vagrancy had nothing to do with groups of ex-slaves wandering off and being completely idle. What remained at issue was *the instituting of a set of behavioral norms* that were designed not only to confine the ex-slaves to the plantations but also to control the behaviors of those who remained on them as part of the reaffirmation of a specific conception of order and what it means to be fully human. For this reason, an Alabama law could declare a "stubborn or refractory servant" to be a vagrant.[51]

This cultural function of the claim to prevent vagrancy and idleness can be seen from further examination of the Black Codes in Mississippi and South Carolina, which amplified the meaning to encompass any action that deviated—literally, wandered away—from the notion of order. In addition to the expected categories of rogues, beggars, vagabonds, and idle persons, vagrants in the case of the former included "wanton, or lascivious persons, in speech or behavior," those who "misspend what they earn," persons who "habitually misspend their time by frequenting houses of ill-fame, gaming houses, or tippling shops" and "dependents," those who could not take care of their families.[52] Without asking what rendered some unable to take care of their families, these laws criminalize what in most instances were effects of the slavery and postslavery political-labor system. Although the Civil War had forced a political reorganization of the Southern states, it had not transformed the conception of order that undergirded it. Carl Schurz remarked upon this phenomenon in his report when he cited the Mississippi assistant commissioner, who stated that White Southerners "still have an ingrained feeling that the blacks at large belong to the whites at large," and even when forced to admit that the Black has become free and "has ceased to be the property of a master," Schurz noted, "it is not admitted that he has a right to become his own master."[53]

The specific political language of vagrancy appeared as well in legislation in the British Caribbean and, as in the United States, was marked by representations that signified symbolic actions that breached social norms. A December 1835 act passed in St. Kitts declared vagrancy as "knowingly spreading any false report to the commission of any act of insubordination." Anyone convicted under this law could be punished with sixty lashes and six months' imprisonment. In Dominica one could become a vagrant simply by making noise in the street. The Jamaica Assembly proposed legislation (eventually disallowed by Parliament) "to restrain and punish Vagrancy" defined as "all persons who run away and leave their wives or children chargeable to any parish, town, or place, without visible means of support," as well as people "wandering abroad lodging in taverns, outhouses, negro houses or in the open air or in huts" — in other words, those not attached to plantations. Moreover, "all persons pretending to be dealers in obeah" or those "not giving good account of themselves" could also be classified as vagrants. This law, passed at the same time as the Jamaica Abolition Act (12 December 1833), embodied more than an attempt to control labor, although this element remained extremely important; by attempting to suppress obeah practitioners, the strategy here went beyond labor questions so that African-derived cultural forms that challenged the Judeo-Christian beliefs could also be suppressed.[54]

Another political claim that emerged in the postslavery era directly reflected an unambiguous attempt to control labor. Although the results differed, in both the British Caribbean and the U.S. South, the immediate response to the emancipation of Black slaves was to encourage the immigration of foreign labor. As early as May 1834 in Jamaica, a planter from St. George's parish, John Myers, had facilitated the immigration of sixty-three Germans.[55] Discussion also occurred of the possibility of importing Maltese and Antiguan (who were not apprentices but reputed to be unconditionally free) laborers in order to replace the native Jamaican laboring population, because, as a committee of planters asserted, "we who know the habits of negroes . . . know that without coercion they will not labor."[56] Over the next few months, Assembly members made several proposals related to immigration, eventually passing in December a law to establish towns for the immigrants.[57]

As a test case, Myers's importation of German laborers (for which he received a bounty of £15 per person plus additional costs totaling £7,590) raised issues that would define the immigration issue in Jamaica as well as in other colonies of the British Caribbean. The handling of the situation with the Germans pleased neither Governor Sligo nor the local politicians. The immigrants complained to Governor Sligo of mistreatment and of having been lied to by Myers. Some became servants, while others worked on his coffee plantation. The inspector general, William Ramsay, conveyed to Governor Sligo that the immigrants had been promised they would not have to work on plantations but rather could work at their respective trades, receiving the supposed high wages to which they had become accustomed at home. They did not have enough food to eat, stating that in Germany they had bread and meat, whereas in Jamaica they "cannot eat plantains and corn rind." The immigrants declared that they would "sooner be killed here at once than return to the Estates to die by Inches." They demanded to be sent home or taken into the police force, which, in fact, did occur for some of them.[58]

Government officials claimed that they learned an important lesson from this first attempt at immigration. The governor's secretary, William Nunes, expressed that he regretted what happened because rather than showing "industry and diligence to the Negroes," the affair "will probably lead them to think their state more than what it really is."[59] Such a sentiment made explicit that the local government's endorsement of immigration stemmed from two objectives: to provide a role model for the former slaves in habits of industry, so they would learn how to work (and, by inference, behave properly) as free laborers; and to show that ex-slaves, although free, should not think they have too much power in defining the new terms of labor.

Out of concern for the welfare of the colonies, the entrepreneur A. A. Lindo wrote letters to Jamaican planters as well as government and business officials in support of immigration. In his correspondence, Lindo stressed the need for emancipation to be carried out "with due interests of [England], justice to the owners, and the well-being of the negroes themselves." He proposed that the way to secure the welfare of the empire would be through the emigration to the West Indies of Europeans, "whose habits of industry and their happy effects to themselves, might lead the negro to fall into them likewise." Arthur Welch, a special magistrate stationed in Manchester, apparently agreed: "The importation of white emigrants will be beneficial as an example to the negroes, who will be pleased to see white men labor; and I consider it will cause emulation."[60]

In his letter to the earl of Aberdeen, secretary of the Colonial Office, Lindo expressed a concern about the state of Jamaica after the transitional period of apprenticeship would come to an end. The issue for Lindo remained "how the advantages, hitherto derived by this country from one of the most important of its possessions, may still be preserved under the new order of things." When considering this "new order of things," Lindo invoked racialized language to justify different treatment, stating that "coercion, beyond what the law allows to be used to incite a white man to labour, cannot . . . be exercised towards a black man." The dilemma then became how were the ex-slaves going to be induced to work, especially considering "the natural aversion of all men to hard bodily labour" and that the Black laborer "will refuse to exert himself beyond what is necessary for procuring such articles as may satisfy his most urgent wants." This situation existed, Lindo claimed, because Blacks could "subsist contentedly on the coarsest food," required "scarcely any clothing," and cared "little about accumulating wealth, for the purpose of acquiring what we deem necessaries and comforts."[61]

Consequently, Lindo proposed, the large tracts of unoccupied crown lands in the interior of the island should be settled by "German, Scotch and Irish peasantry and even small farmers, who cannot make out a subsistence in Europe." This strategy would be a great saving to England and "a blessing to the island of Jamaica; the interior trade of which would be greatly benefited, since a white population will always consume much more of manufactures than the negroes." Moreover, given that "the wants of negroes being fewer and more easily supplied, they will be able at all times to work at a lower rate than the whites." The presence of these immigrants "would lead the negroes to adopt European habits of order and industry" by a "more humane course" preferable to the "the former system of coercion, or to the scarcely less inhuman supiness, that would leave them to run riot in a state of freedom."[62]

Whether the suggestion came from planters or from entrepreneurs, the message implicitly conveyed by the immediate postabolition call for immigration was the extent to which immigrants would be granted the very inducements, such as land, that the planters refused to give the native Black population. A May 1835 memorial presented to Governor Sligo by a Trelawny coalition of "Proprietors, Planters, and others concerned in the management of Plantations" stated unequivocally that "the only chance now left of continuing this Island as a valuable colony to Great Britain, is by the settlement of white families in the interior." The petitioners claimed that because the interior climate was more temperate, it would allow Europeans to perform the required labor for the cultivation of coffee and provisions. It was also contemplated that "the males would form a valuable body of police" and that they may even be used on sugar estates and other plantations, "where, by their industry, they would set a good example to the apprentices." Moreover, with Europeans occupying these lands, "they would prevent the idle and dissolute negroes from making them places of resort when the period of absolute freedom arrives." It became important therefore that the ex-slaves not be able to possess lands, because "[i]f the lands in the Interior get into the possession of the Negro, *goodbye to lowland cultivation, and to any cultivation.*"[63]

Across the Caribbean, planters, fearing the collapse of the estates, claimed that the new terms of freedom, which allowed some women and children to withdraw from field labor, could be remedied only by "a steady and certain command of labour," as with the immigration of foreign laborers. The governor of Trinidad, Lord Harris, unequivocally stated, "I have no hesitation in saying that on [immigration] depends, under God, the welfare of the island." The Combined Court in British Guiana passed a resolution in 1850 to resume immigration after a hiatus because "the agricultural interests of British Guiana are greatly aggravated by the want of continuous labour." Rather than asking what led to such conflicting social and labor relations, planters posited that immigration would become the panacea for the postslavery labor problems that existed across the British Caribbean. The House of Commons Committee on the West India Colonies also assented to this claim: "The most obvious and desirous mode of endeavouring to compensate for this diminished supply of labour, is to promote the immigration of a fresh labouring population, to such an extent as to create competition for employment."[64]

With the financial and political support of the government, Jamaican planters tried more schemes until late in the century to bring in immigrant laborers, most of which ended unsuccessfully. The ex-slaves, of course, protested, noting the political strategy working against their interests. Additionally, many White missionaries vehemently criticized immigration plans, but usually on the basis of preventing the importing of pagan ideas from non-Christian Africans.[65] These attempts included bringing immigrants not only from Europe but also some from Africa (including some liberated slaves from ships and settlers in Sierra Leone), India, Portugal, China, and North America (including a small number of Blacks from the United States). In larger numbers, these populations migrated to British Guiana and Trinidad as well, constituting the most significant labor migration to the British West Indies after the abolition of slavery. Between 1834 and 1865, more than 25,000 laborers migrated to Jamaica, while in Trinidad, twice this number and in British Guiana, five times this number eventually immigrated to these colonies.[66]

Immigration as a solution to labor problems related to the legal emancipation of slaves emerged in the U.S. South in a political crusade within similar terms. The editors of journals like *De Bow's Review* carried on a campaign to bring in foreign labor.[67] Moreover, immediately after abolition, states across the South established agencies to encourage immigration. Georgia, Louisiana, and South Carolina created immigration bureaus in 1866. In the same year, five companies were incorporated in Virginia to facilitate the immigration of White laborers. Later, other states acted likewise: Tennessee in 1867, Arkansas in 1868, Florida in 1869, and Texas in 1871 established bureaus to encourage foreign laborers to migrate to the South. Alabama provided for a commissioner with.agents abroad from 1875 to 1877. In North Carolina in 1869 a land company was chartered to encourage immigration, although an official agency was not created until 1874. In 1873 the Republican government in Mississippi formed a department of agriculture and immigration, upon which the Democrats elaborated in the following decade. An observation in reference to the situation in South Carolina can be generalized to other Southern states: "[T]he great panacea for the political and economic ills of the state was immigration."[68]

As occurred in the British Caribbean, support for immigration came from both sides of the question of abolition.[69] Contemplating what he termed the "higher laws which govern the progress of humanity," the staunch critic of South Carolina's Reconstruction government, James Pike, contended that "on the question of immigration . . . the interest of the State requires it."[70] While certainly it was no surprise that states' rights proponents supported measures to undermine the bargaining power of the ex-slaves, the humanitarian friends of the freedpeople also seemed to agree with the necessity of immigration, ostensibly for different reasons. South Carolina assistant commissioner Rufus Saxton "highly approved" of Scottish and other peoples migrating to the South because "[h]er fruitful fields need cultivation, as they have been left desolate by the war." In a statement ironically resembling that of the Trelawny proprietors, Saxton contended that the lands would remain uncultivated "for a long period of time period unless Emigration is encouraged hither."[71] Saxton's superior, Commissioner Howard, acknowledged support for immigration in a circular letter where he stressed to his subordinates that they were forbidden to invest in projects to encourage foreign labor. Howard stated the specific reason as to why he felt the need to bring in workers from other countries: "In order to meet an emergency, when the whole system of labor was deranged, the Commissioner urged the forming of joint companies, the encouragement of the imigration [*sic*] of those accustomed to free labor, so as to afford promptly, as many examples as possible, of the successful employment of negroes under a free system."[72] Even Carl Schurz, who often astutely pointed out the political strategies of Southerners to keep Blacks subordinated, claimed that, for the South, immigration would "contribute much to the solution of the labor problem."[73]

Although these immigration schemes failed to settle a significant nonnative laboring population in the South, the important fact remained that "the desire was very real," and this aspiration definitely affected the political situation. It seems that whether the Southern labor supply in actuality was insufficient mattered less than "whether the Southern employer thought that it was."[74] For it was on the basis of this belief that those calling for immigration in both the British Caribbean and the U.S. South could claim they were doing so out of an expressed concern for the general prosperity of the society. As Pike's assertion implied, the general well-being of the social order depended on such a solution, a link most clearly made by the free-trade advocate Herman Merivale. Merivale, who later served as permanent under secretary for the colonies, contended that without immigration, which could depress the high wages the Black ex-slaves demanded, the plantations would be destroyed and "the *best interests of humanity* will have received a shock which it may take centuries to repair."[75] This perspective represented more than the ideology of a ruling class (although that it certainly was), as the belief that the interests of humanity were being secured with immigration constituted a genuine understanding of how the society should be governed.

Given the intellectual strategy of linking immigration with the securing of the common good, the use of public funds for the costly projects becomes logical. After passing the act that created the commissioner of immigration, the South Carolina legislature appropriated $10,000 to cover outlays related to this objective. In the Caribbean, local governments risked financial stability in order to facilitate immigration. Trinidad, reputed as one of the more fiscally sound islands, sold £30,000 in assets to cover immigration expenditures. A large portion of Jamaica's debt in the 1840s resulted from expenses related to immigration schemes, a development that, even when combined with other failed attempts, did not prevent the government from reviving this plan in 1852 with another £100,000 loan. As a consequence, immigration had a serious effect on the financial situation of the colonies. By 1858 "Jamaica had spent £231,488 to import immigrant workers and £21,404 for return passages — about ten times the educational expenditures over the same period."[76] Taking into account the inducements given to immigrant laborers that would not be given to the native labor pool, it does seem, particularly in the British Caribbean, that "the freedmen, through taxation, financed the bringing in of laborers whose purpose was to reduce their own standard of living." In an ironic moment, the immigration society in Newberry, South Carolina, recognized the contradiction: "The wages and rations that the Newberry Society prescribed for its charges were nearly twice those of Negro workers, and the fringe benefits — quarters, garden plots, and fuel privileges — were much more generous than those allowed Negroes." Such fiscal policies provoked some humanitarians to suggest that the funds used to underwrite the costs of immigration could have been put to a more constructive use.[77]

Proponents of White immigration to the South often gave the reason for their claim as the need to dilute the potential voting bloc of Blacks should they be granted the franchise. The gaining of suffrage during Reconstruction for Blacks in the United States constituted a significant difference with the emancipation process in the British Caribbean. Yet the way in which the issue emerged in Jamaica paralleled in some ways what occurred with Black Americans in the United States. During the colonial era in the United States, political power was confined to the holders of landed property. Within this political order, many Blacks who owned property voted. As W. E. B. Du Bois noted, "[T]here was not a single Southern colony in which a Black man who owned the requisite amount of property, and complied with other conditions, did not at some period have the right to vote." In some Northern states as well, property-holding Black males could vote. However, a change began to occur with westward expansion in the 1830s when midwestern and southwestern states began to enter the Union. At this time, Blacks who previously met the voting qualification were now gradually being disenfranchised, while states with low populations offered any alien White male the vote immediately upon immigration.[78] While the 1821 New York Constitution continued to allow propertied Black males to vote, increasingly a shift was occurring whereby the political language of "Race" replaced that of property as the qualifier for the vote, in effect, making the symbolic attribute of whiteness into a property itself.[79] Although in some non-Western agrarian societies, the holding of property connoted value, this tradition of linking property to freedom has its origins in medieval conceptions of liberty.[80]

Therefore, later during Reconstruction when Blacks demanded the vote, it would be due to the historic development, first, with the American Revolution and the "rights of man" discourse and, second, with the democratization process that occurred during the 1830s. "I want the elective franchise," Frederick Douglass stated, "because ours is a peculiar government, based upon a peculiar idea, and that idea is universal suffrage." Employing a precise historical analysis, one that also referred to the culture-specific understanding of freedom, he contended that if he lived under an autocratic or aristocratic government, "where the few bore rule and the many were subject, there would be no special stigma resting upon me, because I did not exercise the elective franchise." Yet, in the United States, "where universal suffrage is the rule, where that is the fundamental idea of the Government, to rule us out is to make us an exception, to brand us with the stigma of inferiority, and to invite to our heads the missiles of those about us."[81]

In a parallel situation to the pre-Jacksonian United States, the question of the vote in Britain and its colonial extensions remained restricted to a qualified elite of property holders. Given the vast differences in numbers between White and Black (and, before emancipation, between free and slave), the colonial assemblies represented only a small percentage of the Caribbean population. Once abolition began to challenge the foundation of the social order, however, the Jamaican legislature attempted to mitigate the transformative potential of making Blacks citizens by enfranchising *marginalized* groups (as distinct from the *subordinated* slave population group) such as Jews, Catholics, and "free persons of colour." This process of incorporation was clearly designed to compel these intermediate groups to ally themselves with the slaveholding *Herrenvolk*.

In December 1827 an act was passed "to entitle Jews, born within the legiance of the King's to the rights and privileges of other natural-born British subjects." The law, noting the historical treatment of Jews as discriminatory, stated that "it was expedient that the disabilities under which they have hitherto laboured should be removed." This law complemented one passed a year earlier that repealed the 1711 law prohibiting "the employment in the several Public Officers . . . of any Jew, Mulatto, Indian, or Negro."[82] A December 1829 law made it possible for Roman Catholics, upon taking an oath, to sit and vote in the legislative bodies of Jamaica (the Assembly and the Council).[83] Provided that a free person of color had the requisite property, a February 1830 law removed the "politically-imposed disability" that prevented members of this group from voting.[84]

Soon after abolition took effect, the Jamaica Assembly passed in December 1834 an "Act to amend the Elective Franchise." This law raised the property requirement for voting and holding office. In order to vote, one now had to pay £5 in taxes or £50 in rent, and to hold office in the Assembly, the citizen had to have £300 in annual income or £3,000 in landed property. The next year, the Assembly raised the qualification to vote to £10 in taxes, which apparently was still not satisfactory, for the 1836 session proposed tripling the 1835 qualification. The governor of the island, Sir Lionel Smith, approved the "admirably calculated" alteration, because it would "raise the respectability of Candidates for those Offices." Such an act was needed, Smith claimed, because a threat from the "lower Classes" was occurring with a few leading men, who "with ignorant and violent materials" had "easily found a means of preponderance in Elections . . . by erecting Huts then easily sworn to us as of £10 value." The implication therefore was quite serious, for "[m]en without any ostensible property" had begun to exercise "the Privilege of laying on the Parochial Assessments on those who have Property."[85] The blatant discriminatory intent of the 1836 law forced the colonial secretary to disallow this last act, although the earlier acts remained sufficiently proscriptive to disenfranchise the Black majority.

Ironically, during the same time period, the 1830s, when in the United States Whites employed the political language of race to disqualify propertied Blacks from holding the franchise, in Jamaica, planters used the language of property to disqualify Blacks (as a racially defined population group) from voting. Although property had been important in qualifying those who could vote (only Anglo-Saxon Protestants), after emancipation it was utilized in a more rigorous fashion to disqualify those of the "lower Classes." By the 1860s the percentage of voters, while having slightly increased since abolition, still remained quite small. In British Guiana, 2,046 people out of 270,000 had the privilege to vote; in Jamaica, 3,000 out of 440,000 could vote. Grenada and St. Vincent, with slightly more than 30,000 inhabitants, had only 191 and 273 electors respectively.[86] With a history not unlike that of Black Americans, who with their allies fought so hard to secure the vote, the ex-slaves in the British Caribbean would be disenfranchised until the next century. Whether the qualification was linked to property or based on a racial designation, the intent of the strategy remained the same: a Black electoral bloc could not be permitted to exist. On this point hinged the politics of Morant Bay and Redemption. For although the vote in Jamaica could be extended to the commercial middle classes, as well as to formerly marginalized religious groups such as Jews and Catholics, such could not have been the case for the former slaves.

The issue of franchise, like those of colonial or state government autonomy, labor control, and immigration, remains important for examining the nature of the political context after emancipation. Evaluation of these political strategies in terms of whether the specific project was successful (immigration or Black Codes in the United States, the vote in the Caribbean) responds to only one side of the historical question. As Woodville Marshall has observed, the historical literature, while full of the details of the labor polices after emancipation, remains *"largely silent on the models for these policies."* This assertion can be generalized to these other issues as well. A need exists to understand the conceptual models on which these claims were based, especially given how in both the British Caribbean and the United States the representations in the political languages did not necessarily correspond to the empirical reality. Nowhere is such a dynamic clearer than with the claim that a "labor problem" existed after slavery, defined as a need for "a steady and certain command of labour." Marshall insisted: "This may be a loaded term. It suggests a particular perspective: a labour problem of a particular sort had to exist once the slaves were freed. This was evidently the view of the planters, of the Colonial Office, of the abolitionists: all of them said so, and in this regard their actions matched their words."[87] Thus, defining the issue as a "labor problem" in the historiography could continue the erasure of the perspectives of the ex-slaves. The postslavery political situation hinged upon the reorganization of the society and the terms in which social stability would be instituted. Such, in effect, were the purposes of the political languages of immigration, local autonomy or states' rights, and the franchise.

Nevertheless, in some way all of these strategies served to maintain the plantation system. Consequently, prosperity continued to be defined in terms of the cultivation of crops, with ruin being the destruction of order and stability putatively generated from the plantation social structure. In a rare moment of balance, the secretary of state, Lord John Russell, noted the political strategy implicit in such a formulation whereby "the term 'ruin' is used to designate, not the poverty of the people, not the want of food or raiment, not even the absence of riches or luxury, but simply the decrease of sugar cultivation."[88] It is precisely this conception of the social order, and of the general good, that the ex-slaves challenged from a perspective of utopia, that is, not as escapism or resistance, but rather as the possibility of cultural transformation. Indeed, if the former slave societies genuinely desired an inclusively free society, a new definition of prosperity, one able to include the well-being of the ex-slaves on their own terms, that is, their transcendent political languages, needed to be conceptualized.

Chapter Three

This Work of Civilization
The Secular, Evangelical Mission of the Special Magistrates and the Freedmen's Bureau Officials

The most striking remark which [the custos] made to us on his mode of management was, that the white people on the estates required as much attention and oversight to keep them in their proper place as the negroes.
—Joseph Sturge and Thomas Harvey,
   The West Indies in 1837

It will take many years to make an economical and thrifty man out of a freedman, and about as long to make a sensible and just employer out of a former slaveholder.
—Edward Philbrick, 1865

In an article published several months before the end of the Civil War, Lyman Abbott, the noted minister and general secretary of the American Freedmen's Union Commission, suggested that after the North defeated the South, it would still have to be occupied with ideas to reconstruct it as a "free" society: "We have not only to conquer the South—we have also to convert it. We have not only to occupy it by bayonets and bullets—but also by ideas and institutions." Only a mission of "Southern evangelization," Abbott argued, could make having fought the physical war meaningful: "If we fail in our second task, success in the first will be of little use." This task had earlier been articulated with respect to the cultivation of cotton by Edward Atkinson, one of the Boston investors during the Port Royal experience: "It is already evident that the whole cotton country must be permeated and regenerated by New England men and by New England ideas." In the memoirs of his travels in the Carolinas during the fall of 1865, Sidney Andrews's impressions demonstrated that a general conceptual transformation of the South, which included a change in labor organization, would become the central issue in the reorganization of the region after slavery. Based on "the Northern idea of right and wrong, justice and injustice, humanity and inhumanity," Andrews claimed, there existed enough "work ready for the hand of every New England man and woman who stand waiting" to "bring here the conveniences and comforts of our Northern civilization."[1]

The U.S. federal government delegated much of the task of implanting Northern virtues in the "rebellious" and "backward" South to the Bureau of Refugees, Freedmen, and Abandoned Lands. Central to the Freedmen's Bureau's secular, though no less evangelical, mission remained the instituting of economic relations based on the ideology of free labor. Within the "utopian assumptions" of many officials, once the bureau provided a helping hand to the South, Southern society could then be governed naturally by the invisible hand of the free market: "With the Bureau acting as midwife at its birth, the free market would quickly assume its role as arbiter of the South's economic destinies, honing those qualities that distinguished free labor from slave." Yet the ex-slaves in South Carolina, it has been shown, did not completely adopt the emerging industrial middle-class conception of the social reality. While Blacks rejected the mode of subordination associated with being held as property, they also "challenged emergent claims that subjection to landowners' management and to the discipline of an abstract market constituted freedom."[2]

Although abolition in the English Caribbean did not immediately result from a violent civil war as it did in the United States,[3] the political struggle that brought slavery to an end nevertheless had to be completed with new ideas and institutions in the postslavery context. The British Parliament delegated this role to the special magistrates, those regarded as the "architects of freedom," or, as they have also been described, the "mid-wives" who, like the agents of the bureau, had to assist in giving birth to a new social order. This idea of bureaucratic agents facilitating the ex-slaves' transition from slavery to postslavery fitted within the general intellectual framework that defined the emancipation process in the British Caribbean: "[T]he legal systems of the West Indies and the conceptions of Justice which prevailed there made [the special magistracy] essential." Once the precedent had been established with the 1824 Trinidad Order in Council, which created an office of Protector of Slaves, when the emancipation question later arose in a House of Commons committee in 1832, it was asserted that the appointment of government officials to protect and instruct the ex-slaves would be necessary for the successful implementation of the emancipation process.[4]

The legal acts establishing the special magistrates and the Freedmen's Bureau provide a useful point of departure for examining their respective roles, and how the political languages that underlay their policies would give the emancipation process a specific form. In order to give effect to the 1833 Act for the Abolition of Slavery, according to Section XIV of the law, the king was authorized, or could authorize the governor of any colony, to issue special commissions as justices of the peace to be responsible for "the effectual Superintendence of the said apprenticed Labourers." Only the special magistrates had the power "to punish any such apprentice Labourer for any Offence by him or her committed or alleged to have been committed by the whipping, beating, or Imprisonment of his or her Person." If the employers committed an offense, this also came under the authority of the special magistrates. Moreover, the act stipulated in broad language that "in their Relation to each other, or of the Breach, Violation, or Neglect of any of the Obligations owed by them to each other, *or of any Question, Matter, or Thing incident to or arising out of the Relations* subsisting between such apprenticed Labourers and the Persons respectively entitled to their Services" remained the exclusive jurisdiction of the special magistrates.[5]

After a discussion that extended over more than two years, on 3 March 1865 the U.S. Congress passed An Act to Establish a Bureau for the Relief of

Freedmen and Refugees to be administered under the War Department. In broad terms reminiscent of the British Abolition Act, the first section of the act described the primary task of the bureau as being "the supervision and management of all abandoned lands, and *the control of all subjects relating to refugees and freedmen* from rebel states, or from any district of country within the territory embraced in the operations of the army." With appointments being made by the president, the operations of the bureau were to be executed by a head commissioner and by assistant commissioners located in insurrectionary states. Like the special magistrates, the assistant and subassistant commissioners had to submit periodic reports of the proceedings in their states or, in the case of the head commissioner, the proceedings of the agency. A result of the disruption caused by the war, the act further provided that the secretary of war could issue provisions of clothing and fuel to destitute and suffering refugees and ex-slaves. The fourth and later the most contested section of the act concerned the issue of land, which, under the direction of the president, gave the commissioner the authority to set apart, "for the use of loyal refugees and freedmen, such tracts of land within the insurrectionary states as shall have been abandoned, or to which the United States shall have acquired title by confiscation or sale, or otherwise."[6]

An association with the military often formed a part of the background of the special magistrates and agents of the Freedmen's Bureau. While some of the officers appointed as special magistrates were half-pay retirees from the British army and naval forces, in the case of the United States the bureau came under the jurisdiction of the War Department and some of its agents had served in the Civil War. The military experience would be useful as both of these positions demanded a certain amount of physical exertion. This situation became especially true in Jamaica, where some special magistrates had to visit estates in mountainous regions of the island. These physical demands led many to complain of the inadequate nature of the pay for such arduous duties. On their 1837 voyage in the British West Indies, the English missionaries Joseph Sturge and Thomas Harvey noted the difficulties that came with being a special magistrate: "Their districts are often twenty miles in extent, in a country more mountainous than Wales or Scotland; frequently they cannot obtain houses within them; they are required to visit each estate twice a month; and in order to do this, are obliged to keep from two to four horses, and to incur other charges which their salaries are totally inadequate to sustain." The magistrates received £300 sterling per year, a salary described by one historian as "a niggardly display of imperial meanness, especially in view of the £20,000,000 compensation awarded the planters." However, as a result of the dedicated lobbying of Governor Sligo beginning in November 1834, the Colonial Office finally agreed in July 1835 to supplement the pay of the special magistrates with a £150 allowance for the keeping of horses and for housing-related expenses.[7]

The perceived low rate of pay, coupled with the political tightrope they had to negotiate, made the job of the special magistrates taxing. Richard Chamberlaine, stationed in St. Thomas in the East, contended that the special magistrate could expect cooperation from the planters and succeed in carrying out his duties "only when he renders himself an object of terror to the apprentices." Edward Baynes, located in the parish of St. John, argued that with those in his position being the "objects of so much undeserved jealously and odium," he could think of few services "so harassing and ungrateful as those of the special magistrate." It was a no-win situation, for if the magistrate attempted to administer punishment judiciously, Baynes asserted, "he is instantly assailed and vilified in public journals as endeavouring to relax the reins of discipline." Yet, if he should act as a "strict disciplinarian," Baynes said, adding that "in some districts such a character is highly necessary," the special magistrate "incurs the ill-will of the negroes, who flock by hundreds to the seat of the government to complain of him." The response of many to these pressures, Sturge and Harvey concluded, should "cease to surprise that so many of them have fallen victims to their labours, or have withdrawn in disgust," given "the incessant persecutions of the planters, and the harassing pursuit of their duties, under a burning sun."[8]

Due to the expressed feeling that the Freedmen's Bureau would be a temporary institution, the U.S. Congress made no appropriations for the organization immediately following its establishment in March 1865. Both funds for paying staff as well as the supplies for Blacks and needy refugees came from the War Department. The commissary general of the army furnished rations, the quartermaster provided clothing, and the surgeon general donated medical and hospital supplies. The bureau also derived substantial income from the rental of abandoned estates, which in South Carolina alone amounted to over $6,000 per month by the end of the year. In July of the following year, Congress finally appropriated funds to the bureau, with stipulations for the increase in the number of assistant commissioners from ten to twelve as well as setting the maximum salary for local civilian agents at $1,200 per year.[9]

The terms that would govern the execution of freedom for the former slaves became clear from instructions given in the early stages of the emancipation processes in Jamaica and the United States. A few months after the apprenticeship phase began, Governor Sligo of Jamaica sent a circular letter to the special magistrates outlining their primary duties. The magistrates had to visit each estate within their district at least once every two weeks, keeping "an exact diary" of occurrences on the plantations, especially noting any disputes. The special justices, as they were sometimes called, were to make weekly reports for themselves, which were later sent to the governor in Spanish Town by the first post of each month. A significant part of the job also involved the valuation of apprentices who wished to purchase their freedom, the prices of which were determined by witnesses who could testify to the value of the laborer's services before and after the first of August 1834. Given the often disparate interests of the participants in the emancipation process, valuations, which when finalized issued a "Certificate of Freedom," predictably became contentious.[10]

More important than valuations, however, the administering of punishment became a central requirement for the special magistracy. For this reason, as Secretary of the Colonial Office Edward Stanley noted in his July 1833 address to the House of Commons, military officers, who were accustomed to enforcing discipline, should be encouraged to serve in this position. When dispensing punishment, Sligo reminded the magistrates, the optimal goal remained the securing of as much labor as possible from the former slaves: "In the adjudication of punishment it is recommended that where ever the offence will allow it you should allot the punishment in such a way as to give the estate as much Labour as you can." He stated unequivocally that when it could be done without injury to justice, "the Interests of the proprietor are to be Considered in the punishment." This assertion was not an accidental one, but formed part of the dominant understanding of emancipation, as illustrated by the governor's emphasis on the importance of the Vagrant Acts in a context described as one of freedom. Although the Vagrant Acts contradicted some basic principles of freedom, according to Sligo, they were "intimately connected with that great measure [of abolition]" and therefore should serve for the special magistrates "as [the] Code of instructions and guide in the Performance of [their] duties." The governor did not overlook the coercion (and by inference the attempt to resubordinate the ex-slaves) implicit in these acts, as he gave unequivocal support to these strategies of social control: "It is also the duty of the special magistrate to point out to the Apprentice, how much *it is his interest to Conciliate his Master* by reasonable Concession and a willing performance of that labour, *which if not freely Given, must be enforced by the power of Coercion which has been provided by the Law.*"[11]

In outlining the parameters for punishing the ex-slaves, Sligo's "General Instructions" reflected the tension between personal liberty and subordination defining the postslavery situation. Freedom did not mean the ex-slaves could ignore the commands of the ex-slaveholder; indeed, the former slaves were to "conciliate" them by "reasonable Concession and a willing performance." The underlying implication remained that ex-slaves should not have the expectation that freedom would mean the license to define the situation on their terms, but that a certain obligation remained to the governing powers, illustrating that what the society understood by freedom was a postslavery set of norms that should regulate the thoughts and behaviors of the former slaves.

From the beginning of his tenure as the assistant commissioner of South Carolina, Rufus Saxton remained committed to helping the ex-slaves acquire land, for as W. E. B. Du Bois remarked, he held a "deep interest in black folk." Despite this commitment, Saxton asserted that Blacks should not immediately expect to acquire all their rights as free people: "If you do not obtain all rights this year," he stated in a circular to the former slaves, "be content with part, and if you act rightly, all will come in good time." A month before Saxton issued his circular, Head Commissioner Oliver Howard asserted a similar claim. While instructing assistant commissioners and agents of the bureau to protect the freedpeople from the "avarice and extortion" of dishonest Whites, Howard pointed out that some suffering among the freedpeople may result. He contended, however, that "suffering is preferable to slavery, and is, to some degree, the necessary consequence of events." Within this particular understanding of the past—that is, one defined by the political language of gradualism—the fact that Blacks had already endured more than their fair share of hardship under slavery could not be acknowledged. So, despite the historical record, the former slaves were advised to "be patient and hopeful" for they were being told that "[t]he nation, through this Bureau, has taken your cause in hand, and will endeavor to do you ample justice."[12]

Justice was precisely the issue, as Frederick Douglass noted when he questioned the primacy of humanitarian gestures over measures that could ensure that the ex-slaves would have the right to govern their own lives, a guarantee that could be secured only with equal rights and protection of these rights under the law. Before the end of the war and the creation of the Freedmen's Bureau, Douglass challenged the moral interpretation implicit in much of the later policies concerning the postslavery condition of Blacks: "We would not for one moment check the outgrowth of any benevolent concern for the future welfare of the colored race in America or elsewhere; but in the name of reason and religion, we earnestly plead for justice before all else." The emphasis on justice, that is, politics, rather than moral uplift became central to the debate on a "bureau of emancipation."[13]

Two years after Douglass espoused this idea, Edward Atkinson suggested that, while he supported the concept of such a bureau, he also admonished against a focus on the supervision of Blacks: "Let them avoid over-legislation, too much guardianship, too much taking care, but recognize in the negro a man fully competent to make his own contracts, if protected from injustice and abuse." As an advocate of laissez-faire economics, Atkinson defended the right of individual choice and self-determination, asserting that the only coercion that the ex-slaves needed was "to be paid fair wages for a fair day's work." Douglass and Atkinson's apprehensions were shared by some of the assistant commissioners of the bureau. Clinton B. Fisk, head of operations in Kentucky and Tennessee, noted that the "superintendents will be cautioned against supervising too much," while, in words almost identical to Douglass's, Thomas W. Osborn of Florida contended that the ex-slaves there "need no sympathy above other people, but they require justice at the hands of the people and of the government."[14] Had the federal government and especially the Freedmen's Bureau continued to stress the issue of justice for the ex-slaves, rather than shifting the focus onto the character of Blacks, the postslavery situation, it has been suggested, may have been quite different: "Never before in American history had there been such an organized effort towards such a humanitarian end [as the Freedmen's Bureau]. It was, in short, an endeavor of warm generosity and kind human response to great human need, made without reference to sectional boundaries or political differences. Had its spirit carried over into the realm of politics between North and South during the same period, the nation itself may well have been spared some harsh moments and unhappy memories."[15]

Although the former slaves had not demanded the establishment of an institution like the Freedmen's Bureau, once it was created they supported the organization. However, as a resolution adopted at the 1865 Colored People's Convention in South Carolina illustrated, the ex-slaves emphasized the bureau's duties that involved the protection of their political rights, noting that such an institution would be needed only temporarily until these rights could be completely obtained: "*Resolved,* That we, the delegates in Convention, representing the colored people of the State of South Carolina, do earnestly request the Government to continue the Freedmen's Bureau *until such time as we are fully protected in our persons and property by the laws of the State.*"[16] Black gratitude and support of the bureau, a logical response given the immediate physical needs stemming from the war as well as the White antipathy that persisted after slavery, should not, however, be confused with the perspective that saw this kind of organization as the key to the success of the emancipation process. In the original conception of their freedom, the ex-slaves never demanded the establishment of a supervisory, paternalist organization. And, unlike the slaveholders in the British Caribbean, who were compensated for the abolition of slavery, and those in the United States, where Lincoln attempted to entice border state planters to free their slaves with monetary incentives, the ex-slaves, whose labor beginning with their ancestors extended over several centuries in the Americas, did not receive any direct payment in compensation for their toil.[17] And neither did they ask for such a form of compensation.

What the Black ex-slaves in the British Caribbean and the U.S. South insisted upon was the attainment of freedom on their terms. And because this freedom had to have a political and economic base, it was associated with the protection of rights as well as some kind of landownership. This desire for independence could take different forms. In Jamaica, for instance, the desire for land led in some parts of the island to the formation of free village settlements. The Baptist missionary James Phillippo helped to establish the first of such communities in the hills above Spanish Town in 1835. Although the reports of special magistrates that claimed that the establishment of small freeholders was "rapid and unceasing" seem exaggerated from a historical perspective, nevertheless, given that throughout the republican Anglo-Americas land often served as the basis for political and social independence, many ex-slaves logically felt that only as a freeholder of land "could a man make a home for his family consistent with self-respect." Moreover, as landholders, the former slaves would be able to protect themselves from abuses of the planters and therefore "obtain that measure of independence which could give [them] some bargaining power in the matter of wages."[18]

However, the striving for independence after the end of slavery did not lead immediately to a massive abandonment of the plantations, as historians previously contended. The representation of the plantation as the site of oppression, which the ex-slaves fled once slavery terminated, became an attractive formulation "because it [was] simple and symmetrical, linking revulsion against slavery with the persistence of resistance against it." Yet this emphasis on flight "largely ignore[d] the realities of the blacks' existence and their views about it." Under slavery Blacks had fashioned an alternative lifestyle based on independent production and huckstering. Therefore, given that these survival strategies had sustained families during these times, "[s]uch people would not have been disposed towards suicidal gestures, to an exchange of their considerable investment in provision ground on the plantation for a spot in the bush, if such spots were indeed available."[19]

The soon to be "emancipated" slaves on the Playfield plantation in the parish of St. Mary illustrated the general preference "to continue to live in their old villages on the estates and to cultivate their own provision grounds." Less than a month before the Abolition Act was to take effect, the owner asked the slaves to leave because with "the land having been worn out" he "did not require to[o] many hands upon the Estate." This request was refused by the slaves. In consequence, three special magistrates and thirty-nine maroons from Charlestown came in to assist with the situation. Despite the presence of these mediators (that is, law enforcers), who read an order from the governor of the island, the leaders of this action (described as a gang) continued to defy the request to leave and actually went back to work in the fields. As a result, they were flogged, being given forty-eight lashes by maroons, whose complex relation to enslaved Blacks had been determined by the terms of the treaties with the British government that stipulated they return runaway slaves. Lieutenant Frederick White, the special magistrate in whose district the plantation was located, reported that after the twelfth lash was inflicted, he "asked each one of them if they would go quietly as they had been requested," to which "[t]hey all replied we will not leave this place or words to that effect." Troops were eventually brought in and forced the slaves to leave Playfield plantation, demonstrating that "resistance" did not always have to mean running away but could also be represented by staying and laying claim to the land where the former slaves had over many years made an investment with their lives and labor. Moreover, this incident on Playfield plantation (an ironic name) illustrated the complex understanding of freedom on the part of the former slaves, one in which subordination to earlier terms of slavery could also challenge postslavery planter dominance.[20]

Almost two years after abolition occurred, this sentiment seemed to persist among some of the ex-slaves. John Daughtrey, a special magistrate appointed to the parish of St. Elizabeth, noted that, in regard to the projected change in 1840 in the civil condition of the apprentices, the "more intelligent part of them" had no intention of abandoning the estates: "There are indications already that a considerable number have no intention of withdrawing from the properties to which they are now attached." So as not to convey an "erroneous impression," however, Daughtrey qualified his statement by adding that "this disposition to settle on the properties to which they belong is hitherto very much limited to the places where they are best treated, and to such as are least likely to change overseers." In other words, as he noted, the ex-slaves understood very well their interests: "On points of this latter kind the sagacity and penetration of these people appear almost intuitive; they are seldom found to be wrong."[21]

The Jamaican ex-slaves did leave plantations in some areas in significant numbers, but this "flight" did not begin until the early 1840s. An 1842 investigation conducted by the House of Commons Select Committee on the West India Colonies concluded that, due to the conditions of existence, many Blacks left the estates to find a better life for themselves, a trend implicit in Daughtrey's analysis according to which the ex-slaves remained on estates where they were treated fairly. Thus, as it has been noted, this movement came as a result "not of burning recollections of brutalities suffered during slavery, but rather of the terms of emancipation itself and the behaviour of estate-owners after 1834." When the employers and employees could not agree on terms of labor and tenancy, Blacks did leave, but "only where land for small scale agriculture was available." In other words, rather than "fleeing," the ex-slaves were simply doing what they had always done since abolition, that is, act in accordance with the securing of their well-being. Such a concept may have appeared insurrectionary in a society where Blacks existed to secure the interests of others, but to the former slaves it was the only choice if the freedom was going to have any real meaning. Writing from Clarendon in 1839, Hall Pringle reported that the freedpeople had begun to settle in a village near the Manchester border of the parish. When Pringle mentioned to the ex-slaves that the quality of the land was not very good and the freeholds seemed rather small, they responded that "they only wished for homes where they could not be troubled, and that they might have the liberty of working where they might choose for their livelihood."[22]

The issue of the availability of land for ex-slaves and its relation to the general politics of emancipation has sparked a debate among scholars who study the history of the Caribbean. William Green has argued that the amount of land available, in relation to the population of ex-slaves, determined the quantity of laborers that planters could employ: "In the free West Indies, the supply as well as the quality of labour was mainly determined by two factors: population density and the availability of arable land." He contended that on islands "where the ratio of people to arable land was high," such as in Barbados, St. Kitts, and Antigua, "estate labour was comparatively plentiful" when juxtaposed with other colonies such as Jamaica, Trinidad, and British Guiana, "where the ratio was low." O. Nigel Bolland has challenged Green's analysis, asserting that he abstracted land and labor "from the socio-historical totality which gives them their real meaning," thereby giving a "deterministic, monocausal, and reductionist" explanation of the politics surrounding the abolition of slavery. For Bolland, the "availability of land is primarily determined by the power structure," and thus one would have to examine the political context since rather than being "a geophysical determinant of social life," land is "a factor which is itself socially produced and defined."[23]

Without completely invalidating Green's interpretation, the Colonial Office's position on the question of land for the ex-slaves seemed to have coincided with Bolland's assertion of relying on politics rather than geography to understand the issue of land distribution and ownership. Due to a concern that once apprenticeship terminated in certain localities the supply of laborers would reduce cultivation, in January 1836 Secretary Lord Glenelg suggested that some "precautionary measures" should be taken "in order to guard against that degree of danger to the value of property, or the more permanent interests of society." He contended that in order "to keep up the cultivation of the staple productions, we must make it the immediate and apparent interest of the negro population to employ their labour in raising them." This concern stemmed from an understanding that where land existed "to yield an abundant subsistence to the whole population in return for slight labour," the ex-slaves would have "no sufficient inducement to prefer the more toilsome existence of a regular labourer, whatever may be its remote advantages, or even its immediate gains." Asserting a naturalistic belief in human behavior motivated purely by hunger, Glenelg stated that "should things be left to their natural course," the ex-slaves would not "be attracted to the cultivation of exportable produce, until [they] began to press upon the means of subsistence, and the land failed . . . to supply all its occupants with the necessaries of life." While this impulse might lead to the cultivation of staples, "the depreciation which would take place in property, and the rude state into which society would fall back in the mean time," implied that "measures would have to be adopted to check this apparently natural course."[24]

Glenelg proposed that one of the means to obstruct this "natural course" whereby the supply of laborers diminished involved limiting access to land: "[B]y diminishing the facilities of obtaining land, it may certainly be impeded." This goal could easily be achieved by preventing the occupation of crown lands by people not holding proprietary titles and by placing "such a price upon all Crown lands as may place them out of the reach of persons without capital." The specifics, he added, would necessarily have to be tailored to the local situations. This strategy concerning the politics of geography had an intellectual basis, one that Glenelg explicitly articulated in the circular.

It would appear that a country is . . . in its most prosperous state when there is as much labour in the market as can be profitably employed. In new counties, where the whole unoccupied territory belongs to the

Crown, and settlers are continually flowing in, it is possible, *by fixing the price of fresh land so high as to place it above the reach of the poorest class of settlers, to keep the labour market in its most prosperous state from the beginning.* This precaution, by ensuring a supply of labourers at the same time that it increases the value of the land, makes it more profitable to cultivate old land well than to purchase new. The natural tendency of the population to spread over the surface of the country, each man settling where he may, or roving from place to place in pursuit of virgin soil, is thus impeded. The territory, expanding only with the pressure of population, is commensurate with the actual wants of the entire community. *Society, being thus kept together, is more open to civilizing influences,* more directly under the control of the Government, more full of the activity which is inspired by common wants, and the strength which is derived from the division of labour; and altogether is in a sounder state, morally, politically and economically, than if left to pursue its natural course.[25]

Glenelg's Circular Despatch demonstrated the contradictory nature of those arguing for a laissez-faire approach on one hand and intervention of the imperial government on the other, and especially with respect to Blacks being able to choose how best to secure their well-being. From the perspective of the dominant understanding on emancipation, the ultimate goal remained securing the stability of society (opening it up to "civilizing influences"), and this objective could be achieved, according to Glenelg, only by having as much labor in the market "as can be profitably employed." His analysis therefore preempted the Green-Bolland dispute for, while acknowledging the importance of the geophysical conditions of the specific location, the colonial secretary suggested that these factors could (and should) be controlled by public policies like the ones that had been "pursued with very good results in our North American and Australian Colonies" and, without a doubt, "may be applied with advantage to the West Indies."[26]

In the Southern United States, the ex-slaves expressed a conception of independence in terms quite similar to those of their British Caribbean counterparts, especially with respect to land serving as the basis of this autonomy. John W. Alvord, the Freedmen's Bureau's general superintendent of education, noted the enthusiasm of the ex-slaves in regard to obtaining land: "The freedmen have a passion for land. Where little can be obtained, they are always purchasers." W. E. B. Du Bois suggested that this impulse came from a combination of the intuition of Blacks with what they had learned under slavery:

"Some of them had been given by their masters little plots to work on, and raise their own food. . . . This faint beginning of industrial freedom now pictured to them economic freedom. They wanted little farms which would make them independent." The ownership of land, which for many ex-slaves became synonymous after the Civil War with the demand for "forty acres and a mule," represented "the symbolic and actual fulfillment of freedom's promise." For this reason, South Carolina assistant commissioner Rufus Saxton argued that the settlement of the ex-slaves on forty-acre tracts should be encouraged because making them landholders would be "the greatest step in their elevation," for "[w]hen a man is made a land holder he becomes practically an independent citizen."[27]

From actions taken by both the military and Congress during the war and the first year after abolition, it seemed as if the federal government would carry out this promise. With the passing of the direct tax laws and Confiscation Acts in 1861 and 1862, General Sherman's Field Order No. 15, and Section IV of the act creating the Freedmen's Bureau, the former slaves had good reason to think that they would acquire some landed property. Sherman's order resulted more from a war necessity involving slaves who began to join the Union army's march than from a commitment to justice in the ex-slaves' terms; however, because once articulated the meanings of political languages become diversified, this fact mattered little after officers within the ranks of the bureau vigorously expressed their support for Blacks obtaining land. No one displayed support for Black landownership more than Assistant Commissioner Saxton, who conveyed to Commissioner Howard that the ex-slaves deserved land because with their ancestors they had "passed two hundred years of unrequited toil . . . [o]n this soil." Moreover, because they "have always been loyal to the Union cause . . . and have enlisted as Soldiers in our Country's darkest hours to help fight in her struggle for existence," the U.S. government had an obligation to its most loyal supporters, a point on which Frederick Douglass had always insisted.[28]

During the early days of the bureau, Howard needed little prompting, as he also remained dedicated to seeing that the ex-slaves obtained land. With the more than 800,000 acres of land under the control of the bureau (more than one-third of which was located in South Carolina), Howard issued Circular No. 13 in July 1865, stipulating that assistant commissioners could begin selling or renting land in forty-acre plots to the ex-slaves. This directive was to be executed despite President Johnson's Amnesty Proclamation issued two months earlier, which restored land to Confederate rebels, because Howard felt that the pardon did not "extend to the surrender of abandoned or confiscated property which by law has been 'set apart for refugees and freed-men.'" However, once the president learned that Howard issued the circular without his consent, Johnson thwarted the bureau's attempt to distribute the lands. To make his policy clear, Johnson oversaw the preparation of a correc-tive circular, issued later that year in September, stipulating that the assistant commissioners begin to restore all abandoned and confiscated lands to par-doned Confederates with the only exception being those lands which were condemned and sold by a court decree.[29]

Although Johnson's restoration policy would become the beginning of the end of the hope of landownership for most of the ex-slaves, alternatives that allowed a minority of South Carolina freedpeople to acquire land emerged. In response to efforts of Radical Republicans concerned with the effects of res-toration on the opportunities of Blacks becoming landowners, in June 1866 Congress passed what has since become known as the Southern Homestead Act. This law set aside public lands in Alabama, Arkansas, Florida, Louisi-ana, and Mississippi for settlement by ex-slaves and loyal refugees, causing some to emigrate from South Carolina. The homesteaders could obtain as much as 80 acres (although some in the Senate pushed to increase the maxi-mum allotment to 160 acres), and they did not have to pay the registration fee until the settlers received patents for the land. A problem existed, however, in that the lands were often swampy, being inconveniently located for facilitating transportation (far from railroads) and not being conducive to supplemen-tary modes of survival (far from the coast and rivers where one could fish). The largest amount of homesteading occurred in Florida, where a policy pro-viding rations to settlers had been instituted, thereby diminishing the obstacle of having to earn a living at the same time as they cleared the land for the first crop. Although much of the public lands under the earlier 1862 Homestead Act fell into the hands of speculative companies "furthering the incorporation of Western lands into the Eastern industrial system," it nevertheless provided land to a significant number of (mostly White) citizens. Unlike its predeces-sor, the 1866 Southern Homestead Act afforded land only to approximately 5,000 families and thus remained, according to one historian, "a miserable failure."[30]

Another effort designed to assist the ex-slaves in the goal of landownership occurred with the formation in March 1869 of the South Carolina Land Com-mission. As a result of an ordinance of the recent Constitutional Convention, the Republican legislature appropriated $200,000 to an advisory board to sur-vey and subdivide tracts of land of no less than 25 and no more than 100 acres on which the ex-slaves were to settle. During the first three years, the settlers had to pay only the land taxes and 6 percent interest on the principal of the loan. After three years of continuous residence, the inhabitants then had to begin making payments on the purchase price. This attempt to facilitate Black landownership had minimum success, with only 2,000 families being settled with the help of the Land Commission by 1871, a year after the state government appropriated an additional $500,000 to continue the project. Moreover, corruption schemes also plagued the agency, including one that involved the former bureau assistant commissioner and governor Robert K. Scott. In consequence, the head of the Land Commission changed several times. The instability and corruption of the organization resulted in the same end as previous attempts to assist the ex-slaves with obtaining land: "[T]he story ended as it had begun in 1860 with the restoration of the plantations; by 1890 much of the land commission holdings were concentrated in the hands of a few white families."[31]

The original conception of the South Carolina Land Commission resembled a national Black landownership plan that Frederick Douglass proposed in the same year. The fundamental problem of Reconstruction, Douglass always insisted, was the failure to provide land for Blacks. This concern carried over from the antebellum era when Douglass took a stand against the government's freely granting land to railroad monopolies.[32] Like many of the ex-slaves, he did not advocate confiscation or the free distribution of lands; rather, he suggested that Congress provide Blacks with the opportunity to purchase land on relatively lenient terms, as it had done for other interest groups. After procuring land, the National Land and Loan Company (with a million-dollar capitalization) proposed selling or leasing land to the ex-slaves, while providing them with some start-up funds to begin cultivation. Douglass held no doubts that the plan would be successful, if the ex-slaves were given a "fair chance," asserting that with the abolition of slavery, Congress "gave the Negro the machinery of liberty but denied him the steam with which to put it into motion." If such a plan was not to be implemented, Blacks would be forced to endure abject social conditions: "Unless something of this kind is done thousands [of Blacks] will continue to live a miserable life and die a wretched death," and the very power structure that kept the population subordinated would have continued after abolition; for although the former slaveholders could no longer buy and sell Blacks, Douglass maintained that "they retained the power to starve them to death, and wherever this power is held, there is the power of slavery."[33]

The Postslavery Civilizing Missions

As the emancipation process unfolded in Jamaica, conflicts emerged. Hence, in order to clarify what should be the modus operandi of the special magistrates, Governor Sligo issued at the beginning of 1836 another letter of instructions, which in great detail outlined the specific nature of their duties. Although their decisions on issues such as valuations were to be based on justice and impartiality, Sligo directed them to "remember you are particularly appointed by the law to see that the interests of the apprentices are not neglected." This emphasis, however, did not constitute the dominant thrust of the activities of the special magistrates. From the perspective of these officials as well as of Sligo himself, emancipation meant primarily regulating the lives of Blacks (although in forms ostensibly different from those under slavery) more than granting them liberties and absolute freedoms.

This circular seemed to contradict Sligo's May 1834 letter of advice to the slaves. In the latter, Sligo remarked that, although the king of England had sent him to Jamaica to protect their rights, he noted that His Majesty "has also ordered me to see justice done to your owners, and to punish those who do wrong." The implication here was that the emancipation process would not neglect the interests of the former slaveholders, and thus should be viewed from their perspectives as well as that of the ex-slaves. Moreover, the ex-slaves would have to fulfill their part of the obligation, especially given the fact, according to Sligo, that the British people had demonstrated their support: "The people of England are your friends and fellow-subjects; they have shown themselves such by passing a Bill to make you all free." The responsibility for the rest of the outcome of apprenticeship, and by inference full emancipation, remained on the shoulders of the Blacks: "It will therefore depend entirely upon your own conduct whether your apprenticeship be short or long."[34]

Underlying Sligo's political language of justice for the ex-slaveholders and the character of the soon to be freed slaves remained the question of whether Blacks could actually handle freedom. The latter concern was so prevalent that the British Parliament tied the appointment of the special magistrates and the apprenticeship phase to the abolition of slavery in its colonies. This link occurred because, in addition to providing a cushion for the planters, it was also thought that the ex-slaves needed to acquire certain attributes before being granted "unqualified freedom." The primary objective of the special magistrates therefore became the resocialization of the ex-slave population, what John Daughtrey of St. Elizabeth parish called the "work of civilization and moral improvement." While the special magistrates came from different backgrounds and held varying perspectives on the approach to their job, they nevertheless remained nearly unified in the conception of emancipation that defined the fundamental issue as being the need for spiritual and moral uplift of the ex-slaves. As a result, these officials often described Blacks as a group who had to be "prepared" and "fitted" for freedom.[35]

Writing from the parish of St. John less than a year after the Abolition Act took effect, Edward Baynes illustrated this understanding of his role. Being a special magistrate for Baynes entailed "gradually preparing [the ex-slave] for the change that will take place in 1840, when he will be elevated to the condition and responsibility of a free agent and citizen." Richard Chamberlaine of Clarendon suggested that it was not only the magistrate's duty but it also became the obligation of the gentry to "prepare the minds of the people for the grand change which must take place in their condition in 1840." This task was supposedly not an easy one because, as Baynes noted a year after his initial statement, his effectiveness waned as the typical ex-slave continued to be "as gross and licentious in his private and domestic habits as ever." From two years of observation, Baynes concluded that the ex-slave "had not made a corresponding progress towards fitness for taking upon himself the duties of a free agent and citizen." Fitness also became a relevant issue to other groups in the society, for, as John Daughtrey contended, the managers and overseers who supervised the former slaves should also have to demonstrate a certain "moral fitness" to be qualified to hold their positions of authority.[36]

Within this intellectual context, it can be seen that the idea of apprenticeship for ex-slaves carried a specific meaning. This term has usually been applied to describe the learning of a trade or craft in which a mentor instructs a novice. However, although the ex-slaves may have acquired knowledge of new skills after abolition, for the most part they engaged in the same agricultural tasks that had defined their labor under slavery. The impetus behind the employment of this concept by British government officials widened, in some respect, the traditional understanding of the term. Rather than facilitating the learning of new trades, the intellectuals and politicians who conceptualized the Abolition Act employed the political language of apprenticeship in order to legitimate the belief that ex-slaves needed to be instructed in how to behave as free citizens, central to which was also how they should now conduct themselves as ostensibly free (that is, wage) laborers. Here, one could extend Willie Lee Rose's analysis of the experience in the South Carolina Sea Islands beginning in late 1861 to the situation before 1840 in the British Caribbean. What Rose described as a "dress rehearsal" for Reconstruction after the Civil War in the United States provides the basis for understanding apprenticeship as a more directly executed "rehearsal" for emancipation in the British West Indies.[37]

Given this specific ideological orientation, government officials logically described the apprenticeship phase using specific terms. The idea of probation constituted one of the terms often used to depict the transition between slavery and putative freedom. Sligo defined apprenticeship as a "probationary state" during which the ex-slaves had to prove that they were "deserving of all this goodness"—proof that could be demonstrated with the ex-slaves laboring diligently and following the advice of those appointed to supervise them. Samuel Pryce of Trelawny reinforced the description of this early stage after abolition as a "probationary system." While reporting that the apprentices were "taken good care of throughout this splendid district," Pryce believed nevertheless that it was "difficult to frame human laws to alter human nature." In St. Thomas in the East, Richard Chamberlaine detailed that the "gentry of the country" retained the misguided notion that this "probationary state was established for the exclusive advantage, and as part of the ransom for the emancipation of the slaves," disregarding "its paramount importance as a preparatory system for elevating the former serf, and instructing him in moral duties, and in the obligations of freedom."[38]

The designation of apprenticeship in terms of a trial period in which Blacks had to prove their character suggested an understanding of abolition as a social experiment, a position that some modern historians have reiterated.[39] To the Jamaican House of Assembly, this "mighty and frightful experiment introduced by His Majesty's Government" placed the island in a "dangerous state." However, from the abolitionist-derived special magistrates' perspective, the end of slavery, while still perceived as an experiment, affirmed a humanitarian moral imperative: "The British people naturally feel a lively and deep anxiety in the operation and successful completion of their magnificent experiment—an experiment worthy of the term sublime." Although Chamberlaine remained certain that "this probationary period was a wise and an expedient measure," he also believed that "time has been lost" and "much remains to be done." Given the representation of the immediate abolition era as probationary and experimental, special magistrates intimated that this trial effort could possibly fail. Reflecting a specific understanding of history, John Daughtrey cautioned that too much should not be expected from the ex-slaves. He claimed that "as the consequence of the change, their radical improvement will be a work of slow degrees," and thus "it will require a generation or two" to undo the effects of slavery on the "personality" of Blacks.[40]

The paternalism that characterized much of the behaviors of the special magistrates, while logically derived from the political language of apprenticeship, was paradoxically inseparable from the revolutionary ideology that abolished slavery. Functioning within the abolitionist understanding of slavery, the special magistrates represented the slave system as having damaged the evolution of the character of Blacks. These officials frequently explained many of the problems that occurred during apprenticeship as a consequence, in the words of Daughtrey, of the "deeply-demoralizing system" of slavery, which had resulted in "debasing effects" on the "negro mind." Such an understanding led Richard Hill, one of a few Colored magistrates, to describe the job of special magistrates as "elevating the demoralized out of their debasement." R. Standish Haly, assigned to the Chapelton District in Clarendon, reinforced this line of reasoning when he proposed that the "predominant vices of idleness and petty thefts are clearly the offspring of a state from which [the ex-slaves] can only be said to be now emerging."[41]

The case of Richard Hill demonstrates that it was not only a question of the White special magistrates who harbored paternalist ideas toward the ex-slaves. The first Colored (out of an eventual seven) to be appointed to the special magistracy, Hill led an extraordinary life, having been described as "the most published Jamaican of his time over a broad range of subjects." He corresponded with Philip Gosse and Charles Darwin, publishing articles on natural history in journals in England, France, and the United States. For a year (1837–38), he served in the Jamaican House of Assembly, the lower chamber of the legislature, becoming the fifth person of color to do so. Appointed 28 February 1834 by the earl of Mulgrave, Hill served as a special magistrate for only a few months, resigning in the midst of a controversy involving a constable who gave evidence against William Norcott, a fellow magistrate stationed in the parish of St. James. Despite their disagreement over the Norcott incident, Sligo supported Hill's appointment as the secretary to the special magistrate's department at Spanish Town, and while serving in this capacity, Hill's performance pleased the Colonial Office.[42]

Richard Hill's days as a special magistrate were numbered, according to William Burn, because he became one of those agents who acquired a reputation for clemency of "every idle, shiftless apprentice for miles around." Like his colleague Norcott, who, in the words of Sligo, became "a decided Partizan of the Negroes," Hill refused to approve of floggings of the ex-slaves. Agreeing with Sligo over a century later, Burn argued that due to this approach, Hill seemed "to have lacked the judicial sense" needed in a special magistrate. However, while Hill protested the use of the lash (logical within the anticoercion emphasis of abolitionist thought), in a paradoxical fashion his conception of his role vis-à-vis the ex-slave population partly reinforced the general horizon of understanding. The "moral corruptions of slavery," Hill claimed, "have left traces of the deepest debasement." This influence explained why Blacks emerging from a "schooling of bondage" often had the impression of liberty as a state of licentiousness. Hill hoped that the Abolition Act would change the character and conduct of the ex-slaves, noting that if freedom "has not been accompanied by an elevation of character," the fault lay "in the indelible moral stain which slavery has left behind it, and which must continue to affect a more perfect state of freedom."[43]

If any change was to be effected in what Thomas M. Oliver believed to be the "doggedness usual to the negro character," it would be only "through the judicious management of those placed over them." True to their bureaucratic orientation, the special magistrates ascribed a certain importance to the effectiveness of management in controlling the postslavery behaviors of Blacks. In his district located in Trelawny, Richard C. Pennell described the ex-slaves as being "well disposed, tractable and easily managed." However, when problems emerged, "the fault may be traced to bad management, habitual drunkenness, or opposition on the part of those placed in immediate authority over them." Arthur Welch of Manchester succinctly articulated the issue: "The fact is, on the management depends all." According to Welch, competent management accounted for the difference between estates that produced good crops and those which did not, and such was the case because some managers did not have the ability "to discern where indulgence becomes relaxation of discipline, and discipline becomes tyranny." John Daughtrey stated that planters had often made the argument with respect to individuals among themselves that the success of a season depended on good management, and thus asked, "[W]hy is it unfair or unreasonable in me to apply it to the whole?" For Daughtrey, however, labor management formed only part of the general "moral management of negroes" necessary for the success of the emancipation process.[44]

Central to the issue of management, as Welch's report implied, remained the question of discipline and punishment. Sligo's response to Richard Hill and William Norcott's decision not to sanction floggings of the ex-slaves demonstrated the importance of these concerns for the government. According to the governor, Hill and Norcott "came to a resolution that they would never inflict corporal punishment and up to this day not a lash has been inflicted by either of them." The implication remained that administering punishment became essential to the effectiveness of implementing the Abolition Act, for, as Sligo stated, as "desirable as such an absence of punishment may be, . . . it cannot be considered to be compatible with the due execution of the law." Keeping this in mind, the governor did acknowledge that the planters in St. James "have been in all times notorious for the severity of their discipline with respect to their Slaves, and more cases of oppression have been proved in that parish since the first of August than in any other part of the Island." In fact, this pattern of behavior led him to deprive two Montego Bay magistrates (apparently not special magistrates) of their commissions of the peace. Notwithstanding this knowledge of disciplinary practices in St. James, Sligo still felt that Norcott's treatment of the ex-slaves rendered him "unfit for his Office."[45]

The attitude of the special magistrates toward discipline and punishment, although certainly not uniform, nevertheless demonstrated the nontransformative nature of the system of apprenticeship as a transitional mode to a more comprehensive freedom. Over a year after the phase began, John Daughtrey noticed that the role allocations had begun to settle according to plan: "All parties have become to understand the position in which the apprenticeship system places them; some of them were a long time in learning." Toward the end of apprenticeship, however, Daughtrey argued that unless Blacks were placed "under instruction, and, what is of equal importance, under discipline" many ex-slaves, and especially the children, would remain "just what original depravity, ignorance and slavery have made them." The situation, according to T. Watkins Jones of St. Thomas in the Vale, made the use of force necessary for the successful performance of their jobs: "Coercion and determination on the part of the special justice is certainly called for, and in many instances has had a most salutary effect." Before coming to the parish, Jones noted that the apprentices worked nine hours per day, but had half a Friday, or the whole of each alternate Friday, off of work. This organization of labor had serious effects for social control: "To allow the apprentices three successive days, Friday, Saturday and Sunday every fortnight," Jones contended, "was attended with the worst result; they went an immense distance from the property to which they were attached, for the purpose of seeing their paramours, attending dances, John Canoes."[46] Thus, discipline needed to be enforced not as a response to legal infractions but rather to prevent behaviors deemed inappropriate, especially those practices associated with retention of African symbolic systems, such as John Canoe (Jonkunnu).

To correct the putative lack of discipline of the ex-slaves, Jones instituted a policy "deemed advisable on the part of their attorneys and overseers to work eight hours each day, allowing the apprentice *no Friday.*" Coupled with the issue of corporal punishment, the eight-hour versus the nine-hour system of work constituted a frequent and protracted source of conflict for the emancipation process in Jamaica. Some magistrates, like Richard C. Pennell, agreed with Jones's analysis and asserted that a "great evil" existed because "the apprentices are allowed too much time to themselves." However, others, like Charles Hawkins of Trelawny, could understand the issue from the perspective of the ex-slaves: "I consider the eight-hour system most oppressive on the apprentice" because "the apprentices cannot by that system work their grounds and bring their produce to market on the Saturdays." In addition to employing this strategy of power, he noted, the planters also discontinued the Sunday market. Thus, the question became less one of maximizing productivity, as Hawkins remained convinced that "much less work is performed when the eight-hour system is worked than the nine." Not only did the ex-slaves dislike it, but on properties utilizing the system "complaints are more frequent, and more ill feeling [exists] between the master and the apprentice, it being considered a punishment, therefore naturally resisted by all the means in the apprentice."[47]

Throughout the course of the apprenticeship era, Governor Sligo attempted to intervene on the issue of the nine-hour versus the eight-hour work system. Initially, he concurred with Pennell's opinion, thinking that the "latter was the most humane for the negroes." However, upon reading the reports of the special magistrates "full of complaints against gangs of negroes and individuals for insubordinate conduct, originating in the change from the nine hours' system to that of eight hours," Sligo changed his position. When the planters continued to resist this policy, the governor issued a circular letter in August 1835, recommending to the special magistrates "to endeavor to induce proprietors to adopt the nine hours' system wherever it seemed to be the wish of the labouring classes." Sligo detected the strategy at work by forcing the ex-slaves on the eight-hour system: "That this is done for the purpose of annoying the negroes it is my painful impression." Yet this policy extended beyond mere annoyance, for it attempted to keep in being the system of subordination that had existed under the social order integrated on the basis of slavery.[48]

The political language of independence, which later emerged more powerfully in the U.S. context, arose in the discussion on emancipation in the British Caribbean. Despite the fact that before abolition the society depended, both symbolically and empirically, on the labor of the slaves to structure the social order, this representation of the past suggested that slavery had caused Blacks to be dependent on others. John Gurly, the magistrate who, in Clarendon's

Chapelton District, replaced R. Standish Haly after his death, attempted to account for the "predominant indolence" of some ex-slaves who, he claimed, refused to work and, as a consequence, existed only "by the means of more industrious relatives, or by robbing the provision grounds and cane pieces of their neighbors." Going beyond Gurly's formulation, John Daughtrey expressed the idea that, in particular, ex-slave women had become too dependent on other peoples and thus could not fulfill what he conceived of as their proper duties: "Negro women, who have always been employed in the field, and dependent for everything upon others (an unnatural condition), know in general as little how to treat themselves and their families in sickness, as to perform the most difficult operation in surgery." Daughtrey prescribed humanitarianism as the cure to remedy this affliction: "Philanthropy must desire to see it otherwise." Samuel Pryce generalized this claim to include the former slaveholders, as he felt that it would solve the continued conflicts resulting from abolition: "[T]he introduction of herring allowances . . . is fraught with much mischief, and ought at once to be abandoned, and the apprentice and his master be immediately taught to be independent of each other."[49]

The emancipation process in the United States took a similar emphasis as that of its British Caribbean antecedent, with the focus of its operations becoming the supervision and regulation of the lives of the ex-slaves. George Bentley, historian of the Freedmen's Bureau, reached the conclusion that, after the initial emphasis of securing freedoms for slaves, this objective came to define the modus operandi of the organization: "In its very earliest months the Freedmen's Bureau had been much concerned with restraining the planters from exercising the powers of masters over the Negroes, but soon its attention had turned more to getting the former slaves to work and keep their labor agreements." Bentley argued that although the bureau maintained a strong position against attempts to reenslave Blacks, at the same time its overall goals did not seem to contradict the interests of those with the opportunities to exploit Blacks and their labor: "On the whole its policies, both in administration of relief and in the supervision of labor, had been those that planters and other businessmen desired."[50] This convergence occurred as a result of abolition having components that entailed both economic and social reform.

The perspective that came to define the dominant understanding on emancipation implicit in the postabolition policies of the Freedmen's Bureau had been foreshadowed by two related events which took place during the Civil War. The first was the experience in the South Carolina Sea Islands, usually interpreted as a precursor to the politics that defined the era of Reconstruction, but which could also be described as an "intellectual rehearsal" defining of the ideas that would structure the governmental policies during Reconstruction. Letters and accounts written at the time illustrate that many missionaries, businessmen, and teachers saw themselves as "advancing civilization" and bringing order to chaos, a chaos, they insisted, created by slavery. Edward Philbrick, the Boston investor who bought eleven plantations (and leased two others) in the Sea Islands in March 1863, claimed that the uncertainties associated with immediate emancipation could be put to rest if doubters saw "the ease with which we have reduced a comparative degree of order out of the chaos we found, and see how ready this degraded and half-civilized race are to become an industrious and useful laboring class." For without people to teach the ex-slaves, Harriet Ware concluded, behaviors such as the theft that occurred at the Pine Grove house in December 1862 would continue: "The way in which those people have degenerated [since they left Pine Grove] and these improved since we moved here [Fripp Point plantation] is a proof of how necessary it is that they should have the care and oversight of white people in this transition state."[51]

Edward L. Pierce, the Boston attorney appointed as a Treasury Department special agent for the Sea Islands, illustrated that it was from the inception of the emancipation process that this specific approach to freedom emerged. To address the disruptive situation caused by the war, the secretary of the treasury appointed Pierce to examine the situation and report as to how the ex-slaves "could best be organized for labor . . . their moral nature addressed and their good will secured." It can be seen therefore that from its origins "reconstruction" entailed not only the implementation of a new labor system but also the implantation of a new value system, one designed to transform the "moral nature" of the ex-slaves and, according to this political language, secure the common good.[52]

In Pierce's reports to the secretary of the treasury, the intellectual and political foundations were being laid for the perspective that later came to determine much of the policies of the Freedmen's Bureau. Central to the success of reconstructing Southern society remained the transformation of the ex-slaves: "The laborers themselves, no longer slaves of their former masters or of the Government, but as yet in large numbers unprepared for the full privileges of citizenship," Pierce emphasized, "are to be treated with sole reference to such preparation." This process could be successful only with proper management, which did not necessarily imply that only Whites should prepare the ex-slaves "to become sober and self-supporting citizens," for properly trained Blacks could also serve such a function: "I saw many of very low intellectual development, but hardly any too low to be reached by civilizing influences either coming directly from us or mediately through their brethren."[53]

At the same time, however, the ideology of Anglo-Saxonism,[54] which appeared subtly among Freedmen's Bureau officials, nevertheless held some significance for Pierce. In his search for agents among the Boston and New York missionary–social reform communities, Pierce insisted that a knowledge of farming or cotton culture, while certainly a valuable asset, did not constitute the most important requirement; what really mattered was the ability to supervise: "[W]hat was most needed being the moral power of the presence of a white man on the plantations to guide and direct." The racial superiority implicit in Pierce's assertion did not seem to have been articulated with malicious intent, as it was ironically coupled with a humanitarian sentiment: "I have said that persons accepted must have in the first place profound humanity—a belief that the negro is a human being and capable of elevation and freedom." Philbrick reinforced this objective in his correspondence with Pierce:

> I think my ideas about the necessity of authority have your approval. We find the blacks as dependent as children, and as ignorant of social laws as they are of the alphabet. We must stand in the relation of parents to them until such time as they can be taught to stand alone, and as all parental authority should be tempered by benevolence, sound judgment & firmness, backed if necessary by force, so must this undeveloped race be treated if we mean to make men of them, & without such authority judiciously exercised, we shall just as surely fail as does any parent fail in trying to make useful and self-governing men & women of his children without first teaching them to obey.[55]

The primary goal of the Sea Island experience became to "make men" of the freedpeople, but such reconstruction had to be "tempered by benevolence" while if necessary being "backed by . . . force."

Employing language similar to that of officials in the British Caribbean context, Pierce gave advice to Blacks living on a plantation on Ladies Island. Like Governor Sligo, who implied that the ex-slaves needed to prove that they were worthy of freedom,[56] Pierce contended "that the great trouble about doing any for them was that their masters had always told us, and had made many people believe it, that they were lazy and would not work unless whipped to it." He conveyed to them that "Mr. Lincoln had sent us down here to see if it was so." In parallel language to a proclamation issued by Sir Lionel Smith to the ex-slaves in Jamaica,[57] Pierce assured the freedpeople that success would be achieved if they followed his advice: "I told them they must stick to their plantations and not run about and get scattered, and assured them that what their masters had told them of our intentions to carry them off to Cuba and sell them was a [lie] and their masters knew it to be so, and we wanted them to stay on the plantations and raise cotton, and if they behaved well, they should have wages, small perhaps at first—that they should have better food, and not have their wives and children sold off—that their children should be taught to read and write, . . .—that by-and-by they would be as well off as the white people."[58] Rather than stressing autonomy from the perspective of the ex-slaves, Pierce proposed a gradual approach bettering the freedpeople's conditions, yet doing so with the overall goal of reproducing labor for the plantations as well as the inculcation of specific sociocultural habits through the enforcement (if need be) of disciplined instruction.

The most distinguished group of Northern humanitarians who appeared during the Sea Island experience called themselves Gideonites or Gideon's Band. Many of these young reformers came from Massachusetts, were well educated, and had strong religious and antislavery convictions, sometimes being the children or relatives of noted abolitionists. Although their objectives tended to be articulated in a language punctuated by religious metaphors, the job of these missionaries became increasingly secular. Pierce acknowledged this new role, stating that the missionaries would not be "merely pietists or religious exhorters, but persons of good sense who could mingle with their religious exhortations advice and counsel as to how these people should act in their new condition, that is, be industrious, orderly, and sober." In other words, Pierce contended, they should become "evangels of civilization" armed with a "gospel of freedom . . . enforcing the duties of industry and self-restraint." More than teaching the Word of the Bible, these evangels now had to impart a secular Word, one that involved the inculcation of the social behaviors and labor habits, which was not unrelated to the then emerging industrial organization of the Northern states.[59]

Central to what the Gideonite William C. Gannett defined as "this work of civilization" remained the belief that self-reliance had to be cultivated in the ex-slaves. In a similar fashion to the special magistrates in the British Caribbean, these evangels represented slavery as having made Blacks "accustomed to dependence." Consequently, Gannett suggested that gifts and charity from the government would "only relieve momentary distress at the expense of their manliness and independence." In fact, although governmental supervision may have protected the ex-slave, "it did little to ameliorate his condition; it prevented deterioration, but did not insure progress." Supposedly, the ex-slaves have been "too much coddled and superintended by the Government" and "the best thing our Government can do, for the good of these people themselves, is simply to offer and enforce their acceptance of the advantages of civil law and education." Gannett adamantly opposed measures that gave lands to the ex-slaves, deeming it unwise and injurious. To save the freed-people, they needed to be forced to become self-sufficient: "[T]he sooner the people are thrown upon themselves, the speedier will be their salvation." If this "experiment in American emancipation" was going to have any effect, certain principles would have to be allowed to operate: "Let the natural laws of labor, wages, competition &c come into play, — and the sooner will habits of responsibility, industry, self-dependence & manliness be developed."[60]

It was the rigid adherence to the idea of individual self-exertion as the causal agent for economic success that led to Edward Philbrick's decision to sell lands to the ex-slaves above their market price, a strategy resembling Lord Glenelg's proposal of how to address the question of crown lands in the colonies. Contrary to what his critics claimed, Philbrick contended that he "never considered the question of profit"; rather, he "did not believe in the success of a system of selling to any people any property whatever for less than its market value, with a view to confer a lasting benefit upon them." Such a policy, he felt, would have "a demoralizing effect upon these ignorant people" and "would beget idleness and unthrifty habits when compared with a system by which every man should be required to pay full price." Despite his claim that "no race of men on God's earth ever acquired the right to the soil on which they stand without more vigorous exertions," coupled with *the fact that he purchased the lands below market value,* Philbrick nevertheless asserted that "no man appreciates property who does not work for it." This feeling reflected a civilizing imperative: "If the freed negro is ever to become civilized in any degree, or elevated above his present ignorant and degraded condition, it must be through his own industry." Thus, Blacks should pay as much as ten dollars per acre for land that cost one dollar per acre because they "would be taught a feeling of independence more readily than by being made the recipients of charity."[61] Why railroad companies and Northern speculators could obtain lands well below market value and somehow not have their independence undermined remained outside the terms of a political language designed to integrate an ex-slave population on an inferior basis into an increasingly industrial social and economic order.

The second occurrence that prefigured the parameters of postslavery thought in the United States came with the submission in June 1863 and June 1864, respectively, of the preliminary and final reports of the American Freedmen's Inquiry Commission. These reports, conducted under the auspices of Secretary of War Edwin Stanton, were completed by a three-member committee composed of Robert Dale Owen, James McKaye, and Samuel Gridley Howe, all of whom had established abolitionist and reformist credentials. The commission's findings embodied the complex understanding of emancipation that would govern the process throughout much of the era of Reconstruction. This understanding was characterized by a two-pronged strategy emphasizing both protection of rights and moral guidance in order to ascribe both individual and collective responsibility in addressing the questions arising as a consequence of abolition.

The commission urged that Blacks "should not be treated with weak and injurious indulgence" but rather with "even-handed justice." No special favor, laws, or "a special organization for the protection of colored people" was needed to correct the injustice continually heaped upon the former slaves when essentially "the safeguard of general laws, applicable to all," could remedy the problem. Quoting Tocqueville, the commission declared that without administering justice, there would continue to be no peace: "We cannot expect, in a democratic republic, to maintain domestic tranquillity, if we deprive millions of freemen of their civil rights." In other words, the destiny of the country depended upon the nonhierarchical integration of the Blacks into the dominant society: "We need the negro not only as a soldier to aid in quelling the rebellion, but as a loyal citizens [*sic*] to assist in reconstructing on a permanently peaceful and orderly basis the insurrectionary states." Such a strategy would hopefully lead to a situation "when both shall be free, persistently to endure side by side, and to live together in one common country harmoniously and with mutual advantage."[62]

Although the commission strongly expressed that no special treatment should be accorded to the ex-slaves, nevertheless the final report advocated the formation of a Freedmen's Bureau, but only as a temporary measure. Such an organization was needed "not because these people are negroes," but rather "because they are men who have been, for generations, despoiled of their rights." Having the hindsight of the apprenticeship process in the British Caribbean, the commission members stressed that Blacks should be accorded total freedom: "Extensive experience in the West Indies has proved that emancipation, when it takes place, should be unconditional and absolute." Therefore, it was recommended that this bureau should not interfere with the employers and the employees, especially with regard to subjecting the ex-slaves to compulsory contracts. Moreover, they suggested that federal government not require "directly or indirectly, any statutory rates of wages" or any restrictions on the local movements of the ex-slaves unless these regulations applied equally to Whites. In conclusion, the commission affirmed a laissez-faire approach to dealing with these issues: "The natural laws of supply and demand should be left to regulate rates of compensation and places of residence."[63]

Notwithstanding the advocacy of free-market principles, the commission also asserted strict notions of instructing the ex-slaves in how to behave. Making specific reference to Blacks in South Carolina, the members contended that the ex-slaves could be "reached" and "in a measure reformed, by judicious management." Convinced that Blacks constituted an "untutored race," the reports suggested that the ex-slaves required military discipline, "the great school for giving character to the race." This strategy would be the most effective: "[O]f all the present agencies for elevating the character of the colored race, for cultivating them in self-respect and self-reliance, military discipline, under judicious officers, who will treat them firmly and kindly, is at once the most prompt and the most efficacious." Such a socialization process could induce "habits of regulated industry" and thereby correct the "indolent fashions of dependence" that many claimed the system of slavery engendered. By introducing the "principle of self-support," the commission asserted, Blacks would begin to understand that "emancipation means neither idleness nor gratuitous work but fair labor for fair wages."[64]

By the time the Sea Islands experience ended and the American Freedmen's Inquiry Commission had submitted its preliminary and final reports, the intellectual parameters had been set for the terms that would structure the policies of the Freedmen's Bureau. South Carolina assistant commissioner Robert K. Scott defined the bureau as "an institution, whereby the benefits of a more enlightened civilization were to be thrown upon a people hitherto deprived of the same."[65] However, the agency did not restrict this impulse to the ex-slaves, for White Southerners also had to be socially and morally "reconstructed." Colonel G. A. Williams contended that only after the extension of "civilization and enlightenment" in the South Carolina district of Charleston would the bureau be able to "restrain the disposition on the part of many whites to reduce the blacks to a condition as near that of slavery as possible." It was in such a context that Edward Philbrick had made the claim that "[i]t will take many years to make an economical and thrifty man out of a freedman, and about as long to make a sensible and just employer out of a former slaveholder."[66]

The attitudes of the subordinate field officers (subassistant commissioners, assistant subassistant commissioners, and civilian agents) of the Freedmen's Bureau reinforced an understanding of emancipation that only partially correlated with the perspective of the ex-slaves. Nowhere was the position of these officials more clearly articulated than in their responses to Congressman Thomas Eliot's December 1867 circular letter, which asked whether the Freedmen's Bureau should be continued beyond the then projected date of termination in July 1868. In concurring with the ex-slaves' perspective on freedom, some of the agents suggested that, for reasons of equal protection, the bureau needed to be continued. Samuel Place, an agent stationed in Sumter, gave such a reason: "In justice to the freedpeople the Bureau should be continued as a safeguard to prevent them from being cheated and defrauded out of their labor," noting that the agency should also provide "protection from abuse and outrage[s], to which they are constantly subjected [*sic*] by their former masters, which practice is not the exception, but the general rule in my Sub District [of Columbia]." An agent at Columbia, W. J. Harkisheimer, asserted that it was "sheer nonsense to suppose for one moment that the negro could receive justice before civil tribunals." Given this fact, coupled with the need to ensure that ex-slaves received their fair share from planters at the time of crop division, Harkisheimer deemed "the continuance of the Freedmen's Bureau, or some other auxiliary friendly to the colored man, an urgent necessity." According to J. B. Dennis, who directed the Claim Division that issued rations in South Carolina, with the Freedmen's Bureau "having been instituted for the care, protection, and benefit of the freedpeople, it would be a great injustice to them to take away the last and only real friend they have ever known."[67]

In addition to political claims espoused in the name of the common good of South Carolina, and of the nation generally, bureau officials also proposed a moral and disciplinary necessity for the continuation of the organization. Despite Frederick Douglass's warning, it was within this context that the agents' understanding of their role often departed from that of the ex-slaves. Samuel Place contended that the "principles of humanity" dictated that "the Bureau or some similar system should be continued, until the freedpeople are taught their duties as citizens, the necessity of laboring and providing for themselves and families," ideas "which now so few understand, and will not, until better informed, or forced to do so." State inspector Erastus W. Everson felt that the agency constituted "the best and most direct channel for educating the freedpeople in the principles of industry, frugality, and integrity, and generally improving their condition," because, "if left to themselves, they would (I believe) under the idea (I have often heard expressed during the past two years by leading men and large planters) that an educated Negro will not cultivate rice or cotton, become indolent and given to thieving."[68]

An agent at Orangeburg, William H. H. Holton, argued for the bureau's continuance on the basis of the need not only "to enforce rules of equal justice between employers and their employees" and to speed up the adjudication of disputes but, more important, "to eradicate the improper impressions of liberty and independence, which in many instances notwithstanding three years of freedom, the freedpeople still entertain and associate with emancipation." Holton believed that the ex-slaves needed to be resocialized out of the African-derived cultural beliefs and practices to which the system of slavery had given birth, thus suggesting the bureau had to be maintained out of cultural necessity: "The moral and educational interests of the freedpeople require the beneficial and fostering care of the Bureau or a kindred institution," because abolition "only released in a measure the colored people from the control of their masters" and the Black was "still as formerly a slave to the superstitions, ignorance and vices engendered by long years of slavery." Thus, the job of the bureau entailed disabusing the ex-slaves of such ideas, "for until they are dispelled emancipation cannot be said to have taken effect."[69]

All the officers, however, did not agree that the Freedmen's Bureau should continue after the proposed date of termination. From his more than two years of experience and observations, Martin Delany, the Black thinker who had an unusual political career, including a run for lieutenant governor on a non-Republican ticket, indicated that "in the event of adequate protection to the Freed People, either by the established military or civil regulations, there will be no necessity for a farther continuance of the Bureau, after its expiration by limitation." John William De Forest, the agent at Greenville who published some of his reports in *Harper's* and *Atlantic Monthly*, contended that once South Carolina was represented in Congress and a new state government was organized under the terms of the Constitutional Convention, "the Bureau will not be needed." Lieutenant William Stone, the assistant sub-assistant commissioner at Aiken, supported De Forest's position, stating that "there would be no longer any necessity for this Bureau" if the state courts "had the confidence of the people and would mete out equal justice." Stone believed that law and order could be maintained if the officers "were not afraid of criminals and where the ends of justice rather than personal popularity are sought." Although he dissented from the majority of agents in regard to the duration of the bureau, Stone based his decision on similar intellectual presuppositions, that is, the need to cultivate independence: "It seems to me that it is time that the people, white as well as black, should rely upon themselves in all that pertains to the machinery of Government." He therefore concluded his response by asserting that with a new code of laws, impartial judges, and intelligent jurors, "the future destiny of the colored people can without fear be left to themselves."[70]

As the responses to Congressman Eliot's plea intimated, despite minor intellectual differences among officials in the Freedmen's Bureau, the need to resocialize Blacks, especially with respect to making the former slaves independent and doing so according to their hegemonic conception, became the organizing principle of the policies of the Freedmen's Bureau. This political language, if partially in different terms, also defined the operations of the British Colonial Office and the special magistrates working in Jamaica. Such an understanding can provide the basis for an analysis of the postslavery Anglo-Americas from a new angle—that is, toward the realization that what has been called "the work of reconstruction"[71] in the U.S. context was fundamentally a cultural question, and thus the emancipation of the Black slaves became as much a conceptual project as it was a physical and social one.

Chapter Four

The Vexed Question of Original Unity
*The Political Language of Race
and the Politics of Emancipation*

Human nature has evidently been but little understood here;
perhaps it never was in a slave colony. It is quite overlooked, that
compulsion may exist without coercion, but of a rational, that
is, of the highest and strongest kind, a moral compulsion arising from the pressure of felt wants, whether natural or artificial,
and from the force of attachment to place and neighborhood,
of which the negro mind is keenly susceptible.
— John Daughtrey, special magistrate, 1836

I know, my friends, that in some quarters the efforts of the
colored people meet with very little encouragement. We may
fight, but we must fight like the Sepoys of India, under white
officers. This class of Abolitionists don't like colored celebrations, they don't like colored conventions, they don't like colored Anti-Slavery fairs for the support of colored newspapers.
They don't like any demonstration whatever in which colored
men take part. They talk of the proud Anglo-Saxon blood, as
flippantly as those who profess to believe in the natural inferiority of races.
— Frederick Douglass, 1861

In an important section of his *Autobiography,* Oliver O. Howard reflected upon his tenure as head of the Bureau of Refugees, Freedmen, and Abandoned Lands, reconsidering the question whether after slavery the former slaves should have been granted lands as compensation for their un-requited toil and in order to solidify their then newly established "freedom." While acknowledging that the restoration policy of President Johnson and the resulting inaction of the U.S. Congress represented a "complete reversal of the Government's generous provision for the late slaves," the commissioner nevertheless maintained that in the end, the failure of the ex-slaves to have ac-quired land was somehow more beneficial for them: "After years of thinking and observation I am inclined to believe that the restoration of their lands to the planters proved for all their future better for the negroes."[1] Howard's *Auto-biography* was published in 1907, a fact that makes his statement all the more striking, as he made it after the retrenchment in the 1870s, which brought Reconstruction to an end and issued in the era of Jim Crow, noted for insti-tuting the policy of segregation and a state-ignored (if not indirectly state-sanctioned) terrorism on the Black population group.

Commissioner Howard's contention illustrated the central duality that had plagued the operations of the Freedmen's Bureau from its inception. On the one hand, while Blacks were no longer to be treated as slaves but rather as "free citizens," at the same time many of the bureau's policies implied that the ex-slaves needed to be supervised and instructed in how to conduct them-selves as "free people." This duality derived from the irresolution of a central issue, that of the political language of "race," that is, the belief in the non-homogeneity of the human species, or what Josiah Nott ironically referred to as "the vexed question of original unity." Although most of the bureau officials displayed a sincere willingness to assist Blacks in making a transition from slavery, such a position did not negate the fact that many had not moved be-yond the racial discourse that had structured their lives and prescribed their perceptions of Blacks. In fact, rather than effecting the displacement of the discourse of race that had existed from the "origin of the Americas," the con-ceptual framework of the abolitionists assisted in the transformation of this political language from an agrarian (that is, slave) context to one that fitted into the industrializing and increasingly laissez-faire economic world system.[2]

The line of analysis here is based on C. Vann Woodward's insightful argu-ment that illustrated the complex and contradictory nature of those who supported abolition. Retracting an earlier proposal where he asserted that during the Civil War a third objective, "the boldly revolutionary aim of racial equality," emerged, Woodward suggested that it was "misleading to equate Equality with the commitments to Union and Freedom." That is, to account for the abolitionist impulse, one had to acknowledge the varied, and often conflicting, interests that supported the end of slavery, for as Frederick Douglass noted, "[o]pposing slavery and hating its victims has come to be a very common form of Abolitionism." Many antislavery advocates, especially in the Midwest, favored abolition as a measure to limit the expansion of slavery in order to privilege "free white labor." As antislavery senator Lyman Trumbull of Illinois declared, the Republican Party was "a white man's party" committed to "making white labor respectable and honorable, which it can never be when negro slave labor is brought into competition with it." Free-Soilism did in the end provide an indispensable contribution to the ending of slavery; however, by embracing negative attitudes toward Blacks, this movement, Woodward remarked, "triumphed over slavery in the name of white supremacy."[3]

Though usually not as hostile to the ex-slaves as others within the antislavery faction, those delegated the task of assisting with the transition to freedom nevertheless expressed ideas of Blacks that sustained the belief in the cultural and racial superiority of the White, Anglo-Saxon population group. This discourse was present in the earliest impressions of the ex-slaves recorded by the "evangels of civilization" who went South in the wake of the Civil War. In her *First Days amongst the Contrabands,* Elizabeth Hyde Botume expressed attitudes toward Blacks that would later shape the politics of Reconstruction, especially the ambivalence of the Freedmen's Bureau with respect to the question of "race." While Botume expressed a strong disagreement with government officials who "spoke of the freed people as if they were a herd of cattle," she also argued that because the former slaves "knew nothing of order, or system, or economy of time," the "work of reconstruction was slow and tedious." In consequence, Botume asserted, one "might as well expect a newborn infant to become a man in four years as that this race, newly born to freedom, should become self-supporting and self-protecting at once." Not only did Botume's statements (recorded in her memoir in 1866 and 1867) reflect the paternalism that later characterized some of the reasoning behind policies of the Freedmen's Bureau; she also exhibited conflicting analyses of the factors that continued to lead to the poor living conditions of the ex-slaves.[4]

Acknowledging that many of the ex-slaves were industrious "and tried hard to take care of themselves," Botume asserted that, "[w]hen they failed, it was through ignorance." Displaying the logic of the dominant abolitionist political language, this statement was ironically made immediately after Botume insightfully described the bookkeeping practices by which some plantation store managers kept the ex-slaves impoverished and indebted. Despite such an understanding of the postslavery conditions of Blacks, the ascription of causality to lack of proper training remained the governing mode of interpretation for Botume. As she argued, the "negro mind has never been cultivated; it was like an empty reservoir, waiting to be filled." Notwithstanding her strong support of education for the ex-slaves, Botume reaffirmed the secular, civilizing mission of the new evangels who felt that "plenty to eat would harmonize and Christianize them faster than hymns and sermons; and that needles and thread and soap and decent clothing were the best educators, and would civilize sooner than book knowledge."[5] This understanding remained inseparable from the understanding of the general social order, in which the securing of the material conditions of existence increasingly became the principle of explanation for the motivation of human behaviors.

Whereas in the United States humanitarians and Freedmen's Bureau officials in the 1860s functioned within a well-established intellectual framework where the mental capabilities (and, therefore, the humanity) of the Black population were questioned, at the time of abolition in the British Caribbean a new racial discourse was only beginning to take shape. While the missionaries remained the strongest allies of the ex-slaves, nevertheless, a subtle shift began to occur after 1834 in the missionary discourse whereby, in their embryonic form, ideas emerged that would later come to characterize the postslavery discourse on "race" throughout the British Empire.[6] Robert Stewart has illustrated that initially, at the moment of emancipation, missionaries remained optimistic that they were on "the threshold of a new era in the Christianization of the world." Where the planters received monetary compensation, the missionaries felt the former slaves should be given religion as their form of compensation for the institution of slavery. However, when the ex-slaves did not respond to evangelism at the rate, or in the terms, that the missionaries desired, the hope transformed into frustration, and the ex-slaves' behaviors would be attributed to character flaws. As a Wesleyan missionary remarked, Blacks were "striking examples of the ignorance and depravity of human nature."[7] Thus, while some maintained that the "sloth, lying and deceit" produced by slavery could be erased, nevertheless, by associating these qualities with the ex-slaves and proposing the need for redemptive-rehabilitative strategies, the allies of the slaves gave indirect legitimacy to the proslavery ideology that insisted Blacks could not exist without supervision, as well as discourses that would later be used to justify the resubordination of the Black population group in nonslave terms.[8]

The response of James Phillippo, the noted Baptist missionary, to a query of Governor Sligo provides such an example. The Baptist religion had been the one most closely aligned with the political struggles of Blacks, from the 1831 slave rebellion to that of Morant Bay in 1865. In October 1835, Sligo inquired in regard to "the possibility of educating the Adult Negro population, and as to the prospect afforded, of Adult Negroes being employed in the instruction of their fellows." While insisting that it was not a question of the "intellectual deficiency" of Blacks, as slavery had caused their "physical and mental degradation," Phillippo still contended nonetheless that he "could not but regard all efforts on a large scale, for the education of Adults, as problematical, or as likely to be attended with very inadequate results." After working with slaves for over twelve years, the missionary concluded that "so dull are they of apprehension from long habits of mental insolence, . . . any scheme for their letter instruction on a large and national scale, (should any such design be contemplated) would prove abortive." Educating the young remained the only hope for future prosperity, but even this became a problem, as they lacked "mental and moral discipline" from being "trained up in such habits of vice & idleness."[9]

Although somewhat at odds with other public statements, Phillippo's discourse forecasted the tension that would define the conception of the ex-slaves held by the special magistrates and other officials of the Colonial Office. Besides having a "total ignorance of the art of teaching," Blacks were unqualified to teach because they "manifest a degree of vulgarity and other evidence of partial civilization, in their ordinary intercourse." Convinced that slavery had exerted such a negative influence on Blacks whereby they became "[a]ccustomed from infancy to an offensive exposure of their persons, and to work and live together, almost in a state of nature," Phillippo contended that "it can scarcely be expected that they should be keenly alive to a sense of shame." Even when the ex-slaves married, which might seem to imply an adherence to the behavioral prescriptions of the missionaries, these were only faint attempts, as he believed they could not sustain "well organized and well regulated families." Moreover, Blacks did not have "an aptitude in communicating knowledge," and when they attempted, Phillippo claimed that it was "proverbially ostentatious, mystical, ambiguous, indirect, and verbose." Blacks could not distinguish truth from falsehood because the mind of the ex-slave continued to be enchanted by superstition, which the power of Christianity was only beginning to demystify. As a consequence, Phillippo believed that it would require "considerable exertion and the lapse of considerable time to overcome" this problem and to achieve the "production of moral good."[10]

James Phillippo's argument would be echoed later by the special magistrate John Daughtrey, who expressed, also out of a putative concern for the former slaves, that teachers could not be found among the Black population. Although Daughtrey favored compulsory education for the children of ex-slaves, he contended that it would be "in vain to look for teachers in the island, they must be supplied from the parent country." For unless teachers were sought from outside of the island, a situation would result whereby only the most intellectually fit would survive, and the children "whose parents are lowest in the scale of intelligence" would simply lose out. One can see from Phillippo's and Daughtrey's claims that a belief in genetic inheritance was beginning to take shape as the emancipation process unfolded.[11]

Thomas Holt has argued that in close step with the transformations stemming from abolition, "British elite ideology and official policy moved from non-racist to racist premises, at the same time that the destruction cleared the way for that elite's more robust embrace of imperialist ambitions." The complex, if not paradoxical, legacy of abolition remained that the "racism that made it possible to think of people as slave labor gave way to a racism that freed individual slaves while justifying the domination of entire nations." Frequently, even when the government agents involved in the emancipation process attempted to espouse a "liberal democratic ideology," it would reinforce the general racial discourse. This dynamic emerged, Holt insisted, as the logical and systemic result of the intellectual framework within which the dominant understanding of emancipation was conceptualized: "Something was amiss in the very project of emancipation, in the very premises on which it was founded."[12]

The British Caribbean Context

More than a decade before Thomas Carlyle argued that where "a Black man, by working about half-an-hour a-day (such is the calculation), can supply, by aid of sun and soil, with as much pumpkin as will suffice, he is likely to be a little stiff to raise into hard work,"[13] T. Watkins Jones gave a similar idyllic account of the conditions in his district in St. Thomas in the Vale. Jones stated that the ex-slaves seemed "perfectly contented" with their situation, being "extremely healthy" and "not distressed during working hours." However, he did not feel that the ex-slaves, while living under such conditions, were becoming more productive: "[S]till I think they are not increasing in industry." The masters and managers on the plantations were "very kind and indulgent," giving clothing allowances and medical care in excess of what the law allows. Combined with the "grounds and provisions in abundance, . . . two or three horses to carry their provisions to market" as well as dogs, goats, and poultry "to an unlimited extent" made the situation enviable:

> The negro, if it be not his own fault, can be the happiest of all working peasantry, living in a climate where clothing is almost superfluous; working but 40½ hours during the week; his master obliged by law to find him all the necessaries of life; the multiplicity of cooling nutritious fruits and wild vegetables, which abound in this country, gives him an opportunity of living for six months without the slightest exertion on his part to cultivate them. No tax collector waits at his door; no sheriff to arrest him for debt; no wood-ranger to prevent his collecting as much fuel as he pleases; all that is asked of from him is, to work diligently for his master, and steer clear of theft.

Despite the Edenic setting ("where clothing is almost superfluous"), crime continued to occur, leading Jones to conclude that "every vigilance and exertion should be used to put an end to a crime so baneful to the interests and peace of the colony."[14]

The issue of crime raised by T. Watkins Jones appeared in many of the reports of the special magistrates, but while some lamented the supposed increase, others understood the "fear of crime" language (if not hysteria) as a political strategy of the planters that evaded other systemic issues. Edward D. Baynes contended that although many asserted that crime was on the increase on the island, "[n]othing can be more contrary to the fact." Those making such claims, "purposely or wilfully conceal, that infractions of the law have only lately, in these colonies, become, in all instances, a matter of judicial animadversion and public notice." Under slavery, "all but enormous and atrocious offences were visited by domestic discipline, and that, in multifold instances, even these were never punished at all." Therefore, "the increase in cases brought before the tribunals is . . . in this country no indication of the increase of crime." Concurring with Baynes, Henry Walsh argued that "[c]rime in this country was formerly hidden to a certain extent, and in like manner hiddenly punished." However, since abolition, crime had taken on political overtones: "[I]n former days, if a slave stole a few canes, or I would see one appropriating, say took a few canes, it was not considered an offence; but now everything is high treason." According to Walsh, time and the resocialization of the ex-slaves were the solutions to this problem: "[T]his can only be remedied by religion, education and age, in the existing laws, and such addition as the British Government may judge expedient to a new peasantry uneducated."[15]

The crime debate really took on political overtones in October 1836 when a Middlesex County grand jury inquiry (essentially a platform for planter concerns) issued a report contending that an increase of crime resulted from the manner in which the special magistrates administered the law. Three magistrates, William Ramsay, Richard Hill, and G. Ouseley Higgins, penned a joint letter to Governor Sir Lionel Smith in order to address the manner in which they felt their character and integrity had been attacked. Although they did not agree that an increase in crime had actually occurred, for the sake of argument, the magistrates granted this point. Nevertheless, they maintained the problem stemmed from the actions of the planters that undermined "those common bonds of mutual dependence and support which form powerful links in uniting communities." The planters' strategy included forcing pregnant women to "repay" the time "lost" in childbirth, withholding provisions from the former slaves, and then reducing the time allotted for cultivating provision grounds (which tended to be located several miles from the plantations). Moreover, the magistrates proposed, it was "not only the fear of famine which compels the negro to become, first a trespasser, and then an avowed thief," but this necessity "is accelerated by his peculiar position under the restriction of police law." Police officers routinely stopped the ex-slaves, and if they did not produce tickets demonstrating that they could sell specific commodities for their subsistence, their provisions could be confiscated. Such examples led the special magistrates to conclude that, "[i]mpelled by his wants, and harassed by vexations of the law, is it to be wondered that the ignorant negro (demoralized by slavery) should take advantage of his position . . . to plunder his neighbor, and to slaughter his sheep and oxen for food."[16]

Other noble attempts like that of Ramsay, Hill, and Higgins were made in response to discipline and punishment around the issue of crime. On several occasions Governor Sligo issued letters and circulars to the special magistrates with regard to the use of corporal punishment, especially when it concerned ex-slave women. Publicly working freedwomen in chains or flogging them in workhouses recurred as a point of contention between the special magistrates and the planters. In the parish of St. Mary, overseers and managers of plantations would have all the hair of women cut off for reasons, they argued, of cleanliness. However, as Governor Sligo aptly noted, "it never was done during slavery, when the proprietors were possessed of a much deeper interest in the health of the slaves than they are now." The real issue remained, as the governor stated, the attempt to reexert a certain power over the ex-slaves: "I have come to the painful conclusion that it is done on purpose to annoy the apprentices."[17]

Notwithstanding these astute insights, many of the special magistrates adhered to the belief in a strict policy of discipline and punishment, and this philosophical position undermined the freedom the ex-slaves could have been accorded. Although he opposed the mixing of prisoners regardless of offense and objected to hard labor for ex-slave women, William Marlton of St. Mary nevertheless justified the system of punishment. Admitting that the original Abolition Act probably did not stipulate that the ex-slaves be placed in chains for minor infractions, Marlton countered that "the special justice has often no alternative, there being no place of confinement on many estates," believing that there existed a way in which the punishment could "be sufficiently severe without adhering to old views." Governor Sligo apparently agreed in this instance, and for reasons that he felt were racially and climatically based. In defending this policy to the Colonial Office, which had grave concerns about it, Sligo asserted that, while he would work toward substitutions for corporal punishment and the abolition of the use of confinement, these measures, which might have seemed cruel, did not have the same affect on Blacks: "I am bound to say, that simple confinement is not at all the same punishment to a negro that it is to an inhabitant of a colder climate; they do not feel so acutely the deprivation of society; even solitary confinement is here a very inferior mode of punishment; and confinement in the workhouses, unless accompanied by diminution of food or hard labour, possess no horrors for them."[18]

The claims of Sligo and Marlton as well as the statements in the joint letter of Ramsay, Hill, and Higgins exemplified much of the paradoxical nature within the philosophical position of the special magistracy, which emphasized the reformation of the character of the ex-slaves in a context that was supposed to be one of freedom. Nowhere was this belief with its racial overtones more clearly illustrated than with respect to the issue of the apprenticeship of ex-slave children. Writing from the Manchioneal District in St. Thomas in the East in March 1835, J. Kennet Dawson argued that it would take an act of the legislature "to secure the bringing up of the children under six in the habits of industry, as well as morality of conduct." Dawson contended that such a situation existed because the parents "decidedly refuse all assistance from their masters, and will not listen to any terms of apprenticeship, but seem to wish to bring up their children as slaves to themselves."[19]

R. Sydney Lambert of St. Mary concurred. According to Lambert, the free children remained "in a state of utter idleness" because their parents exhibited "a great reluctance to their application to any useful employment." James Harris represented the situation in the Santa Cruz District of St. Elizabeth in parallel terms, contending that numerous ex-slave children were "growing up in idleness, filth and ignorance" because their parents, who often neglected them, "will not allow them, on any consideration, to perform the slightest work, either on the property to which they are themselves attached, or elsewhere." Not unlike the claims of proslavery advocates, Harris alleged that the ex-slaves' idea of freedom consisted "in a total exemption from all labour and care." Consequently, he proposed an action to be taken in order "to remedy this great evil" and to prevent the "baneful and desperate state of society which will ensue upon many thousands of children grown up in habits of idleness and ignorance." He suggested that other proprietors should follow the model of the planter and senior magistrate of the parish, James Miller, who, with the consent of the parents, instituted a program where "a portion of each day is dedicated to instruction, moral and religious, and the rest to industrious labour." [20]

While many of the special magistrates would have agreed with Harris's suggestion, some went even further in proposing more extreme measures to be adopted. For instance, Edward D. Baynes suggested that mandatory attendance at Sunday and evening schools for all those under twelve would help the situation, but what the ex-slave children really needed was to be removed from their homes: "It is also expedient, that as many of the children as possible should be separated from their parents; unless this be done, nothing short of fatuity can look for moral improvement." If such a policy were to be implemented, the parents would be allowed to visit their children on Sundays, but Baynes insisted that "on no account should the children be permitted to go home" because only by removing the ex-slave children from the "contagion of example" will this "rising generation . . . possess advantages not yet enjoyed by the negro race." A year after making this proposal in his December 1835 report, Baynes recognized that the government was not moving in this direction, but, reinforcing an intellectual trend emerging in Europe at this time, he continued to advocate for institutionalization of ex-slave children in labor asylums: "I take the opportunity of repeating an opinion I have expressed in a former report, that whatever system may be adopted, it will fail in the great end of enlightening and improving, at an early period, the negro population, if many of the children as is practicable are not separated altogether from their parents, by the establishment of houses of industry, or of similar institutions, in the various districts of the island." According to Baynes, such drastic measures became necessary because it would take a long time "before the peculiar habits, vices and superstitions, the natural offspring of slavery, and a state still half savage, will be entirely extinguished in their posterity." In other words, the decision not to institute such policy would have enormous repercussions for the evolution and development of the ex-slave population: "If some system of this kind is not tried, I see no prospect of their advancing for a long time, *in the scale of human beings;* and if it be adopted, it will soon satisfactorily solve the problem of their natural equality or inferiority to the white man."[21]

Expressing this opinion in more than one of his reports, John Daughtrey agreed with Baynes's contention that ex-slave children should be removed from their parents. For Daughtrey, the condition of the free children constituted "one of the most depressing circumstances connected with [the special magistrates'] very onerous and anxious duties." In order to counteract the "growing up in total ignorance, and in habits of indolence and dishonesty," the British Parliament needed to arrange "their separation from their parents" and institute "regular employment as well as instruction." The issue of education, Daughtrey proposed, would "tend to their civilization, and remotely to something better" by allowing the ex-slave children to be "trained in entirely new principles and new habits." However, if the children attended school but continued to live with their parents, in an environment where nothing "like a strict and sacred regard for either honesty or truth" exists, "what they gain in moral sentiment at the school they will lose at home." Like many of his counterparts who ascribed what they defined as problems as resulting from slavery, Daughtrey attributed the situation to their former condition, stressing the need to protect the young from the continuation of a kind of cultural pollution. "Duplicity in one shape or other forms a component part of the character of the emancipated negro. I by no means wonder at it; the fruit is the natural product of the seed and the soil; but is it not of the first importance, in any attempts to benefit their offspring, to rescue them from such inevitable contamination[?]"[22]

Whereas many special magistrates felt that separating the children of ex-slaves from their parents should be coupled with education, Arthur Welch, stationed in the parish of Manchester, remained suspect of such a proposition. Describing the free children as "idle and ill clad," Welch stressed to the governor that "[t]his subject calls loudly for the consideration of your Excellency." While attendance at church exceeded capacity, school attendance in Welch's district remained low. And, although he favored the erection of more schools, he felt that it would have to be in connection with some form of work: "Mere literary education, unless combined with agricultural labour, will do little for the ultimate benefit of the country." Welch felt that those of the younger generation should be instructed in how to be industrious and provident, that is, made "useful members of society." The task, however, would not be an easy one, for "in a semi-barbarous country like this, to give children [such] an education . . . will just make them self-opinionated, and think themselves superior to their parents, and too clever to earn their bread by the sweat of their brows." Welch contended that this effect could already be seen in the free people of the island, and thus "what the free people of the lower orders here are now, the free children will be hereafter."[23]

Not all of the special magistrates agreed that the children of ex-slaves should be apprenticed into another form of indentured labor. Some totally rejected this idea and corroborated the perspective of the ex-slaves on this issue. The Montego Bay magistrate, William Carnaby, sympathized with parents who would not apprentice their children, despite the liberal allowance managers offered in return: "[I]t must be evident that such children are much better employed obtaining education, to enable them to become good members of society, than labouring at the tender age of eight." As other special magistrates had noted, William Marlton found that the parents in his district in St. Mary had a "decided aversion to let the free children do any work for the estate." However, his characterization of the parents' capabilities differed from most accounts. According to Marlton, the free children were "easily supported by their parents," and he encountered only one instance where the parents were unable to support their children. The children in his district were clothed and had medical assistance when they became ill. This situation existed because the parents agreed to give up the half day per week on the estates.[24]

Richard Chamberlaine noted that the complaint of the proprietors in his district in Clarendon of the disinclination of the parents to apprentice their children derived from "the desire to keep up the strength and cultivation of their properties at the cheapest rate after unrestricted freedom shall be proclaimed." Yet Chamberlaine insisted that, "so far from being blamable for this unwillingness," the ex-slaves deserved praise: "[I]t is characteristic of their foresight, and incontestably proves that they are inferior to none in the value and importance which they attach to freedom." Agreeing with Chamberlaine, S. R. Ricketts provided the strongest dissent from the majority opinion that attempted to encourage the apprenticing of the children of the former slaves. Asserting that "the love of offspring is generally a strong feature of the negro character," Ricketts argued that the fact that the parents rejected all overtures for their children to work for wages demonstrated "the judicious discrimination of maternal care, which deprecates the former system of children at the tender age of seven or nine years engaging in severe field-labour, before their physical capabilities were properly developed." Ricketts stressed the physiological effects of slavery on the former slaves, that of decreasing population as well as people of adult age "exhibiting the appearance of mere children." To counteract such a process, he favored the complete "exemption from labour (except in the cultivation of provisions and domestic matters) of all free children to the age of 15" in order to "ensure a healthy and athletic race of labourers."[25]

Rather than being concerned with making them into laborers, Ricketts suggested that the legislature should follow the parents' wishes and turn its attention to the education of the children. Admitting that most planters and special magistrates would consider it proof of industry and goodwill if the parents hired out their children, Ricketts offered a different interpretation: "I contend that . . . their time would be better employed in learning those truths and duties which are essential to their happiness, as ignorance and indolence will ever be found inseparable companions." If allowed to go uninstructed — and Ricketts claimed such allowance was "itself the fruitful source of crime" as the ex-slaves did not fully "understand the advantages and duties of a denizen" — the blame would have to be placed on those whose responsibility it was to educate the former slave population: "[W]hen all the evils which will arise from the neglect of education are felt, and doubly felt when the severe discipline of the system is removed, no blame can be attached to the parents; but great will be the responsibility of those who allowed the larger portion of the community to remain in ignorance; and those who neglected to provide for the storm, are assuredly in danger of reaping the whirlwind."[26]

The issue of apprenticeship of the children of the ex-slaves encapsulated the racial attitudes implicit (and sometimes explicit) in the political discourses of the special magistrates. Even those who seemed to have argued against the proposals of separating children from their parents and apprenticing them did so on the basis of creating a better "race of labourers," rather than seeing the symbolic importance attached to not having one's children submitted to a new form of indenture that resembled slavery. As John Daughtrey, himself an advocate of child apprenticeship, remarked, ex-slave parents were "jealous of every thing that seem[ed] to place their free children within the powers of others." However, his statement illustrated the difficulty for the agents and other governmental officials in accepting that the ex-slaves often subordinated economic concerns to social and political freedoms and thus did not necessarily behave according to the prescriptions of the free-labor, free-market system, that is, as *Homo oeconomicus*. This position led some of the agents of emancipation to imply that the ex-slaves, suffering from what some might call "false consciousness," did not understand their own social reality, and consequently needed to be instructed as to how best to secure their interests. James Harris of St. Elizabeth best articulated this understanding: "The negro character is fond of novelty and change"; thus, he does not understand "the nature and extent of the injury he inflicts on himself." The St. David special magistrate, Patrick Dunne, remained an exception to this rule, arguing that rather than behaving irrationally, former slaves were "fully aware of their rights, and tenacious in upholding them." Dunne, in fact, was struck by their perceptivity: "[I]t is surprising, debarred as they have been with but few exceptions, of the blessings of education, to see how acute and sensible they are."[27]

An underlying racial discourse also emerged in the descriptions of the social and cultural habits that emerged within the activities of the ex-slaves, especially with regard to the work and leisure patterns of the former slaves. The cultural and aesthetic forms of the ex-slaves, such as John Canoe (Jon-kunnu), could not be understood within their specific historic and cultural context but rather, within the logic of the governing political languages, had to be stigmatized as pagan rituals that needed to be eradicated. At the beginning of 1836, Governor Sligo was happy to report that this practice had begun to decline: "It has been generally remarked, that there has been this year by far less of the John Canoeing and the barbarous accompaniments which heretofore have been practised at this season." Two years later, Governor Sir Lionel Smith made a parallel statement: "I am delighted to say there has been this Christmas a considerable decrease of followers in those disgusting Bacchanalian processions in the towns, the remains of African superstition and slave policy" — a change that Smith attributed to an "improvement to the increase of Christian knowledge."[28]

Functioning within a *Homo oeconomicus* definition of being human, some of the special magistrates felt strongly that the ex-slaves should spend as much time as possible working in the fields. Since such labor supposedly had redemptive qualities, if the former slaves did not agree to specific policies, force should be employed. To this effect, T. Watkins Jones supported "coercion and determination on the part of the special justices," as well as a change in his district from the nine-hour to the eight-hour system so as not to allow the ex-slaves a larger block of time to themselves: "To allow the apprentices three successive days, Friday, Saturday and Sunday every fortnight, was attended with the worst result; they went an immense distance from the property to which they were attached, for the purpose of seeing their paramours, attending dances, John Canoes, &c." Ignoring this measure that circumscribed their freedom, the ex-slaves continued to take the alternate Friday without having the official approval of the special magistrate or the overseer. This action led Jones to solicit the assistance of the police, and, by making "some severe examples," he was able to force the ex-slaves into compliance. Such discipline and punishment were necessary because "the negro's mind is not strong enough, nor is he possessed of rationality sufficiently, to submit tacitly to a deprivation of that to which he has hitherto been accustomed." In consequence, this disciplining of the ex-slaves produced a positive psychic effect for Jones: "I cannot conclude without expressing my sincere pleasure at seeing the plough used most successfully in this parish for the purpose of making cane holes." [29] Here, one can see the "new image of man" that abhorred slavery and coerced labor but still derived pleasure from seeing Blacks engaged in labor, symbolizing that the world was properly ordered.

With regard to an issue that recurred in other historical contexts, that of controlling the free time of workers, Trelawny special magistrate R. C. Pennell agreed with T. Watkins Jones, asserting that the free time allotted to the ex-slaves remained an important concern: "The great evil, in my humble opinion, is, that the apprentices are allowed too much time to themselves, more than is necessary for the cultivation of their grounds." [30] Some special magistrates felt not only that the ex-slaves should spend the majority of their time performing agricultural labor (to induce "habits of industry") but also that they should do it cheerfully. [31] Such an attitude referred to the centrality of the belief in labor as a source of value, almost as an end in itself. This vision remained distinct from that of the former slaves who, in a large part, saw labor as a means to an end—that is, provisioning for their material conditions of existence and, therefore, providing the economic basis of their social freedom. Whereas some special magistrates insisted upon the ex-slaves laboring out of a disciplinarian impulse, whereby they would be taught specific cultural values, and thereby reproducing the notion of social order, others wanted the ex-slaves to labor because of an adherence to the philosophical premise that human "nature" automatically led to the desire to maximize profit.

From within the latter perspective it became no accident that some of the special magistrates equated civilization with the satisfaction of, in the words of John Daughtrey, "artificial wants." Hall Pringle of Hanover contended that with the proper inducements, the former slaves did not display "any signs of laziness." Given "that they have been accustomed all their lives to labour, . . . they are already so far advanced in civilization, that they will gladly labour for its luxuries." Although he departs somewhat from Pringle's analysis, Pennell also believed in the power of money as the great socializer. A month after making the preceding statement, Pennell claimed that the ex-slaves "cannot be said to be an industrious people, although the love of money, in which they fully participate with Europeans, would lead one to hope they will gradually become more so."[32]

It was often thought that money, evidenced by paying the ex-slaves' wages in cash, could be used to counter the idleness that it was continuously claimed they associated with freedom. Arthur Welch of Manchester suggested that the "importation of white emigrants," combined with cash payment for labor rendered, could transform the ex-slaves: "We may reasonably hope that a better example [immigrant presence] during the term of apprenticeship and the being actually paid in money the moment the work is done will greatly tend to dissipate these false notions of independence." According to Welch, these "false notions" came from the attitude toward labor held during the era of slavery: "In former times every white man considered himself above manual labour (field labour at least), and in consequence the climax of freedom was invariably made to consist in the most absolute and unqualified idleness." However, due to human nature, money could change this situation, for as Welch believed, "the old adage of 'money will make the mare go,' is as applicable to the negro as any other class of human beings."[33]

What David Brion Davis identified as a "new image of man," where being human was increasingly defined in purely naturalistic terms, was elaborated by some of the special magistrates and, indeed, remained central to the implementation of the project of emancipation. John Daughtrey's assertion that "compulsion may exist without coercion" implied that the objective of the slaveholders to compel Blacks to work was not necessarily wrong, but the strategy in how such compulsion was to be achieved was not effective. Daughtrey admitted that a preference of many ex-slaves to work for hire on other properties "clearly prove[s] . . . that the negro is capable of being stimulated to labour by the ordinary motives which actuate our common nature." There was nothing "extraordinary or unreasonable in this," he asserted; it was a simple question of considering the "natural motives" existing within all humans. In language that Adam Smith and other commercial abolitionists would have staunchly supported, Daughtrey insisted that labor problems occurred because "every thing that has the resemblance of compulsory labor" was irksome to the former slaves, a logical response given the history: "[S]lavery has made it so: it has given to labour, executed under superintendence, the air and impression of a penalty." A new strategy must now be employed, that is, as St. James special magistrate R. S. Cooper proposed, "the hope of reward," which "operates more powerfully than the fear of punishment as a stimulus to labour." Using such a technique, Daughtrey stated, "artificial wants [could] become in time real wants." This new form of coercion would help "to civilize" the ex-slave: "Every step they take in this direction is a real improvement."[34]

One can therefore see the extent to which attempts were being made to socialize the former slaves in terms that would eventually come to define the industrialization process. Without using specific terms, such as labor constitutes the source of all value, the special magistrates nevertheless affirmed the dominance of the political language that later organized the social reality of not only those in the colonies (even if in different terms) but also those in the metropole. This political language, while having forged the transformative abolitionist movement, paradoxically produced contradictions, whereby the same terms could be employed to resubordinate the former slaves. Despite claims to the contrary, many of the ex-slaves did demonstrate a sense of entrepreneurship in the postslavery context, especially with respect to the use of their provision grounds. Such a practice remained in part responsible for the conflict that occurred at Morant Bay. Yet, when the ex-slaves did not behave rigidly on the basis of the *Homo oeconomicus* premise, the special magistrates felt a need to prescribe a cure for this putative affliction. Due to the profoundly symbolic attachment to freedom, after purchasing their freedom many would not hire themselves out for wages because they were no longer bounded by the terms of apprenticeship. Alexander MacLeod of St. Dorothy commented on this phenomenon: "[F]rom one end of Jamaica to the other, not a single free person is to be seen working in the field for wages." Thomas Davies made the exact observation in his district in St. Mary: "[I]n no one instance have any who purchased themselves consented to work at any field-labour." MacLeod's remedy, which concurred with "the planters in the view they take of the present situation," was to bring in immigrant laborers. "Without considerable exertions and sacrifices on the part of the mother country, such as an immense immigration by Parliamentary aid, and a material reduction in the duties in the principal articles of colonial produce," he concluded, "the landed proprietors and planters of Jamaica are threatened, at the termination of apprenticeship, with general ruin."[35]

Alexander Fyfe displayed a similar attitude toward the ex-slaves when they did not behave in the ways in which he thought they should. On some of the plantations in his district, in order to receive extra allowances, the ex-slaves chose to work forty-five hours per week (nine per day with half the alternate Friday off). Fyfe supported this work schedule, and even in instances when the overseers did not want to accept this system, he used his power to insist that it be followed. However, when the ex-slaves preferred to work only forty and one-half hours per week (having a half day off every Friday), which meant giving up these allowances, Fyfe again asserted his power as a special magistrate because he did not agree with this viewpoint: "[W]hen they persist in relinquishing these allowances, and in claiming the four and a half hours, I shall allow the overseer to work them on the eight hours a day system." Fyfe was probably aware that few of the ex-slaves preferred the eight-hour to the nine-hour system, but their preference did not concern him, as he was attempting "to induce them to give the four and a half hours for indulgences."[36] Again, he believed that he understood the interests of the former slaves better than they did.

Rather than working them on a nine-hour system with the alternate Friday off, which would have been a compromise to both sides, Fyfe gave the impression of wanting to punish the ex-slaves for not seeing this situation from his perspective, although when implementing this policy he maintained that he operated purely out of "motives of humanity." Many children were dying from lack of medicine and medical attention (one of the allowances), and this occurrence resulted, Fyfe believed, from the refusal of the mothers to give up their four and a half hours, which would have given them this allowance. However, Fyfe's contention could be contested, for the issue remained, as he stated himself, "extra labour for the extra indulgences"; it would be highly unlikely that the mothers, who did so much to protect their children, would willingly jeopardize their health. Moreover, with extra time many of the mothers would have been allowed more time to nurture and care for their sick children; yet, within an understanding of freedom defined primarily by labor, such an idea was not conceivable.[37]

R. S. Cooper noted instances in his district in St. James parish when the former slaves did not necessarily behave according to the premise that "money will make the mare go." Cooper stated that, "as has occurred under my own eye," the ex-slaves would refuse "to work for their master, and hire themselves, for *even a smaller sum,* to a neighbor." However, rather than accuse the ex-slaves of behaving irrationally, Cooper understood that the question of just and fair treatment could easily outweigh any pursuit of material reward on the part of the former slaves. He did not agree that the ex-slaves would not work for wages in their own time; most would, "provided a suitable inducement is held out to them i.e. fair wages offered, and *honestly paid* when accepted."

When complaints are made by the planters that the ex-slaves did not show up for work, in every one of Cooper's cases, with one exception, he discovered that the ex-slaves had been cheated in the payment of wages. For this reason, Blacks had been forced into relying upon themselves, and refused to work for wages in their own time, because they had better financial prospects: "Sometimes the negroes decline working on certain days because those days are destined to be employed in the cultivation of their provision grounds, or carriage of their produce to town or market, which pays them better than a day's hire."[38] In other words, even if the ex-slaves were behaving in order to acquire money, but chose different means, some magistrates, unlike Cooper, could not recognize it.

The central issue remained, as Edward Baynes pointed out, that "labour cannot, at the same time, be voluntary and compulsory." The issue of labor, however, was only a part of the equation, as evidenced by the special magistrates and the government's attempt to control the social milieu of the ex-slaves, such as the domestic habits and cultural forms like obeah and John Canoe celebrations. As Thomas Davies asserted, "[V]isible improvement in morality . . . must go hand in hand with industry." Baynes's statement described the contradictory nature of the task delegated to these agents during the emancipation process. Yet this contradiction was foremost an intellectual one. While most of the special magistrates would have probably agreed that there were no natural or genetic differences among population groups, at the same time they made statements that implicitly questioned the mental capacity of Blacks. Baynes himself had already espoused doubts about the cognitive ability of Blacks, which he argued in terms of "race" and "class": "There are doubtless among them individuals not inferior in intelligence and acquirement to the European peasant, but the proportion is by no means large." Claims of the special magistrates such as "the weak minds of the negroes," or representations of the ex-slaves as "savage," "half-savage," "semi-barbarous," having a "naturally idle disposition," all served to verify that the "vexed question of original unity" had not been completely resolved with the abolition of slavery.[39]

The U.S. Context

Earlier, it was argued that the preliminary and final reports of the American Freedmen's Inquiry Commission served as intellectual precursors to the conception of emancipation that defined the postslavery political situation in the

United States. This claim can be extended as well to the "vexed question of original unity," that is, the political language of "race." In some respects, these reports advocated pioneering, if not revolutionary, ideas regarding the treatment of Blacks. As an example, on the question of Black enlistment in the Union forces, the commission displayed an astutely nuanced analysis of the dynamics of this issue. The members argued that for a couple of significant reasons "a considerable portion of the Union armies should be made up of persons of African descent." One reason came from the lessons of the past: "[T]he history of the world furnishes no example of an enslaved race which won its freedom without exertion of its own." If the struggle for abolition in the United States was not marked by "servile insurrection" in addition to civil war, the commission contended this fact was due more to an absence of "revenge and bloodthirstiness" that characterized the Black population, rather than any lack of courage or other qualities needed in combat. From the experience of those Black troops already engaged in battle, it was noted that the soldiers displayed the necessary qualities for battle. Thus, the preliminary report concluded that "in such warfare it is fitting that the African race seeks its own social salvation. The negro must fight for emancipation if he is to be emancipated."[40]

In addition to this historic reason, a general societal concern for the future of the country also impelled the inclusion of Blacks into the armed forces of the Union. The commission intimated that the well-being of the Black population could not be separated from the well-being of the nation as a whole: "If, then, emancipation be the price of national unity and of peace, and if a people, to be emancipated, must draw the sword in their own cause, then is the future of the welfare of the white race in our country indissolubly connected with an act of justice on our part toward the people of another race." Such a relation affirmed that, in order to preserve the social order and move into the future, this "struggle for good or evil" had to be resolved: "Then is it the sole condition under which we may expect — and if history speak truth, the sole condition under which we shall attain — domestic tranquillity, that we shall give the negro an opportunity of working out, on those battlefields that are to decide our own national destiny, *his* destiny, whether as slave or as freedman, at the same time."[41]

This potentially transformative attitude toward Blacks that appeared throughout the preliminary and final reports of the commission had another complex, though logical, side. Although the reports strongly disagreed with the premise of the natural inferiority of Blacks, the commission at the same time affirmed the belief in characteristics that could be ascribed to "race."

Cited at length, the commission confirmed the insight of Douglass that some abolitionists spoke "as flippantly" of their "Anglo-Saxon blood" as those who believed in the natural inferiority of Blacks:

> The Anglo-Saxon race, with great force of character, much mental activity, an unflagging spirit of enterprise, has a certain hardness, a stubborn will, only stronger than its social instincts. The head predominates over the heart. There is little that is emotional in its religion. It is not devoid of instinctive devotion, but neither is such devotion a ruling element. It is a race more calculated to call forth respect than love; better fitted to do than to enjoy.
>
> The African race is, in many respects, the reverse of this. Genial, lively, docile, emotional, the affections rule; the social instincts maintain the ascendant. Except under cruel repression, its cheerfulness and love of mirth overflow with the exuberance of childhood. It is devotional by feeling. It is a knowing rather than a thinking race. Its perceptive faculties are stronger than its reflective powers. It is well-fitted to occupy useful stations in life; but such as require quick observation rather than comprehensive views or strong sense. It is little given to stirring enterprise, but rather to quiet accumulation. It is not a race that will ever take a lead in the material improvement of the world; but it will make for itself, whenever it has fair play, respectable positions, comfortable homes.[42]

The political language of "race" should not be seen as separate from the emerging naturalistic self-conception that arose in the postslavery United States, in which the integration and stabilization of the society became increasingly described in laissez-faire terms. Reflecting this mode of thought, the commission articulated the central belief in labor as a structuring principle of society, and thus implied that slavery, which stigmatized labor, had to be abolished in order for civilization to develop and evolve: "The greatest social and political problems of the world connect themselves more or less intimately with the subject of labor. A people who regard work as degradation, though arts and letters flourish among them, are but emerging from barbarism." More than the position accorded to women, the commission argued that the "grade of civilization" can be measured by labor "from which, in one shape or other, the world receives everything of good, of useful, of beautiful, that charms the senses of ministers to the wants of man; to which we owe life, and everything that makes life desirable." This phenomenon supposedly resulted from the nature of all humans: "One of the most universal objects of human desire and of human endeavor is the acquisition of property."[43]

To a certain extent, South Carolina assistant commissioner Rufus Saxton agreed with the commission's perspective with regard to major concerns that needed to be addressed in the postslavery context. Saxton concurred with the commission's assertion that implementation of a labor system became the main issue after the end of slavery: "The great question which, of course, lies at the foundation of all the efforts of the government to promote the well-being of the freedmen, through the agency of this bureau, is the labor question." However, because Saxton espoused a different representation of human nature, his analysis diverged somewhat from that of the commission. Rather than assuming that humans had a natural disposition to labor, Saxton contended exactly the opposite: "The difficulty which has been found in the way of the immediate solution of this important question has been the natural disinclination of all the human race to labor, unless compelled to do so." According to Saxton, Blacks differed in no respect from others in this matter: "This disinclination is shared by the freedmen in common with other races of men, and so far as my observation extends, to no greater extent." As slaves, Blacks could not have been industrious, because "the only stimulus to work was the fear of punishment."[44]

Saxton's partial dissent from the perspective of the American Freedmen's Inquiry Commission led him to depart radically from the kind of thinking that eventually became the modus operandi of the Freedmen's Bureau. Recognizing that the Sea Island ex-slaves had "their hearts set upon the possession of these islands," Saxton proposed that "a practical solution of the whole question of lands, embraced in Special Field Order No. 15, may be had by the appropriation of money by Congress to purchase the whole tract set apart by this order" or, after a "fair and liberal assessment" of the value of the land had been made, by paying the landholders this sum. Should the property owners prefer the land to the money, "then pay the money to the freedman who occupies [the land]." Saxton stressed that "this arrangement would satisfy the freedmen and some of the former owners." However, his proposal—which essentially implied that those upon whose labor the society had for so long depended would have been compensated for their toil—would have to be rejected as the condition for sustaining the conception of the postslavery United States, which, while no longer organized by the coerced labor of Blacks, nevertheless mandated their symbolic and empirical subordination. As a result, the politics of emancipation would be defined by the continued avoidance of this issue, an absence that the political language of "race" increasingly justified.[45]

Given this situation, negotiating the labor question logically became the nexus where the racial notions of officials of the Freedmen's Bureau can be detected. The major question resulting from the near total collapse of the commitment to the ex-slaves acquiring land was whether, after the restoration of plantations, the ex-slaves could now be induced to work for wages on them. This situation led to the question of forming contracts, an issue that emerged only in the postslavery case of the United States. D. T. Corbin tried unsuccessfully "to dissuade [the ex-slaves] from settling in the fine lands and advised them to labor on the plantations for good wages." Inspector General C. H. Howard toured South Carolina toward the end of 1865 and noted as well that many of the ex-slaves did not want to sign contracts for wages: "There was a universal reluctance to the renewal of contracts with their former masters and hence desire to wait till the end of the year when they intend to seek other places." While planters remained in favor of the ex-slaves agreeing to contractual labor "on the ground that there would be a great deal of disturbance at the end of the year," Howard found "that there was not always the disposition on their part to conciliate their freed workmen." Such an attitude led to conflict: "For instance some Freedmen refused to renew the Contract with the employer unless he would change the overseer; but this he refused to do." As a result, even some Whites admitted that only the military officials and bureau agents "have any influence with the colored people to secure Contracts or counteract erroneous impressions because the Freedmen have no confidence in those who have been slaveholders."[46]

As Howard's analysis suggested, bureau officials easily acknowledged the responsibility of the planters in failing crops within the state. In his district of Edisto, Subassistant Commissioner J. M. Johnston reported in May 1867 that the crops "looked remarkably well [and] show that little has been lacking on the part of the laborers." In the few cases where crops were "in a backward condition," Johnston contended that it could be traced "to some default on the part of the Planter: lack of furnishing prompt payment of wages, which of course compels the freedman to seek employment elsewhere, to enable him to procure his daily bread." Following a similar line of reasoning, Assistant Commissioner Robert Scott asserted that when landholders could not produce a profitable crop, it was due to a certain lack of understanding: "In very many instances where planters have failed to realize a paying crop, the failure is easily traceable to ignorance of the free labor system and general mismanagement." Mistreatment of the ex-slave workers formed a central part of this supposed ignorance: "[I]n attempting to secure by unfair contracts more than would justly revert to them, [the planters] have overreached themselves." This strategy forced the laborers to leave in search of better conditions, a situation that prompted Scott "to deduce the principle . . . that a contract unfair to the laborer is unprofitable to the planter."[47]

Scott's understanding of the postslavery situation differed from that of his predecessor Saxton in the extent to which he supported the ex-slaves, as can be seen from the conclusion of his circular letter. Scott ended the letter with an appeal to the ex-slave population that typified the contradictory nature of Freedmen's Bureau operations. In terms reminiscent of the discourse of apprenticeship in the British Caribbean, Scott implied that the ex-slaves needed to prove they were deserving of freedom: "I would say to the freedpeople [i]t is incumbent upon you to show the world that you are worthy of this freedom which your country has bestowed upon you." Blacks could best demonstrate their worthiness by adhering to the behaviors prescribed by the new secular missionaries: "To this end it behooves you to labor industriously; to lead a strictly honest and virtuous life; to abide faithfully by the obligations of the contract you enter into; to be honest and thrifty in all your transactions[;] to observe the sanctity of the mar[r]iage [relations;] and by every means in your power to secure education to yourselves and your children." Scott admonished the ex-slaves to treat their employers with respect and to obey all lawful orders, and in return the employers would treat them fairly: "[I]t will be for your interest to so conduct yourselves as to deserve his respect and regard." Ironically, the role of the planters coincided with that of the agents of the Freedmen's Bureau, as they were represented also as being able to instruct the ex-slaves: "It will be the duty as it is certainly for the interest of the planter to practically acknowledge the freedom of the laborer in its fullest sense as guaranteed by law—to kindly and in a friendly spirit, correct those erroneous ideas of license and independence which the freedpeople too frequently associate with freedom; and to teach them the obligations imposed upon them by citizenship."[48]

As Scott's letter demonstrated, agents of the bureau often minimized the political conflict implicit in the emancipation process and, as a result, suggested that the ex-slaves needed to be socialized into adopting new values and behaviors, especially new habits with regard to labor. George Pingree, the subassistant commissioner for the district of Darlington, contended that if the ex-slaves were only "true to themselves" with "hard labor and strict attention to duty," they could "expect to prosper, and receive the solid benefits" of freedom. According to Pingree, some ex-slaves thought that contracts were "binding upon their [e]mployers but not upon themselves." Consequently, if the laborers left the estates, he would have them arrested and "obliged them to return to their first [e]mployer, where they had signed a contract." Pingree's analysis and response to social conflict demonstrated an imbalance that operated in the governing conception of emancipation, for rarely (if ever) were planters arrested for nonpayment of wages, a frequent occurrence across the state. Combined with the knowledge of the tactics of the planters, which included turning ex-slaves off of plantations before harvest in order to avoid having to pay them and, as Pingree noted in his report, the "common practice" whereby the planters "threatened to shoot Freedmen for the most trivial offenses," rational reasons existed in most instances for the ex-slaves to quit the plantations. Yet when it came to disciplining or punishing planters for provocations or for outright breaches of the social-labor contract, bureau officials would claim they were powerless and could not change the situation.[49]

In many cases, the hands of the bureau agents were tied, and they could do little to assist the former slaves. A. E. Niles recounted in very moving terms a sense of powerlessness in the face of the treatment of Blacks: "Toward the Freedmen there is much bad feeling, and but for the presence of our small garrison I can hardly see how he would manage to live. The men that understand the Freedmen to have or that they are entitled to any more rights than a horse are Exceptions to the general rule. We can do but a part of what we should do. A freedman is now standing at my door, his tattered clothes bespattered with blood from his head, caused by blows inflicted by a white man and with a stick and we can do nothing for him."[50] With such insight, it appears increasingly ironic that many agents would ignore the social and political conflict of the emancipation process.

The neglect by many Freedmen's Bureau officers of the political dimension implicit in the postslavery situation became the condition of possibility for many to argue for the need for a new civilizing mission. Within this context, the signing of labor contracts, a process usually interpreted from a purely economic point of view, can be seen to have been a part of a larger project of "cultural reconstruction." According to Ralph Ely, only by signing contracts could the ex-slaves expect to receive their "just rights," for as distressing as the conditions for the ex-slaves were, it would be "unjust" for the bureau to "compel the Planters to care for them longer." Thus, Ely hoped that Blacks would "now see the folly of not making contracts." Precisely for this reason, D. T. Corbin devoted most of his time "to the enlightenment of the freedmen and advising and superintending the making of their contracts."[51]

Such a viewpoint impelled some officials of the Freedmen's Bureau to describe the failure to sign contracts as an evil. H. W. Smith suggested that evil "must necessarily follow a failure on the part of employers and freedmen to enter into contracts." In his subdistrict of Georgetown, A. J. Willard noted that he "corrected" the evil which emerged during the year, which resulted from the ex-slaves and "their unwillingness to do anything except cultivate and harvest their own little lots." Rather than placing the emphasis on contracted labor for the planters, the ex-slaves divided the lands among themselves, which may have provided them with more independence. However, Willard strongly felt that he had to put a stop to it, contending that "[s]uch a system cannot be maintained for any length of time, as it is contrary to the Laws of Nature and civilization as I understand them."[52]

While the evil to which the Freedmen's Bureau officials referred may have been the suffering and consequent social problems (like crime) that they felt would have been the result of not having a successful crop, this idea was not always evident. F. W. Liedtke justified to his superior why he approved of a contract that "so manifestly intended to swindle the freedpeople out of their rights." Liedtke reported that he had questioned the former slave, John Rawlins, as to whether he fully understood the terms of the agreement. Rawlins, who Liedtke described as being "very anxious to enter into the contract," stated "that, if left alone, he was sure to work all the open land." However, Liedtke was concerned that Rawlins had an insufficient number of workers, and although he should have somehow foreseen the problem, because Rawlins was so confident, he "trusted his intelligence and energy." Liedtke declared that it was certainly not his intention to do anything to injure the ex-slaves; rather, he was attempting to do what he thought best for them: "There are people near Entaw Springs living in the woods, who have settled there against the will of the owners and against my advise [*sic*]. These people live in a state of barbarism and plant not more than one or two acres to the hand, in such a way that in my opinion they will not make more than one bushel of Corn to the hand, but still they refuse to accept any reasonable Contract, thinking that if the[y] work for themselves, they will be better of[f]."[53]

Liedtke's primary concern, that the ex-slaves should be provided with guidance under supervised, contracted labor, was an idea shared by some of his counterparts. Like Liedtke, out of a genuine concern for the well-being of the ex-slaves, W. P. Richardson issued regulations for the production of corn in his district: "The recommendations contained in [this circular] have been made upon mature reflection, and are believed to be for the best interest of the freedmen." The principal objective of the circular involved securing food, clothing, and shelter for the ex-slaves, necessities that Richardson felt were not attainable "under any other system of contracting," and which the ex-slaves did not know how to obtain for themselves: "Many intelligent and industrious negroes might very well be allowed to work for wages in money, or for a share of the crop, but the greatest number would unquestionably be brought into a state of destitution, by their want of economy, prudence and foresight in providing for themselves and families. It is therefore recommended that they be protected from this, by stipulating for these things in the contract. When they have had more experience in taking care of themselves, and more fully comprehend the necessity of providing for their future wants, such restrictions may become unnecessary."[54]

From the perspective of the ex-slaves, the contract system became dysfunctional, and by 1868 there was even an open acknowledgment of its failure. Like the bureau's Commissioner Howard, many believed the free market would induce harmonious relations between the planters and the ex-slaves. Yet as early as 1865 a report indicated that with these contracts the planters were trying to recreate a situation "as near to the condition of slavery as possible." In Edgefield County, 60 percent of the contracts contained words that implied subservience of the ex-slave to the ex-slaveholder. Echoing the Black Codes, these contracts represented more than attempts at labor exploitation, as they often stipulated "standards for the freedmen's behavior in his own life and towards other people." More than 50 percent of the contracts in Abbeville County contained clauses that attempted to regulate the personal activities of the ex-slaves, a goal shared by the agents of the Freedmen's Bureau. Only in rare instances "did the contracts yield authority to any of the freedmen," and these infrequent occurrences were usually accompanied by the employers taking great pains to protect their interests. As a result, the contract system "served to reinforce the employer's control over every aspect of the freedmen's life."[55]

Despite evidence that suggested that the postslavery social and labor system operated to the disadvantage of the ex-slave population, officials such as Liedtke maintained the central issue as being a lack among the ex-slaves of "foresight in providing for themselves" for the future. In a manner parallel to the political languages of the special magistrates, agents of the bureau, like Edward O'Brien, felt that for such a reason, the ex-slaves needed to be taught to think of the future: "My opinion is based on actual facts and figures and until these people are taught to provide for the future they will not be successful in working land on shares." J. S. Power succinctly articulated this resocialization mission, which implied that if the ex-slaves were taught to be "thrifty accumulators," they could in the end depend upon themselves: "It has been my constant endeavour to impress upon their minds the importance of industry, and frugality, and to explain to them the necessity of fulfilling their agreements to labour faithfully and diligently while I gave them to understand they must now rely upon themselves." This task was not an easy one, as the ex-slaves had to learn the cost of living, something that slavery, according to George Pingree, allowed them to ignore. Responding to the dispute between the planters and the ex-slaves concerning the bookkeeping practices of the former, Pingree disregarded the political implications of the conflict and asserted that because slaves had been furnished food, clothing, shelter, and medical attention, they "cannot now begin to realize how much it costs to live."[56]

Behind the statements of O'Brien, Power, and Pingree and the language of the contracts remained an ambivalence concerning the issue of "race." Although most of the agents of the Freedmen's Bureau rarely made explicit statements with regard to the basic humanity or mental capacity as being genetically based, most of the policies, which emphasized instruction and supervision (rather than justice and equal opportunity, as Frederick Douglass insisted), did in fact imply the idea that Blacks could not know what was best for them. Officials of the Freedmen's Bureau felt that slavery had damaged, if not destroyed, the character of Blacks, and thus they had to become agents of socialization to humanize Blacks. The idea remained the most fundamental throughout the ordeal of emancipation.

At the outset of this process, W. F. Young espoused this position when he described his job as being a "helper, teacher and friend of the colored man . . . to whom he can look to for encouragement and sympathy, *in his efforts to become a man*." Bureau agents were to encourage Blacks in this endeavor because, according to William Stone, "the stronger race" does not have a "natural right to oppress the weaker [or] to take advantage of his ignorance." Like many of his counterparts, Stone did not even question the existence of a "stronger" or a "weaker race," but genuinely considered that he paid Blacks a compliment when he acknowledged being impressed with the progress that the ex-slaves had made, especially "in view of their ignorance and the imperfect development of their reasoning powers." However, this putative humanization process or cultural reconstruction would proceed slowly, for, according to J. E. Cornelius, "Bigamy, Adultery, fornication and theft" had "become almost a second nature to them."[57]

John William De Forest, the agent at Greenville, seemed to have agreed with Cornelius's Lamarckism. According to De Forest, the question was moot as to whether Black children could learn as quickly as White children: "I should say not; certainly those whom I saw could not compare with the Caucasian youngster of ten or twelve, who is 'tackling' French, German, and Latin; they were inferior to him, not only in knowledge, but in the facility of acquisition." De Forest explained this supposed inferiority in terms of the Lamarckian notion of the inheritability of acquired characteristics, a central assumption, historians have noted, of Black social uplift proponents. "In their favor it must be remembered that they lacked the forcing elements of highly educated competition and of a refined home influence. A white lad gets much bookishness and many advanced ideas from the daily converse of his family. Moreover, ancestral intelligence, trained through generations of study, must tell, even though the rival thinking machines may be naturally of the same calibre." As a result, Blacks could never be considered to be intellectually on par with Whites: "I am convinced that the Negro as he is, no matter how educated, is not the mental equal of the European." Even the humanity of Blacks continued to be called into question: "Whether he is not a man, but merely, as 'Ariel' and Dr. Cartwright would have us believe, 'a living creature,' is quite another question and of so little practical importance that no wonder Governor Perry wrote a political letter about it." Reiterating the position of the special magistrate S. R. Ricketts, De Forest believed that the fundamental issue remained that if measures were not taken to resocialize the ex-slaves, the general society (which he understood to have been generically White) would suffer the consequences: "Human or not, there he is in our midst, millions strong; and if he is not educated mentally and morally, he will make us trouble."[58]

After studying the life and work of De Forest, a sympathetic biographer, when confronted with his view of Blacks, was compelled to conclude that "[s]uch were the convictions of man entrusted with the reconstruction of race relations in South Carolina." Frederick Douglass had already detected this perspective before the Civil War among some abolitionists. Douglass felt that these attitudes undermined the principles of abolition and constituted what he defined as an unholy alliance, "an outrage on humanity and a sin against God." In the end, Douglass contended this "false reform . . . will curse more than it will bless." Once again, Douglass prophesied coming events, for due to the irresolution of "the vexed question of original unity," the former slaves were forced to challenge what was defined as a "reign of terror," one that would endure well into the next century.[59]

Chapter Five

Delusions of a False Canaan

On Morant Bay, Redemption, and
the Incomplete Victory of Emancipation

Looking at the matter simply and solely with a view to the interests of the negro, it is now beyond a doubt ascertained that his condition has been incalculably damaged by the very measures which were adopted with the exclusive purpose of improving it. . . . No person can now rise in Exeter-Hall and deny that in every single department of the system it has been a total failure. We do not say this in any triumph or with any spite. We simply wish to establish the proposition that our scheme must be totally changed if only for the sake of the negro himself.
— *The Times* (London), 6 January 1848

The unchanging verdict was [i]n favor of the Southern Gentleman. The Black Man—whom the Gov[ernmen]t of the US had declared "Free" [s]ighed that the long-cherished Word— "Freedom" when realized meant a fabric without foundation— a guarantee without faith—a proposition without support—a right without privilege—and a testament without a legacy— and [s]aid "Would to God! you had allowed us to remain in Egypt in our bondage—and not have deceived us by delusions of a false Canaan."
—J. M. Johnston, Freedmen's Bureau agent, 1867

In 1838, when the apprenticeship stage terminated two years earlier than anticipated in the British slave colonies and the era known as "full freedom" began, officials of the government maintained the assertion that it was still necessary to instruct the former slaves in certain cultural habits. As a consequence, some continued to feel compelled to advise the ex-slaves on how to conduct themselves. The island governor, Sir Lionel Smith, offered his recommendations in a proclamation issued shortly before the abolition of apprenticeship was to take effect. The governor insisted that he was giving the apprentices "a great blessing," claiming that it was in their interest to be "civil, respectful, and industrious." He stated that in this new context of "freedom," the former slaves needed to become self-reliant: "Remember that in freedom you will have to depend on your own exertions for your livelihood." Smith counseled the ex-slaves that if they could agree with the terms of labor, then they should remain on properties with their former slaveholders; but, in instances when there was not agreement, the governor did not offer any recommendations. Yet he did insist that for those who supposedly did not want to work, force would be used against them: "Idle people who will not take employment, but go wandering about the country, will be taken up as vagrants, and punished in the same manner as they are in England." Stressing that the former slaves should recall the "large price" paid by the English for their freedom, Smith suggested that by following his simple advice, they would be guaranteed success in the new social order and the general public would become the better for it:

> [The English citizenry] not only expect that you will behave yourselves as THE QUEEN's good Subjects, by obeying the laws, as I am happy to say you always have done as apprentices; but that the prosperity of the island will be increased by your willing labour; greatly beyond what it ever was in slavery. Be honest towards all men — be kind to your wife and children — spare your wives from heavy field work, as much as you can — make them attend to their duties at home, in bringing up your children, and in taking care of your stock — above all, make your children attend divine service and school. If you follow this advice, you will, under God's blessing be happy and prosperous.[1]

On this occasion, the active and outspoken special magistrate, Edward Baynes, took it upon himself to publish some advice for the ex-slaves in his periodical, the *West Indian and Jamaica Gazette*. Baynes also framed his comments in the context of serving the public good, contending that he was able to point out "the faults on both sides . . . so that each being brought to see their respective errors existing difficulties may, with a little concession, be removed, and the stream of events flow quietly in its natural channel." Affirming a sentiment that seemed to have been widespread in the postslavery era, Baynes argued that due to a "natural disinclination to labour" some ex-slaves had persuaded themselves that "freedom consists in an exemption from work." In language like that of other special magistrates, and not dissimilar from that which Thomas Carlyle would later employ, Baynes contended that some of the ex-slaves "would sit down in their huts, or lie basking in the sun all day, until aroused by cravings of nature." This group of ex-slaves, he asserted, had a tendency to "drag on without cares for respectability, or attention to personal comfort or decency," and led "a miserable and disgraceful existence, profitless to themselves, useless to the public, and displeasing to God, who has said that man must 'eat bread in the sweat of his face.' "[2]

Although he contended that those embodying these characteristics were few among the ex-slaves, Baynes, like Smith, stressed the behaviors of this putative minority group, relating them to others of which he felt the general ex-slave population also needed to be disabused. Some ex-slaves "err in demanding exorbitant wages." According to the special magistrate, such behavior could have serious consequences for the stability of the social order, as it can result in land lying uncultivated. As a consequence, the livelihood of both planters and laborers would be ruined; for the latter the "advance in the career of civilization" would be impeded, plunging the former slaves "anew into the state of darkness and barbarism, from which [they] are now so happily emerging." The situation therefore called for the ex-slaves to accept their position in the social structure, especially because it has been ordained by God: "You have a right to wages for your labour, for your labour is your property; your employer is entitled to profit from his lands, for they are his property. He and his wife and children, as well as you and your families, have the means of living suitably to *the station in this life in which it has pleased God respectively to place you*."[3]

The statements of Sir Lionel Smith and Edward Baynes clearly demonstrate that at the outset of "full emancipation," as was the case during the era of apprenticeship, government agents had a tendency to deemphasize the institutional forces that gave rise to and sustained the postslavery social hierarchies. Moreover, in instances when a reference was made to the history of the colonies before the abolition of slavery, the centrality of the unpaid labor of the slaves, which led to a massive accumulation of capital for the mother country, was rarely recognized. A clear illustration of this perspective can be discerned from the governor's statement in his proclamation that the ex-slaves would now have to depend upon their "own exertions for [their] livelihood." In making such an assertion, he denied the possibility that the general society had depended on the labor of the slaves. The former slaves in Jamaica would have probably agreed with the statement made by a counterpart in the United States. Responding to Commissioner Howard's concern about the ex-slaves being able to take care of themselves, one remarked: "I always kept master *and me.* Guess I can keep *me.*" Such a perspective challenged the one implicit in the governor's stressing the "large price" paid by the English people, when the slaves also paid a price, one that directly led to the enrichment of the British Empire. Thus, rather than a recognition of the importance of the Black presence to the society, the former slaves were left with the advice of Baynes, being told to make a "little concession" by accepting "the station in this life in which it has pleased God . . . to place you" in order that the emancipation process could "flow quietly in its natural channel."[4]

What flowing "quietly in its natural channel" meant varied depending upon the perspective with which one viewed the process of emancipation. From the viewpoint of the former slaves, it does seem that given the intractable nature of the policies of both the Colonial Office and the local government in Jamaica, the emancipation process was compromised from the beginning. And yet, even between these political factions, disagreements and conflicts arose that struck at the heart of the meaning of freedom. Regardless of which side of the spectrum, the position of the ex-slaves would still not be represented. The dispute over the Colonial Prisons Act provided such a case in point.

The Act for the Regulation of Colonial Prisons was passed as a result of Captain J. W. Pringle's 1838 report on prisons in the West Indies; and while it referred specifically to the issue of prison reform, it also became the symbol of a much larger issue. Beginning his analysis with Jamaica, which deserved "chief notice" because of its "great extent and population," Pringle concluded that "the system of discipline carried on both in gaols and houses of correction . . . hardly hold[s] out a chance of bringing about reform in the character of the inmates." Brutal customs such as "chaining prisoners in couples by collars round their necks" and cutting off the hair of inmates, including that of women who were accused of only minor offenses, served more than the purpose of punishment, as such practices were also intended to degrade the prisoners. Pringle suggested that the West Indies prison system should adopt the "separate system" of the United States that he had seen in operation in Philadelphia and in other penitentiaries, where the prisoners worked in their cells, and the whip was never employed. The "silent system" on which Caribbean prisons was based, where the prisoners slept and ate in solitary cells, but worked together under strict discipline without being allowed to communicate (hence the name "silent"), lent itself to indiscriminate use of the whip by the keepers.[5]

Coming on the heels of the highly contested early termination of apprenticeship, the passing of the Prisons Act by the imperial Parliament became the final straw for the Jamaica Assembly, which in response refused to continue conducting its legislative business. Henry Taylor, a senior clerk in the West India Department from early in the emancipation period until 1872, who became "a barometer for official thinking," acknowledged that the conflict over reorganizing the prison system had very little to do with what was alleged in the dispute but rather had much larger political implications: "Their [the Assembly's] refusal to do business is no doubt founded, in reality, less on the parliamentary interference with the prisons than upon their desire to evade giving an answer to the specific applications about to be made to them for laws of protection for the negroes." The issue of local legislative autonomy, and thus political control over the ex-slave population, remained at the heart of the disagreement over the prison system.[6]

Henry Taylor proposed recommendations to address the political conflict, in a memorandum often cited by historians. The main question for Taylor remained "whether the West Indian Assemblies be or be not, by their constitution and the nature of the societies for which they legislate, absolutely incompetent and unfit to deal with the new state of things." Although the immediate crisis referred to Jamaica, the response should be extended to the other colonies as well, given that "the general features of society are the same throughout the West Indies." Employing the conceptual vocabulary of classical republicanism, Taylor contended that the West India legislative assemblies (of which Jamaica was the most exemplary) could not be trusted to secure the common good: "We see the virtue of the members corrupted, the revenues of the island diverted from their proper application, and the Government left without the necessary resources for administering justice, spreading instruction, preventing crime, and administering to the public welfare in the most important and vital points."[7]

The former slaves also could not be trusted to represent the common good: although emancipated, they were "still in the depths of ignorance and by their African temperament highly excitable." According to Taylor, Blacks had "neither property nor knowledge, and cannot therefore have political power, or communicate it through any exercise of the rights of a constituency." Although it might seem logical to institute a representative democracy, he suggested that such an act would lead to a Black and colored oligarchy, which "would change the complexion of the evil to be dealt with, but not reduce the magnitude. The mass of the population is, and must long be, ignorant and bedarkened." In the final analysis, no one in the colonies should be entrusted with representing the political interests of the general population: "[W]hether the men who sit in the Assembly be white, black, or coloured, they will inevitably be irresponsible and unrepresentative of the interests of the people."[8]

Agreeing with the abolitionist interpretation of the slave system, Taylor ascribed the inability of both ex-slaveholders and ex-slaves to hold political office to this legacy of the past. It was claimed that slavery had so retarded the educational development of Blacks "that it was thought by the Governor that their own friends would not wish to see the Assembly chiefly composed of them." To correct the situation, the former slaves needed to be resocialized and "made fit" for the duties of citizenship. The planters could not be charged with this mission given that the lingering effects of slavery had caused them to be "proud and stubborn and at all times inaccessible to any motives connected even with justice or humanity to the negroes, let [a]lone their advancement in civilization and qualification for civil rights." The character of the Jamaica Assembly, exemplified by its refusal to enact "indispensable measures required at the outset of the career of improvement," only confirmed for Taylor that this body was "eminently disqualified for the great task of educating and improving a people newly born into freedom as it were."[9]

For Taylor, what remained a central concern did not differ in objective from the official understanding of emancipation; the difference lay in the method. The overall objective of securing political stability could be achieved only by abolishing the assemblies and substituting them with legislative councils based on the model in crown colonies, like that of Lower Canada. "That assuming the objects of the government to be necessary to the establishment of the liberty and promotion of the industry of the negroes, and that the habits and prejudices, if not the interests, of the planters are strongly opposed to them, then the only method of accomplishing them effectually and completely . . . will be by exerting at once and conclusively a power which shall overrule all opposition and set the question at rest." Although some cabinet ministers supported this idea, Colonial Secretary Lord Glenelg did not enthusiastically endorse the proposal. The consequences of a policy of conciliation, Taylor wrote years later, could be seen with the Morant Bay rebellion.[10]

The very posture against which Taylor protested, that is, a policy of conciliation, seemed to have been exactly the one adopted by officials of the Colonial Office.[11] This strategy became evident with the first governor appointed in the postslavery era, Sir Charles Metcalf. Coming out of retirement from long and distinguished service in administration in India, Metcalf became governor in September 1839. Reflecting on Metcalf's administration a couple of years later, James Stephen, who served in the capacity of legal adviser and permanent under secretary of the Colonial Office for many years, noted that a shift had occurred in the approach to dealing with the local government in Jamaica: "Lord Normanby, the Marquis of Sligo, and Sir Lionel Smith especially, regarded the Assembly in the worst possible light. Each began with Courtesies and conciliation. Each ended by denouncing the Assembly as a Body of men who were equally unworthy of Confidence in their individual and collective character. . . . Sir Charles Metcalf reverses all this. He makes himself Sponsor to the utmost extent for the integrity, the intelligence and the public Spirit of the Assembly. His Despatches claim for them almost unlimited confidence, and describe them in terms such as they would themselves select for their own eulogium." According to Stephen, "[d]iscord has ceased, and the scene is one of unbroken mutual [c]onfidence," a situation that resulted from Metcalf's predecessors having governed before complete abolition in 1838, whereas, "after Freedom has been entirely established, [Metcalf] has no such cause of irritation." Because the "great abuse is extinguished," the governor insisted that there would be more progress "by propitiating the good will of the Assembly, even at the expense of acquiescing in many bad measures," rather than "rejecting all such measures at the expense of one protracted quarrel with that House."[12]

Metcalf's early impressions, recorded just a few weeks after his arrival, forecasted the Colonial Office's acquiescence to the Jamaican planters from the inception of "full freedom," which, despite the government's intentions, led the former slaveholders to feel justified in their often unfair treatment of the ex-slaves. In his 16 October 1839 despatch to the colonial secretary, Metcalf relayed his understanding of the problems in the island, offering some solutions, and these ideas would lay the foundation for the interpretation of the situation in Morant Bay. According to Metcalf, because during the era of slavery the practice of granting grounds to the slaves had developed, once slavery ended this practice continued with the effect of rendering Blacks "in a great degree independent of labor, and enabled them to hold out for terms." As a result, some properties were ruined and the wages of the ex-slaves "have been hitherto settled more at the will of the laborer than at that of his employer." The situation would continue as such, Metcalf claimed, "until a great increase of the laboring population shall make labor cheaper, or until laborers shall be more dependent on labor, or until such a number of properties shall be thrown out of cultivation by the impossibility of meeting the expense." In response to the "power of the labourers over wages," Metcalf admitted that the planters would charge rents without "reference purely to the value of the house and grounds." This strategy sustained "much irritation and litigation" between the planters and the former slaves, although Metcalf hoped that in time the situation could be settled on the basis of mutual interest.[13]

Repeating a claim that was heard from the 1831 rebellion, and that would be heard until the insurrection at Morant Bay, the governor asserted that an obstacle to the resolution of "[t]his natural struggle between proprietors and laborers" stemmed from the presence of the Baptist missionaries: "The Baptist missionaries have made themselves particularly obnoxious to the proprietors by the advice and aid which they are supposed to have given their laborers." In order to be fair to the ex-slaves, Metcalf acknowledged that "it was natural that the laborers should seek the advice of the pastors and ministers who had evinced a great interest in their welfare," and possibly without such advice "the emancipated population might have fared worse in their dealings with their former master, or might, from disappointment, have followed desperate courses." Nevertheless, although he saw some good in the actions of the Baptists, the governor felt strongly that "it is an evil whenever the ministers of religion deviate from their purely religious functions to take part in the strife and broils of political parties."[14]

In addition to the Baptist missionaries, the special magistrates, who after August 1838 were called stipendiary magistrates if they continued in their position, also presented a problem for social stability. "The stipendiary magistrates are a class, with individual exceptions, offensive to the proprietary interest." Metcalf contended that after the transformation that resulted from the abolition of slavery, the appointment of the special magistrates "became a second revolution in the island." In essence what the governor asserted with specific reference to Baptist missionaries could be applied to anyone who gave the impression of supporting fair treatment of the former slaves: "It seems very possible that the intervention of a third party between the two immediately concerned, giving its support to one, may have prevented a settlement that would otherwise have taken place favorable to the other, or equally fair to both."[15]

As his comments implied, Metcalf suggested that part of the solution to the problems would have to include bringing in foreign laborers. Five months later in another despatch, written after a tour of the island, the governor spoke more forthrightly. The shortage of labor stemmed from two causes: "the actual want of population and the facility with which the population can support themselves without labouring in the service of others." This situation could be remedied only "by the natural increase produced by time, or by extensive immigration, which is a question beset with many difficulties." Although various immigration schemes had been tried, and failed, the governor insisted that if properly executed, such a plan could work: "My own desire would be to see the elevated parts of the island peopled by our own countrymen leaving the lowlands to the negroes." The former slaves seemed to prefer these lands, the governor thought, where "Europeans cannot I perceive be located as labourers consistently with the preservation of their health." As a condition of their immigration, the governor insisted that "[h]ouses must be prepared for them in the hills ready to receive them on their arrival."[16]

Reiterating a point made in his 16 October despatch, Metcalf again assailed the influence of the Baptist missionaries. On one hand, the governor admitted that he could not determine the charges leveled against the missionaries, for while he regretted that some became "formentors of discord," he noted that in other parts of the island where the Baptists had less influence, the same problems arose. On the other hand, however, Metcalf continued to launch his attack. "As minister of religion and instructors of youth," the Baptists did not present a problem; yet, as a political body, the governor felt they were "designing and turbulent, as well as dangerous to the public peace from the influence which they have acquired."[17]

Metcalf was certainly not the first official to attempt to blame the Baptist missionaries for the conflicting postslavery social relations. Just a couple of months before Metcalf's arrival, the missionary Thomas Abbott found himself refuting such an argument being made by planters. Writing to the secretary of the Colonial Office out of a "sense of justice" and "on behalf of the deeply injured peasantry," Abbott insisted that contrary to press and planter "misrepresentations," which even led the governor "to issue a proclamation which casts unmerited censure upon our peasantry," the claims of the former slaves remained logical and reasonable. After having interacted with more than 10,000 ex-slaves across the island, he had no hesitation "in saying that the charges preferred against them as a body [had] no foundation in truth."[18]

The proclamation to which Abbott referred had been recently issued by Sir Lionel Smith in order to correct the "delusion in the minds of the negroes as to a right to their houses and grounds." Following Smith's precedent, Metcalf also stressed in his despatches that this issue served as the largest source of conflict. "The payment of rent, or in a greater degree the vexatious manner in which it is generally imposed, is almost universally a source of great dissatisfaction on the part of the peasantry." Metcalf claimed that the former slaves believed "that a law would come from England giving them their houses and gardens free of rent," a belief stemming from habits acquired during the era of slavery: "They held their houses and grounds in a state of slavery free from any charge. They cherished the idea that a change to freedom was to be in every respect an improvement."[19]

If his congregation of 3,000 members could be seen as representative, Abbott asserted, the former slaves "neither suppose that they have a right to the houses and grounds they occupied during slavery, nor believe that a law is to be sent out from England to give them the said houses and grounds." Although "the attachment of the labourers to the places of their birth, and to the burial-places of their ancestors or offspring, is so strong that they would rather make any sacrifice than leave them," many former slaves understood the attempt by some estate managers to exploit their sentiments. Abbott stressed, however, that when reasonable conditions were offered, the former slaves would comply: "I have not met with any who have been unwilling to pay a fair rent for their houses and grounds, or to work for those who will treat them as human beings, for equitable remuneration." Even Metcalf admitted that he had heard of specific examples of ex-slaves paying as much as fifty dollars Jamaican (thirty pounds sterling) for an acre of land, demonstrating, as occurred later in the Sea Islands experience, the length to which some would go to secure a material and symbolic basis for their independence.[20]

In other words, when some ex-slaves would not pay rent, Abbott contended, this refusal was based on the feeling that the price was too high; likewise, when they deemed the terms of labor unfair, they would not agree to work. Officials should not have been surprised at such a response, Abbott asserted, for "similar feelings are manifested by freemen in other countries," and thus the former slaves should not be blamed "for daring to maintain their rights," which was tantamount to being treated as fully human. Abbott did not deny that he felt some of the ex-slaves were "idle, dishonest, and unworthy members of society." Yet he contended such a group was not restricted to the Black ex-slave population: "That there is at least an equal proportion of this stamp in the other classes of the community, who have fewer excuses for their crimes, is painfully manifest," not to mention "that the same may be said not only of the peasantry and mechanics, but of the aristocracy of highly-favoured England." Thus, he concluded that "where they are treated well they behave well; and while they reasonably seek to be paid for what they do, they are willing to pay for what they get."[21]

Some officials in the government clearly understood that the planters attempted to use the payment of rent for housing as part of a political strategy to maintain the kind of relations that had existed during slavery. Yet the response of the Colonial Office demonstrated that from the early period of "full freedom," the imperial government wavered in its support of the former slaves. Like the transition from slavery to apprenticeship, the shift from apprenticeship to complete abolition was accompanied by the passage of new laws. Across the Caribbean, legislatures again submitted laws governing the organization of the society, and again some of them the Colonial Office was forced to disallow. During the first legislative session of Metcalf's administration, the Jamaica Assembly passed laws related to vagrancy, trespassing, the bearing of firearms, the formation of a militia, as well as others that dealt with various aspects of colonial life. Despite the Colonial Office's disapproval of specific acts as well as public criticism from supporters of the ex-slaves, Metcalf still asserted without contradiction that "[w]ith respect to the laws passed during this session I am not aware that any of them are iniquitous."[22]

Metcalf based his interactions with the planters in Jamaica on a policy of "conciliation and mutual cordiality and co-operation." The imperial government, despite its intentions, adopted a similar policy, and therefore much of the Colonial Office's approach could be classified in such terms. For instance, when the Jamaica Assembly refused to conduct business in protest of the passing of the Prisons Bill and Sir Lionel Smith dissolved the Assembly, disregarding the recommendation of officials like Henry Taylor to make the island a direct crown colony, the British Parliament chose to suspend the constitution of Jamaica for five years. Later, this penalty would be reduced, a response that reinforced an ongoing inconsistent public policy in regard to the local legislature, whereby the central government would censure the local government and then appease it.[23]

As noted, by the 1840s James Stephen openly stated that the Colonial Office was going to adopt such a policy, even if it meant having to accept measures of the Jamaica Assembly to which some may have had strong objections. Stephen's position was particularly notable because he had become known for his antislavery views and, in other contexts, his defense of the personal liberties of the former slaves.[24] Yet it would be the support of the planters' positions that came to define the policy of this era, as evidenced by the 1842 report of the House of Commons Select Committee appointed to inquire into the situation in the West India Colonies. This investigation centered on relations between employers and laborers, the rate of wages, the nature of the supply of labor, and "the General State of their Rural and Agricultural Economy." In order to avoid postponing their findings until the next session of

Parliament, "the evils and inconveniences" of which they felt "greatly counter-balance any benefits which could result," the members of the Select Committee restricted themselves to resolutions. On the whole, these resolutions reaffirmed the often contradictory nature of what was to have been conceived for the ex-slave population as freedom.[25]

The Select Committee's report maintained that the emancipation of the slaves had been productive with regard to the "character and condition of the Negro Population." In every colony there had been "improvement in the character of the Negro," which could be illustrated by the display of certain behaviors, including "an increase and increasing desire for religious and general instruction; a growing disposition to take upon themselves the obligations of marriage, and to fulfill the duties of domestic life; improved morals; rapid advance in civilization, and increased sense of the value of property and independent station." Yet with this positive change in the habits of the former slaves came "a very great diminution in the staple productions of the West Indies" in British Guiana, Jamaica, and Trinidad—an indirect affirmation that the prosperity of the colonial economy depended on the subordination of the Black population. Employing language that bore a striking resemblance to Governor Charles Metcalf's analysis of the social problems in Jamaica, the Select Committee claimed "[t]hat the principal causes of this diminished production and consequent distress are, the great difficulty which has been experienced by the Planters in obtaining steady and continuous labour" as well as "the high rate of remuneration which they give for the broken and indifferent work which they are able to procure." The reason for the inability of planters to secure "steady and continuous labor" stemmed from "the easy terms upon which the use of land has been obtainable by Negroes."[26]

Adhering to the idea of the determinate nature of geophysical factors, a thesis adopted by some modern historians, the Select Committee contended that the inexpensive price of land was "the natural result of the excess of fertile land beyond the wants of the existing population," and this "cheapness of land has thus been the main cause of the difficulties which have been experienced." Defining the social situation in terms of an "excess of fertile land" that was too cheap would necessarily lead to policies that were not in the interests of the former slaves. While the report cautioned the planters to institute "moderate and prudent changes" in their interactions with the ex-slaves, a more comprehensive solution would lay in the promotion of "the immigration of a fresh labouring population, to such an extent as to create competition for employment." Using the most diplomatic language, the last recommendation made by the Select Committee involved "the early and careful revision" by the local legislatures of the laws regulating the relations between employers and laborers.[27]

From an examination of the structure of as well as the questions posed by the Select Committee, it would be difficult to avoid concluding that support for the planters from the imperial government had been solidified. The Select Committee obtained its evidence from witnesses who had an interest in the situation in the respective colonies; for the most part this meant proprietors or managers of estates. Although others who supposedly doubted "the extent of the present difficulty and distress in the West Indies" were also questioned, such as missionaries, these witnesses clearly constituted a numerical and intellectual minority. Despite the attempt to have varying viewpoints represented, it did seem contradictory, if not politically treacherous, that those most concerned, the ex-slave population, were not consulted. Their absence could possibly be explained by the simple fact that the witnesses gave their testimony in England; however, it would not have been a problem for members of the House of Commons to have journeyed to the colonies to question some former slaves in order to hear their perspectives on the social situation following the abolition of slavery.[28]

In consequence, the Select Committee adopted primarily the planter perspective on social relations in the postslavery period. The well-known Baptist reverend William Knibb became one of the few who provided an alternative viewpoint among all the witnesses who testified regarding the condition of Jamaica. Reaffirming the assertions of his missionary counterparts, Knibb's testimony confirmed that the ex-slaves understood well their interests and behaved in a logically consistent manner to secure them. Rejecting the terms of the planters, Knibb insisted that no irregularity in the labor habits of the ex-slaves existed: "[W]herever fair wages have been offered, and those wages have been regularly paid, there is no want of continuous labor." In the earlier questioning of island agent William Burge, a member of the committee, Sir Charles Douglass, noted that the report of the stipendiary magistrates Richard Chamberlain, John Gurly, Henry Kent, and others suggested that "labour may be had for fair wages and kind treatment." Reverend Knibb noted that a problem arose on the part of the planters, where due to a want of capital the laborers were often not paid on a regular basis. For instance, on the Penn Estate in the parish of Trelawny, the workers had not received their wages for three or four months, a situation that could be found throughout the island: "[The Penn Estate laborers] have walked to the court-house, time after time, to obtain [their wages], but have not received it; and in almost every parish there will be estates, and there are estates situated similarly."[29] Again, the former slaves found the legal system, which could often be tenacious when it wanted to convict the former slaves of property crimes, would often be unresponsive when the ex-slaves were themselves the victims of civil violations.

Moreover, with respect to the claim that the wages demanded by the ex-slaves were too high, a fundamental inconsistency emerged on the part of the planters. During the apprenticeship era, when the apprenticed laborers wished to purchase their freedom, planters valued their labor at the minimum daily rate of two shillings and six pence in Jamaican currency or one shilling and six pence in sterling. The maximum value placed on the daily labor of the slaves was three shillings and four pence or two shillings sterling. Knibb noted that the ex-slaves watched the valuation proceedings closely: "[I]t was all done in open court, and being deeply interested in it, [the apprentices] would generally communicate it one to another." It stood therefore to reason that the former slaves would claim this rate as the minimum for which they should be paid after 1838, but many planters claimed this rate (the very one they had determined) was too high to pay the ex-slaves. From the perspective of the planters and the Select Committee, this profound contradiction could not be recognized. Moreover, it would have been too much of a stretch to have suggested that because the former slaves, unlike the former slaveholders, had not been compensated for slavery, any high wages could have been construed as at least partial restitution for their unrequited toil; but this realization also could not have been conceived within the dominant understanding of emancipation.[30]

Another contradiction emerged in the context of the Select Committee's report. From the early 1830s, when abolition seemed imminent, the political leaders of Jamaica had insisted upon their local autonomy. This issue came to a head with the conflict over the Prisons Bill, which provoked a constitutional crisis in the late 1830s. However, when the Select Committee interviewed William Burge, he insisted, as had been done many times before, that immigration remained "the only remedy for the evil under which Jamaica labours," and that the enterprise should be undertaken by the imperial government: "The whole scheme of immigration should be committed to and undertaken by the Government, commencing from the period when the emigrant consents to emigrate, and continued until he has arrived and been suitably located in the colony." Burge contended that immigration represented a "public benefit," one without which the ex-slaves would suffer even more: "The further evil would be, that the civilization of the negro population would be arrested: they could not be raised to that condition in society which they are capable of reaching, if the colony be placed in such a state that it cannot carry on its government, and the white population are obliged to withdraw their capital from it. The welfare and civilization of the emancipated negro are as much dependent on the prosperity of the colony as the white proprietor himself."[31]

The support of Metcalf and the Jamaican planters implicit in the Select Committee recommendations represented an intellectual and political retreat from the attempt to reconstruct a postslavery society in which the interests of the Black population group would not continue to be subordinated to those of the former slaveholders: "On every issue the British Government retreated from positions it had taken during the initial year of freedom, conceding points of principle and positions of power to the planter élites." For instance, although the framers of the Abolition Act had already contemplated the gradual elimination of the special magistrates after the apprenticeship phase, Metcalf's proposal to abolish the agents served to endear him to the planter class. This adoption of the planter interpretation of the social context came to dominate the analysis of the imperial government, and thus the former slaves again found themselves struggling against a social structure opposed to their interests.[32]

A few years after the 1842 Select Committee issued its report, the House of Commons reconvened its Committee on Sugar and Coffee Plantations in 1848 to examine the condition of such estates across the colonies. While acknowledging the severe effects of the 1846 Sugar Duties Act, the report gave the impression that problems in the colonies stemmed from abolition, a measure in actuality that was forced on the planters by the imperial government. Reinforcing the planters' understanding of the social situation, the committee argued that emancipation "was carried into effect without sufficient provision having been made for providing many of the Colonies with an adequate command of free labour." This situation consequently led to a very high rate of wages as well as "the cost of production [being] unduly enhanced." In fact, Colonial Secretary Earl Grey argued that high wages, in addition to the harmful effects on the system of production, also injured the social development of the ex-slaves. "The high rate of wages, it is clear, far from contributing to the real welfare or to the civilization of the Negroes, has, on the contrary, as might have been expected, from the sudden change in their position, tended to give them habits of idleness, and to produce that demoralization of which idleness, amongst men of whatever race or of whatever rank, is the invariable source."[33] If such was the operating definition of the cause of the problems confronting the colonies, then the solution prescribed became inevitably clear: low wages, immigration, and laws enacted against vagrancy and squatting.

Because the former slaves did not passively accept these terms, the uprising at Morant Bay became the logical and systemic outcome of the local and imperial public policy pursued in the postslavery period. In other words, the seeds of the Morant Bay rebellion had been planted when the abolition of slavery was conceptualized and implemented in terms that continued to circumscribe the freedom of the ex-slave population. As officials and proprietors readily admitted, the ex-slaves always asserted themselves to ensure their interests were being met. Governor Metcalf described it most accurately when he stated that the character "acquired by the people in their transition from slavery to freedom, seems to be more that of independence than of submission to the will of others." When being interviewed by the 1842 Select Committee, Samuel Barrett supported the idea that a new law was needed to compel the ex-slaves to labor, because with the freedpeople one had to prove an agreement existed, "which is a very difficult thing to do with the negro, for he will not sign any agreement." Barrett's reaction reinforced the fact that the former slaves clearly understood and then rejected the attempt to resubordinate them in terms resembling those of slavery, but it did not, on the other hand, seem to render redundant the question of whether they were capable of handling freedom.[34]

Despite their efforts, from the 1830s on it can be argued that the former slaves never received the full support of the imperial government. The planter representation of the population group may have suffered an interruption, but in the postslavery context this ideology was quickly reestablished and institutionally affirmed, albeit in different terms. Although it may seem obvious from a historical standpoint that a connection existed between imperial and local policies and the development of the social situation, such a perspective did not appear to many at the time as desirable. For instance, many actually believed that the former slaves were better off than laborers in England, if not elsewhere in the world. Not surprisingly, Governor Metcalf articulated just such a viewpoint: "The ease, independence, and other advantages enjoyed by the labouring population, are not, I believe, surpassed by those of the same class in any country on the face of the earth." This understanding he asserted on more than one occasion. Yet what may have surprised some was that William Knibb, who had played a central role in the formation of free village settlements and was an ardent defender of the former slaves, also stated that the English laboring population would be doing well if they "were half as well off" as the Jamaican laborers.[35]

Moreover, the planters saw the relative improvement in the living standards of the ex-slaves as an indication that their wages were too high, and, after much complaining, they were finally able in the mid-1840s to reduce the pay of their laborers. This strategy of compelling labor at certain wages occurred across the Caribbean, creating conditions that led to protests and riots in some instances. Workers' protests in British Guiana in 1842 and riots in 1856, the "Guerro Negro" incident in Dominica in 1844, the riots in St. Vincent in 1862, the Confederation Riots in Barbados in 1876, and the laborers' protests in Tobago in 1876 all demonstrated that the "problem of freedom" was not specific to the conditions that led to Morant Bay.[36] Despite the somewhat different origins of the labor disputes elsewhere in the Caribbean, Morant Bay symbolized that unless issues such as wages and labor control were fully addressed, there could be far-reaching consequences.

The uprising at Morant Bay seemed to have come from the reporting of these conditions as much as the actual conditions themselves. That is to say, the letters of Baptist missionaries from 1864 to 1865 sparked much of the controversy in the island, although there was not a strong Baptist presence in the parish of St. Thomas in the East. In January 1865 the secretary of the Baptist Missionary Society, Edward Underhill, wrote Colonial Secretary Edward Cardwell to convey to him the desperate situation in Jamaica. A drought had lasted more than two years, wages had fallen again, and, with the Civil War in the United States, supplies from abroad had become extremely expensive. Quoting another missionary, Underhill argued that none of these factors could be said to have caused the present conditions, but rather they had "given intensity to suffering previously existing." In addition, the former slaves were being taxed at an astronomical rate, forcing them to shoulder much of the island's tax burden.[37]

Underhill's letter was later passed on to Governor Edward Eyre, who had it circulated among the political leaders of Jamaica. The letter stirred public opinion on the island and led to the formation of what have been called "Underhill meetings," where ex-slaves and middle-class colored reformers met to demonstrate their support of the claims Underhill had made in his letter. At these meetings, participants often drafted letters to the governor of the island and the queen, requesting relief for the dire situation in which they found themselves. One petition, signed by the "poor people of St. Ann's Parish," implored the queen to rent them crown lands in order to alleviate their poverty. When he forwarded the "poor people's" statement to the queen, Governor Eyre included a note stating that the petition was the fruit of Underhill's letter as well as circulars of the Baptist Missionary Society, which had "a very prejudiced influence in unsettling the minds of the peasantry."[38]

The response of the queen, drafted by Colonial Office bureaucrats, affirmed the official position on emancipation that had become embedded in the structure of the thought of the imperial government by the 1860s. This perspective identified freedom purely with laboring on the estates and therefore could not see the ex-slaves' conception of liberty, which did not necessarily equate freedom with labor on the plantations. As a consequence, this understanding placed the onus for the social conflict on the ex-slaves' refusal to make the productivity of the plantations (as opposed to securing their well-being) the priority, which the ex-slaves were to have done at the discretion of the planters: "The prosperity of the labouring classes, as well as of all other classes, depends in Jamaica, and in other communities, upon their working for wages, not uncertainly, or capriciously, but steadily and continuously, at the times when their labour is wanted, and for so long as it is wanted." The letter of advice further asserted that if the ex-slaves adopted such an approach, the plantations would become more productive, which would allow the planters to pay them higher wages "for the same hours of work than are received by the best field labourers in this country." Reinforcing the recurrent claim that the situation of the Jamaican ex-slaves was not really so desperate, and thus they should be thankful, the queen's reply insinuated that they could easily then achieve a high standard of living "as the cost of necessaries of life is much less in Jamaica than it is here." Moreover, Blacks would have the satisfaction of knowing that they prospered "from their own industry and prudence" rather than "from any such schemes as have been suggested to them."[39]

The queen's reply demonstrated that the official understanding of the social situation could not effectively address the systemic problems confronting the colonies. For in the letter of advice, which Henry Taylor played a central role in constructing, the complexity of the situation in Jamaica had to be ignored. Most of the sugar plantations had been abandoned by this time, and given that many ex-slaves could not depend on them even if they had wanted— given, for instance, the irregularity of payment of wages—it seemed highly unlikely that working the plantations would increase their wages. Implicit in the reply was that a sufficient opportunity existed that could allow the former slaves to provision for themselves, if they only agreed to provide "steady and continuous labor." By this time, the intellectual preconditions that would lead to the Morant Bay insurrection had been firmly established.

To assert the kind of analysis that directly addressed the social context, George William Gordon, a colored member of the House of Assembly who owned land in St. Thomas in the East and a loyal supporter of the interests of the ex-slaves (having even changed his religious affiliation from Church of England to Native Baptist), initiated the preparation of a response to the queen's letter of advice. Gordon also attempted to raise money in order to send a delegation to England to make an appeal to the queen, and thus circumvent the power of the governor, who had become his political enemy. Events came to a head when on a market day, Saturday, 7 October, the Court of Petty Sessions convicted a boy of assault against a woman. A man present in the court, Geoghegan, said to the young boy that he should pay the fine (four shillings) but not the extra costs (twelve shillings and six pence). A disturbance erupted that prevented the court from continuing with its proceedings.[40]

On Monday, warrants were issued for the arrest of Paul Bogle, a Native Baptist preacher and landowner in Stony Gut (five miles from Morant Bay) who was alleged to be the leader of the disturbance. The attempt to take Bogle and his associates into custody the following day was thwarted by 300 to 500 supporters who overpowered the police officers. The participants had it conveyed to the proper authorities that on the next day they would appear at the vestry to make clear their grievances. They sent a petition to Governor Eyre to inform him that warrants had been issued against innocent persons and that they were compelled to resist, especially given "the mean advantages that ha[ve] been taken of us from time to time." The petitioners pleaded for protection; if refused, they would be forced "to put our shoulders to the wheel, as we have been imposed upon for a period of 27 years with due obeisance to the laws of our Queen and country, and we can no longer endure the same." Governor Eyre responded in typical fashion, claiming that the petitioners were being misled by "evil-disposed and designing men." The impasse led to the uprising, which precipitated a brutal repression.[41]

Without going into the details of the event, which have been excellently chronicled elsewhere,[42] it is important to emphasize that the issue of *being heard* was a central one. For the imperial government's refusal to grant any legitimacy to the political and intellectual assertions of the former slaves (who were overtaxed and underpaid) certainly contributed to the escalation of conflict. Underhill astutely evaluated the situation: "It is obvious that, at this moment [when Bogle and others submitted the petition to Eyre], kind treatment and an effort to deal impartially with grievances, which unquestionably had just foundation, would have averted the calamity that fell on the magistrates and community of Morant Bay." But, in order to have responded in such a way, Eyre would have had to admit that the grievances had "just foundation," an indication that a different set of political languages to understand the postslavery social situation (indeed, to understand the general social reality) would have been necessary in the imperial policies.[43]

To understand events surrounding the uprising, in 1866 the members of Parliament appointed a Royal Commission to inquire into the origins of the disturbances in Morant Bay. On the one hand, the Royal Commission provided a strong critique of Governor Eyre's use of martial law to effect such a brutal repression. The Royal Commission claimed that while there were large numbers involved in the disturbance and an even larger number of those who "availed themselves of a time of disorder to plunder their neighbor," the punishments "seem to us to have been far greater than the necessity required." While the initial actions of the rebels at the Court House as well as the spreading of the uprising into the estates in the parish had led to 18 deaths and 31 people wounded, the response of the government, much of which seemed to have been guided by a racial hysteria, led to 439 Blacks being killed, 1,000 dwellings burned, and at least 600 people flogged. Those following the order of Governor Eyre behaved, particularly at Bath, the commission added, in a "positively barbarous fashion."[44]

On the other hand, however, the Royal Commission remained unable to move beyond the limitations of the official understanding of emancipation. In fact, even its disdain for the excessive use of physical force correlated with the logic of antislavery thought, which often protested the use of physical coercion but also remained unable to see the new postslavery forms of coercion. According to the commission, the immediate cause of the disturbance was a "planned resistance to lawful authority." The principal objective of this "planned resistance" seemed to have been "the obtaining of land free from the payment of rent," although the report admitted that a "want of confidence generally felt by the laboring class in the tribunals" also provided "additional incentive to the violation of the law." The commission saw no legitimacy in the political claims of the former slaves, stating that "it did not appear to us that the rate of wages was low" or that "there was unfairness on the part of the managers of estates in the payment of wages."[45]

At this moment, it became clear that the "problem of freedom" had come full circle. For the Baptist missionaries—from Thomas Abbott in the 1830s, to William Knibb in the 1840s, and to Edward Underhill in 1860s—insisted that the former slaves would have been willing to rent land for reasonable costs as well as work on estates for reasonable wages paid on a consistent basis. The land question was especially important in a political system where the franchise was determined by the possession of real estate. In fact, underlying the brutal repression at Morant Bay and, in particular, Gordon's execution was the issue of land. Becoming the leader of the Town Party (versus the Country Party, which supported the interests of the former slaveholders), Gordon had won his seat in the Jamaica Assembly in 1863 on the basis of the support of the peasant or working-class ex-slaves who met the qualification for the very restricted franchise.[46] As it was earlier noted, just before the onset of abolition, intermediate groups such as Jews, Catholics, free persons of color, and the middle classes were increasingly incorporated into the political structure by being granted the power to vote. Gordon, Bogle, and their supporters were attempting to extend this privilege to the ex-slaves.

Yet, for a society integrated on the basis of the disenfranchisement of Blacks, such an idea was unthinkable. Indeed, a month after the occurrences at Morant Bay, Governor Eyre spoke to the Jamaican legislature and insisted that the recent conflict should serve as evidence of the growing threat (specter of another Haiti) that Blacks would gain suffrage and therefore take control of the island. On the basis of this fear, it was easy to convince both parties in the Assembly to commit an act of "political suicide" and to petition London to govern the island directly as a crown colony.[47] Thus, as would later be the situation with Redemption in South Carolina, it became increasingly clear that *a Black ex-slave electoral majority could not be tolerated* in Jamaica or in any state of the United States where Blacks were a numerical majority. Indeed, this argument can be generalized to explain other postemancipation contexts in the Americas: when Black political parties emerged demanding rights implicit in the abolition of slavery, such as in Cuba and Brazil, they were suppressed; in the case of the former, party members were massacred. The 1912 killing of hundreds of members of the Partido Independiente de Color by the Cuban army and *voluntarios* "made clear to all Afro-Cubans that any further attempt to challenge the social order would be crushed with bloodshed."[48]

In another moment of insight coming from the government, one echoing Lord John Russell, Lord Elgin, the successor to Sir Charles Metcalf as governor of Jamaica, discerned the central problem. This dilemma resulted from the absence of a unified understanding of the common good, one that would have to mean "that the material prosperity of communities . . . is attainable by other means than the systematic violation of the highest moral obligations." While Elgin acknowledged there to be "a practical antagonism between the moral and intellectual claims of one class and the material interests of the other," there needed to be the "discovery of some common ground on which intelligent and conscientious men representing these apparently conflicting interests might meet to concert measures for the common good." Although an official once again realized that the dominant understanding of maintaining order being based on a "systematic violation of the highest moral obligations" could easily become counterproductive on many levels, such an insight was not operationalized as the modus operandi of the government.[49] Although a political revolution had taken place, only a partial intellectual one had occurred for the situation of the former slaves, who, despite these changes, remained outside the dominant society's sanctified universe of moral obligation.

Toward Intellectual Redemption in the United States

The retreat from emancipation in the United States took a similar course in some ways as it did in the British Caribbean, although significant differences remained. As can also be said of the influence of special magistrates, it would be difficult, indeed useless, to blame the agents of the Freedmen's Bureau for the outcome of emancipation, as they functioned within the available political languages used to understand the postslavery social context. Nevertheless, it has been worthwhile to describe in detail their role in the way that emancipation evolved, for by stressing the importance of making contracts to labor on plantations as well as instructing the ex-slaves in discipline and other sociocultural habits perceived as necessary, they deemphasized the manner in which the former slaves conceived of their freedom as well as the role of the social and political system, which continued to reproduce the subordination of the Black population group.

The way in which the Freedmen's Bureau handled the issue of distributing rations illustrated how some agents could overlook—and, in some instances, neglect—the political context of struggle. Upon his assumption of the position of commissioner of the Freedmen's Bureau, Oliver O. Howard made clear in his first circular letter his belief that the "demands for labor are sufficient to afford employment to nearly if not quite all the able bodied refugees and freedmen." Thus, the charge of the agents remained the introduction of a system of compensated labor, correcting "the false impressions sometimes entertained by the freedmen, that they can live without labor," and eliminating "the false pride which renders some of the refugees more willing to be supported in idleness than to support themselves." Although Howard stipulated that "a generous provision should be made for the aged, infirm and sick," the able-bodied "should be encouraged, and, if necessary, compelled to labor for their support."[50]

Howard's line of thinking was certainly followed by some of his subordinate officers in the Freedmen's Bureau. In his communication summarizing bureau operations in the Aiken District for October 1866, Lieutenant Walker noted that both Captain C. R. Becker, subassistant commissioner for Abbe-ville, and Lieutenant G. P. McDougall, subassistant commissioner for Ander-son, reported that in their respective districts labor was plentiful, and only idleness prevented the freedpeople from obtaining employment. George E. Pingree, subassistant commissioner for Darlington, proposed in his July 1867 report that the government issue rations during the following year only to the old, sick, and crippled. Pingree acknowledged that over the past year he had issued rations to many able-bodied ex-slaves, doing so "because they had neither money nor credit" and "their Crops would have been abandoned without help, and [he] believed it to be better to assist them in making a Crop, that they might not be objects of Charity next year." However, he contended that despite his efforts he knew that some had swindled him "and idleness and laziness has been the result," a situation the agent thought existed because "the people here have not pride in the matter, and will beg rather than work."[51]

Some agents who thought the distribution of rations caused idleness and laziness saw the problem as being restricted to a minority within the ex-slave population group. Marion agent J. E. Lewis remarked that "[m]uch complaint is made that whenever corn is issued gratuitously the labor of the District be-comes demoralized." However, he asserted that "this is true to a certain extent and to a certain extent only." Agreeing that he found among both Whites and Blacks some who after receiving rations "lounge about the village until the issue is ended," these represented "but a small proportion of the laborers of the District."[52]

On the other hand, John William De Forest took the argument of the distri-bution of rations as demoralizing to an extreme. De Forest sincerely believed that feeding the former slaves would induce idleness and thus, when he first arrived, refused to distribute rations, insisting on principle that he remained "merciless toward the few for the good of the many, refusing to feed the suf-fering lest I should encourage the lazy." The cure for this affliction, De Forest told the ex-slaves, was to obtain work: "Regular labor is the only thing that will keep you from suffering." Given the dire circumstances of some of the ex-slaves and refugees, De Forest was forced to distribute some rations. As a result, he developed his own system for issuing provisions to the needy. This method involved sending rations specifically to farming precincts in order to assist with the growing of crops as well as collecting lists of destitute persons whose situation could be verified by "respectable neighbors" so as to help only those with the greatest want. De Forest felt that even this measure, which alle-viated suffering for many, also "encouraged beggary and idleness" and thus it "did good and harm in equal proportions."[53]

While extreme, De Forest's position was not unrelated to the policy of the Freedmen's Bureau. On 22 August 1866, Commissioner Howard issued Circular No. 10, which stipulated the halting of the issue of rations of one bushel of corn and eight pounds of pork per month to every adult (and half of this amount to every child) with the exception being "the sick in regularly organized hospitals, and . . . the orphan asylums for refugees and freedmen." Because this policy blatantly ignored natural factors (such as tornadoes and insects), not to mention politics, which led to the destruction of numerous crops, this draconian measure created such distress that Congress passed a bill on 30 March 1867 to relieve many of the destitute in the South. The question remained, however, upon what premise was such a policy as Circular No. 10 predicated.[54]

Michael Katz has traced the discourse on poverty from early in the nineteenth century into the twentieth century. He noted that public officials during this time "attempted to distinguish between the able-bodied and the impotent poor," later transmuting "these categories into the moral distinction between the worthy and the unworthy, or the deserving and undeserving poor."[55] One of the major concerns of the agents of the Freedmen's Bureau was that rations be distributed only to those defined as deserving of assistance, those "worthy objects of charity." This position Commissioner Howard made clear in one of his early circulars: "Great discrimination will be observed in administering relief, so as to include none that are not absolutely necessitous and destitute." These usually included the physically disabled, the aged, the sick, as well as orphaned children too young to work, and sometimes former slaves who had obtained permission to return to their homes.[56]

The assumption remained that if one was able-bodied, then one should be able to obtain employment, but circumstances often prevented those able to work from finding employment or, if they could find it, remaining at their place of employment. G. P. McDougall observed that in his district of Anderson most of the employers as well as the workers violated the terms of their labor contracts. The employers did not adhere to the terms out of "a desire to swindle the Freedmen out of their portion of the crops," while the former slaves broke the contracts in order to secure opportunities to do better, for "in many cases they have failed in raising their crops, and are unable to fulfill their contracts from not having provisions to live on the remaining portion of the year." A few months after making this report, McDougall noted that, while the situation had improved for the freedpeople, a demand for labor remained because the planters were not offering very good wages.[57] Captain E. R. Chase found it difficult to ascertain who had not lived up to the terms of the labor contracts as complaints came from both sides. He noticed, how-ever, that many of the complaints came late into the season, which led him to formulate a certain conclusion: "From this fact alone I would say that the em-ployer is to blame for during the working months of summer, he had hardly any fault to find with his employees; but now when the crops are ready to be housed, it rather hurts him to give the share to the Freedmen that his Labor entitled him to, and is very willing to give evidence against him and find fault now that the labor season is comparatively speaking over." Chase had no doubts that some of the freedpeople without cause did not fulfill the terms of their contracts; however, some "were compelled to break their contracts by being driven away from their plantations by 'bushwakers & murderers'" in addition to the violation of contracts by the employers that impelled some to leave.[58]

Moreover, given that at the end of the year many of the ex-slaves found themselves in debt (and most still landless), it seemed logical that some re-fused the terms of the new labor system. Well into the emancipation process, agents of the Freedmen's Bureau were reporting that the freedpeople con-tinued to have a difficult time making ends meet. Responding to the Decem-ber 1867 congressional inquiry regarding the termination of the bureau, Wil-liam J. Harkisheimer claimed that one would think that after two years the ex-slaves would be able to provide for themselves. Yet he noted that the small-ness of the preceding year's crop had left the freedpeople "as destitute now, as they were at the close of the war." William Nerland summarized the situation in the Barnwell District for 1867: "The freedmen worked hard during the year many of them to find themselves at the end of the year without provisions and without a cent of money." Like Harkisheimer, Nerland lamented the un-fair division of crops that also seemed to have taken place during the year. J. E. Lewis found the situation so bad in Darlington that he felt it necessary "to cause the crops to be impounded to prevent overreaching [and] dishonest planters from swindling the laborers out of their share." Lewis projected that by the end of the year many of the ex-slaves would find themselves in debt "and the larger proportion of them will barely [have] earned a subsistence." The problem was compounded, both Nerland and Lewis pointed out, with the heavy taxes that the former slaves were also expected to pay.[59]

The case of Flora Murphy illustrated that the legacy of slavery rendered some women with children incapable of being self-supporting, according to the terms of some bureau agents. Murphy requested rations because, as she stated, "I wish the assistance of the Bureau to obtain justice for myself and children." She affirmed that "[w]hile the property of said John Horlbeck and subject to his authority I became the mother of two children *by him,* Jimmy now six years of age and Milly, four years of age." Now that she was no longer a slave, Murphy remained unable to secure any help from the children's father: "Since I have been made free . . . John Horlbeck neglects and refuses to render me any assistance to support myself or children." While she certainly sought aid from the bureau, Murphy's idea of justice entailed Horlbeck being held partially responsible for his actions: "I am poor, and I ask that he may be compelled to contribute something towards the support of his and my children."[60]

Although cited as an individual example, Murphy's situation was probably not unique among ex-slave women. As her case illustrated, adopting the position that, if able-bodied, one had to be employed (or then be defined as a vagrant) minimized the political context that complicated postslavery social and labor relations. Many so-called able-bodied freedpeople did not have employment because they left plantations due to the unfair treatment they received, or they were ejected by the planters, or some left because of the lack of consistent payment of their wages. As the freedpeople often noted, at the end of the year, they still were in debt; thus, within their understanding of what has been termed free-labor ideology, it made no sense to endure the labor for no reward. Although some of the agents certainly acknowledged the complex reasons for many of the ex-slaves not being able to labor consistently, the emphasis of the bureau's operations remained getting them to labor, and not addressing the political and social system that produced the problem.

As stated earlier, it would be useless to fault the Freedmen's Bureau for the eventual retreat that occurred during emancipation, because the organization was not designed to address the systemic problems that emerged in the wake of abolition. Like the special magistrates, this institution was established to facilitate the transition to a postslavery society, and thus its purposes remained integrative rather than transformative. Yet such an assertion does not imply that aspects of its policies as well as the actions of some of its agents did not represent a significant departure from the slavery order of things. As was the case in the British Caribbean, however, much of the responsibility lay with the way in which emancipation was conceptualized and then implemented by the respective central governments. Although in the United States there seemed to have been more possibilities for social change than in the British Caribbean, where support for the planters never really wavered, in the final analysis, a policy of conciliation, not unlike that of the British imperial government, came to define the politics of emancipation.

Part of the problem with Reconstruction emanated from its base of support. Outside of the Radical Republicans, many Whites in the North endorsed the abolition of slavery only as a measure to blunt the power of the South, not to promote the social and political equality of Blacks. For the situation to have been otherwise, the North would have also needed to be reconstructed. As a consequence, when the former slaves and their more radical allies fought for the right to vote, it became expedient to support the enfranchisement of Blacks: "The majority of northerners had not enthusiastically embraced emancipation before, nor did they embrace enfranchisement now, but they were convinced that southern black enfranchisement could prevent a conservative comeback and would keep the Republicans in power throughout the South and in Washington." The implication remained that the struggle of the ex-slaves had been made secondary to the political subordination of the Southern power structure, a contention that does not necessarily minimize the importance of the strides made during the era of Radical Reconstruction, but rather suggests that these advances cannot be separated from the self-interest of the North's attempt to secure its political hegemony over the South. Indeed, in history, triumphs have often been inextricably linked to the tragedies. For in the end it would be such a strategy that logically resulted in a "retreat from reconstruction," that moment when the political interests of the North no longer coincided with securing civil rights for the former slaves.[61]

The phenomenon of the Ku Klux Klan in South Carolina brought to light most clearly both the triumphs and the failures of the Republican Party's attempt to ensure freedom for the ex-slaves. The Klan emerged in the state two years after its original appearance in Tennessee in 1866, doing so precisely after Blacks had been enfranchised in South Carolina. Thus, at its origins, the actions of the Klan can be seen to have been political in the larger sense of the term, "for it sought to affect power relations, both public and private, throughout the South," although the group may not have been organized in the formal political sense. The ultimate goal of the Ku Klux Klan remained the regulation of the status of Blacks, an objective most clearly articulated in the related group known as the "Regulators." The Klan attempted to achieve its goal not through the institutional political party system but rather through violence and intimidation, and yet its actions served the interests of the Democratic Party, which wanted to restore the antebellum social and political system.[62]

Most of the Klan activity took place in the up-country region of South Carolina, especially in the counties of Abbeville, Chester, Edgefield, Spartanburg, Union, and York. Whereas Blacks outnumbered Whites in the low country, in the upper piedmont (taken as a whole) Whites outnumbered Blacks, demonstrating that there was no correlation between Black presence and racial animosity. While some Democrats (and later some historians) ascribed the impetus of the Klan to the anxiety and frustrations of poor and working-class Whites, as Georgia assistant commissioner Davis Tillson stated with respect to "Regulators," they were "not mere outlaws, but sons of wealthy and influential families"; or, as a Georgia bureau agent also observed, the "most respectable citizens are engaged in it." Nonetheless, it was probably not irrelevant that nonslaveholding White subsistence farmers had been increasingly displaced with the penetration of railroads and the augmentation of cotton production.[63]

From early in the Reconstruction process, many agents of the Freedmen's Bureau requested the need for troops because violent outrages against Blacks occurred so frequently. As Francis Simkins argued, "[T]he far greater portion of the violence against prospective voters was executed by persons who either were not familiar with the workings of the Klan, or felt that their purposes might be accomplished without taking the trouble to use the ritual and disguises of the order." In fact, it would be everyday, ordinary White citizens "moving in the daylight without disguises" who would perpetrate most of the violent outrages against the former slaves. Nevertheless, not unlike later federal responses to violations against Blacks, it was only with the utterly brutal, flagrant outrages committed by the Klan that the national government felt compelled to intervene in the local affairs of South Carolina during 1870 and 1871.[64]

Congress began by passing a series of Enforcement Acts in 1870 and 1871, the latter of which is often referred to as the Ku Klux Klan Act. The 1870 act prohibited state officials from discriminating among voters on the basis of "race, color or previous condition of servitude." The act also made it a federal crime for any person to "prevent, hinder control, or intimidate . . . any person from exercising or in exercising the right of suffrage," including through force, bribery, or threats. Moreover, "if two or more persons shall bind or conspire together," that is, form a conspiracy, "to prevent or hinder [a citizen's] free exercise and enjoyment of any right or privilege granted by the Constitution," they could be prosecuted under federal law. This measure also gave the president the power to appoint election supervisors who could bring federal cases of election fraud. In 1871 Congress passed two other Enforcement Acts, one supplementary to the 1870 act, which ensured federal control over election procedures, and the other to enforce the Fourteenth Amendment, a section of which gave the president the authority to suspend the writ of habeas corpus. This act also made specific crimes committed by individuals that would normally have been adjudicated under state laws now punishable under federal law.[65]

These acts certainly marked a departure in U.S. constitutional law. Earlier laws such as the Civil Rights Act (1866) and the Reconstruction amendments to the Constitution had left the power of enforcement of the infringement of the civil and political rights of Blacks under the control of local and state officials. With the measures passed in 1870–71, it had now become a federal crime to attempt to deprive Blacks of their constitutional rights. However, the way in which enforcement was executed in response to the actions of the Ku Klux Klan reaffirmed that an ambivalence continued to define the level of commitment the republican federal government had for the advancement of the political rights of Blacks.[66]

The national government could not have been unaware of the outrages from the beginning of Reconstruction that were being committed against Blacks. In fact, agents of the Freedmen's Bureau had insisted in their reports on the necessity of a military presence to counteract the violence and the infringement of the political rights of Blacks. George E. Pingree claimed that his presence without troops did more evil than good and lamented his powerlessness with respect to addressing the outrages committed against Blacks: "It makes my heart-ache to see so many of the poor Freedmen come in here from miles away in the country — covered with marks of brutal treatment — afraid to remain with their families for fear of being shot dead in cold blood, and I am obliged to turn them off, with but slight hopes that their cruel wrongs will be rightly addressed." As a solution, Pingree proposed that "prompt arrest and punishment" would "cause the whites to respect the rights of the freedpeople."[67]

Historians have argued that violence of the Ku Klux Klan coincided with the enfranchisement of Blacks, which resulted from the passage of the Reconstruction Acts.[68] While it might be a decontextualized overstatement to suggest that "Negroes were as often the aggressors as were the whites,"[69] it nevertheless remained true that the ex-slaves did not always cringe in fear of the attempts to deprive them of their rights and, in some instances, even organized militias to protect themselves. Beginning in the wake of federal occupation in 1865, and spreading in the following year, quasi-military Black companies attempted to affect the social and political conditions of the ex-slaves, doing so at a time when ex-slaveholders and Freedmen's Bureau agents stressed social deference. Repudiating alarmists' claims of violence and insurrection, these societies held assemblies that attempted to govern working conditions as well as the functioning of the public affairs of local neighborhoods, such as street cleaning, raising funds for emergencies, attending to matters of health, and police protection from thieves. At times overzealous, some groups undertook to enforce political loyalty with physical assaults or by destroying the livestock and farms of Blacks who did not vote for the Republican Party. When local officials claimed ignorance in terroristic raids of the Ku Klux Klan, these leagues would often investigate the situation. However, the form of popular justice in which some league members engaged differed substantially from Klan vigilance, as a result of their consistent engagement with civil institutions and their arrests and detentions. These local leagues served a myriad of functions, being "part political machine, part labor union, part popular tribunal, part moral or intellectual improvement body, part renters' association, part retail cooperative." Whatever the minor indiscretions, had the federal government or the general society provided such services for the ex-slaves, there obviously would have been no need for the creation of these societies.[70]

After the state legislature passed a militia law authorizing Governor Robert K. Scott to purchase 2,000 stands of arms, the objective of these groups took on an official dimension. In fact, it was on the basis of the strength of these groups that Governor Scott solicited aid in early 1870 to ensure a large number of Republican voters for the fall election. Scott also used the Black militias to control his political adversaries as well as to reward his allies, to whom he gave the highest positions. Between the 1868 and the 1870 elections, Governor Scott maintained an adamant position against the Klan, evidenced by his willingness to employ Black militias to decrease the group's activity. However, after the 1870 elections, in order to placate Whites, Scott began disarming the militias, and thus left the ex-slaves somewhat defenseless. After a riot occurred in Chester County in the spring of 1871, Scott ordered the disbandment of the militia under the command of Major John C. Reister, "to the cheers of his Conservative neighbors." As a result, the Klan continued its raids despite the presence of a federal garrison in town. Klan incidents in both Union and York counties also led the governor to disarm the county's militia companies. In York, known for particularly notorious incidents, this decision only strengthened the Klan, as the guns that were stored in several places throughout the county would be confiscated by Klan members, allowing the group to rearm itself.[71]

The arrival of additional federal soldiers in February 1871 did not necessarily lead to a decline in Klan violence. In Yorkville, while there were no additional raids on the city itself, in the country the raids "became more frequent and bloody than before." With federal laws against the Klan on the books, it still remained extremely difficult to persuade federal officials to prosecute the perpetrators of violent offenses against Blacks, especially given that the closest deputy U.S. marshal and U.S. commissioner in Columbia made themselves unavailable when Major Lewis M. Merrill, under whose command the South Carolina units fell, attempted to contact them. Merrill, who arrived in the state at the end of March, initially believed that most of the accounts of outrages against Blacks had been exaggerated. However, after seeing the extent of the Klan violence, and in York the extent of the support among the White residents for the terrorist group, Merrill recognized that without more federal intervention the situation would only worsen. As a consequence, in October 1871 President Grant suspended the writ of habeas corpus in nine counties in the state and thus began the suppression of the Ku Klux Klan.[72]

Only after Congress had been inundated with reports of violent outrages against Blacks and White Republicans in the South did the national government decide to intervene to subdue the Klan. Beginning with a joint committee created in March 1871, Congress held hearings, took testimony, and eventually brought some members of the Klan to trial. While President Grant, like many moderate Republicans, was appalled by the lawless situation created by the Klan, he nevertheless remained ambivalent about intervening, not wanting to be perceived as a military despot. Grant exercised his executive authority in South Carolina but refused to do so in Florida and Louisiana precisely because of this apprehension. The underlying issue of states' rights versus the sovereignty of the federal government still had not been resolved, although when a partial resolution came years later it did not serve the interests of the former slaves.[73]

The scope of the Ku Klux Klan trials was unlike anything else in U.S. history. By the end of November and after making arrests for only a few weeks, Governor Scott reported that over 600 people had been arrested. Although hundreds (especially the more wealthy and influential Klansmen) escaped prosecution by fleeing the state, over 112 Klansmen pleaded guilty during the November 1871 term. Of these, five cases went to trial, all of which the government won, either by confessions in the courtroom or by guilty verdicts. The trials had a devastating effect on the organization, as the Klan ceased to wreak havoc throughout the state, at least until its resurgence at the turn of the century.[74]

However, one does not have to agree with the critique offered by the supporters of the Democratic Party that the trials were merely attempts to maintain Republican dominance to acknowledge the complex and contradictory results of the Ku Klux Klan trials in South Carolina. It has been argued that while the government succeeded in prosecuting some Klan members, this "did not bring in its train any correspondingly greater constitutional support for black civil rights" and thus a paradox emerged whereby "at the same time the Klan faltered, the constitutional position of black rights waned." This effect resulted from the judges' rejection of the innovative interpretation of the Constitution offered by the government lawyers Daniel T. Corbin, former Union officer and later federal district attorney, and Daniel H. Chamberlain, the state attorney general and later governor of the state, both of whom had worked closely with the U.S. attorney general, Amos T. Akerman, in formulating this strategy.[75]

As Grant's hesitation to intervene in local politics suggested, at issue remained more than a simple question of law and order but rather the recurring question of the rights of the states versus those of the federal government, the issue that in fact had caused the recent Civil War. Corbin and Chamberlain attempted to argue that the Bill of Rights, which was usually invoked against the federal government, could also be applied against states and individuals because the Fourteenth Amendment had incorporated the Bill of Rights into its provisions. Also the meaning of "state action," which the defense insisted meant actions of the state, Corbin and Chamberlain wanted to broaden to include inaction on the part of the state. The final constitutional argument advanced was related to the Fifteenth Amendment, which the prosecution contended had granted Blacks the right to vote, a right that the federal government was obliged to enforce against the states.[76]

The judges who presided over the Klan trials, Hugh Lennox Bond (a Grant appointee) and George Seabrook Bryan, were able to convict the Klan members without adopting the arguments of the prosecution. The first case to come to trial was that of *United States v. Crosby,* which involved the Klan raid on the family of Amzi Rainey in York. With the help of his comrades, Crosby abducted Rainey from his home after they had beaten him in front of his family and shot and raped his young daughter. Of the eleven-count indictment, the judges supported only two, those that involved the attempt through force and intimidation to conspire to violate the 1870 Enforcement Act, thereby violating Rainey's right to vote. The "novel proposition that the Constitution through the fourteenth and fifteenth amendments had granted Rainey certain positive civil and political rights" was rejected. In slippery, hair-splitting legal language, Judge Bond ruled that "[t]he right of a citizen to vote . . . is not granted to him by the Constitution. . . . All that is guaranteed is that he shall not be deprived of the suffrage by reason of race, color, or previous servitude."[77] Such a jurisprudence, of course, facilitated the resubordination of Blacks within legal terms for, as the prosecution's interpretation suggested, inaction is also a form of action that can have serious consequences.

The outcome of the Crosby case typified the political duplicity of the Republican national government and others who wanted the Klan violence to halt. Essentially, the federal government failed to protect Blacks in the South, a situation that also left some White Republicans vulnerable. Officials reacted, as in the case of Governor Scott (who did receive criticisms from other Republicans), only when elections could be affected or when the situation became so dire that it embarrassed the party. This dynamic emerged because Reconstruction, to borrow an apt phrase, was a "reluctant revolution." From the time of President Lincoln and the issuance of the Emancipation Proclamation, which, as he unequivocally stated, came only as a war measure, to the other measures of Radical Reconstruction, such as the Fifteenth Amendment, which while it barred racial qualifications for voting, did not do so with respect to other barriers such as the poll tax and literacy requirement, the Republican Party seemed willing to sponsor only a partial transformation.[78] But, then, inertia remains a powerful political force.

Nevertheless, some of the policies implemented by the Republican Party would have probably worked if they had simply been enforced more effectively. "Perhaps, as often happens with American lawmakers, Republican congressmen had fallen victim to their own hopes by quickly passing a law and expecting it would somehow enforce itself." This hesitance occurred paradoxically with the Enforcement Acts, which themselves were often *unenforced.* Yet, to have fully enforced these laws would have meant resolving another "vexed question," that of states' rights versus rights of the federal government; for whenever this issue emerged, the Republican Party skirted it. For behind this political language lay a racial ideology whose purpose remained that of subordinating Blacks.

Even for some radical allies of the former slaves, it was becoming increasingly clear that issues confronting Blacks had always been an appendage to the larger goal of subduing and reconstructing the "rebellious South." The Radical Republicans whose power began to wane as time went on remained the exception to this rule; but they were a minority within the party, and only for a brief moment did their position control the direction of the party. Moreover, a significant amount of Radicals defected and voted for Democrat Horace Greeley in the 1872 presidential election, demonstrating the total collapse of the commitment to securing freedom for the ex-slaves. This shift also occurred among the once dedicated antislavery advocates as they "shared in the mood of national reconciliation."[79]

The fallout from the Klan trials reinforced the precipitous decline in the support of the political interests of Blacks. The stiffest sentences awarded, five years' imprisonment with a fine of $1,000, in no way could have been construed as cruel and unusual punishment, considering some Klansmen had been convicted of murder. They were unusual only in the sense that Whites had rarely been convicted and forced to serve time for violating the rights of Blacks. Nevertheless, President Grant began to pardon the convicted Klansmen, because the Republicans had won the recent election and "there was no point in risking a negative public reaction by pushing the matter [of the rights of Blacks] further." In South Carolina alone, more than 1,091 prosecutions were suspended and pardons had been accorded to some of the most serious offenders, a process that continued until 1875. Some of the pardons had even been initiated by supporters of Blacks. In July 1872 the veteran abolitionist Gerrit Smith visited the penitentiary in Albany where some of the convicted Klansmen had been sent to serve their time. After talking with the prisoners, he wrote a letter to President Grant stating they deserved pardons as most of them were ignorant and somehow had been fooled into joining the Klan. Attorney Corbin and Commander Merrill also supported clemency for some convicted Klansmen, although they were more selective in their recommendations, suggesting that some should remain in prison, and even that others not yet brought to trial should still be prosecuted.[80]

This policy seemed to have been implemented on a national level. In 1876 the Supreme Court reversed a lower court decision in *United States v. Cruikshank,* a case resulting from the bloodiest massacre during Reconstruction in Colfax, Louisiana, where historians have argued that from 100 to 280 Blacks were slaughtered. The government had been able to obtain only three convictions in the case, and now these had been nullified because the wording in the 1870 Enforcement Act had failed to specify race as the motivation of the rioters. In South Carolina, the government also became more emboldened. Governor Chamberlain succeeded in 1875 in blocking the appointments of two elected Black judges, William J. Whipper and Franklin J. Moses Jr., claiming that their serving would endanger "civilization." While the governor's actions angered Black Republicans in the state, it pleased most Whites and most Northern Republicans as well.[81]

Blacks in South Carolina did not passively accept the process of retrenchment evidenced by some who attempted to go on the offensive. In September 1876 Black Republicans attacked Democrats (White and Black) who were leaving a gathering in Charleston. In October another incident occurred, in which a group of activists fired into a meeting in a village near the city, a situation that ended in the deaths of five Whites and a Black. Black Republicans really resented the presence of Black Democrats. One such Democrat was Martin Delany, the former agent for the Freedmen's Bureau and, more recently, candidate for lieutenant governor. Delany had once been popular with Blacks, being able to negotiate conflicts between the ex-slaves and the ex-slaveholders in the Sea Islands. However, his political opportunism enraged some who claimed that a White man had a legitimate reason to be a Democrat, but no Black man had any such reason. This contention echoed one expressed during the Morant Bay rebellion in Jamaica. When the rebels were confronted with the question of killing a Black person who had collaborated with the planter regime, some stated that although he had Black skin, he had a "white heart" and thus had to be subjected to the same treatment.[82]

This process of resubordinating the Black population had been called Redemption by its advocates, a concept that seemed most logical within the context of what was occurring. While the North and the South reconciled their differences (however provisionally), Blacks were no longer needed politically to serve the interests of the party. President Grant said it best when in private he confided that the Fifteenth Amendment "had done the Negro no good, and had been a hindrance to the South, and by no means a political advantage to the North." Like the British Parliament, the U.S. government had deluded Blacks into a "false Canaan," creating a situation of granting freedom but then not completely supporting it. Moreover, as a Supreme Court justice declared with regard to the reasoning behind finding the 1875 Civil Rights Act unconstitutional, Blacks should not be "the special favorite of the laws." This statement echoed one made by an agent of the bureau, William Stone, who also claimed that Blacks should not be subjects of "special legislation." The inescapable paradox, however, remained that slavery had been a juridical institution and therefore had done precisely what the Supreme Court justice and Stone abhorred—that is, it had made Blacks subjects of "special legislation."[83] It had also done the same for many Whites, granting them privileges of voting, landholding, and even, within the free-labor ideology, job-holding. What remained at issue was a conception of the past and of the present social order inscribed by political languages that could not recognize the importance of Blacks to the formation and reproduction of the society.

Conclusion

The Paradox of Emancipation
and the Limits of Abolitionist Thought

For in history, time supplies the continuum but not the principle of change. To discover that principle, it is still necessary to do as so many of the West Indian historians did—to seek beyond the narrative of events, a wider understanding of the thoughts, habits, and institutions of a whole society. In the society itself, in its purpose and its adaptive process, will be found the true genesis of its history.
—Elsa Goveia, *Study of the Historiography*
  of the British West Indies

Away back in the days of bondage they thought to see in one divine event the end of all doubt and disappointment; few men ever worshipped Freedom with half such unquestioning faith as did the American Negro for two centuries. To him, so far as he thought and dreamed, slavery was indeed the sum of all villainies, the cause of all sorrow, the root of all prejudice; Emancipation was the key to a promised land of sweeter beauty than ever stretched before the eyes of wearied Israelites. . . . Years have passed away since then. . . . In vain do we cry to this our vastest social problem. . . . The Nation has not yet found peace from its sins; the freedman has not yet found in freedom his promised land.
—W. E. B. Du Bois, *The Souls of Black Folk*

If history can be defined as "an intelligible story of how men's actions produce results other than those they intended," then such can be said to be the history of emancipation. To understand these unintended consequences, it is often necessary, as Goveia intimates, to go beyond the "narrative of events" and examine the "thoughts, habits, and institutions of a whole society."[1] Such has been the approach in the present study. It has attempted to illustrate that the institutions put in place after the abolition of slavery in Jamaica and South Carolina were inextricably bound up with certain thoughts—namely, a specific notion of order and of what constituted the general good.

The investigation began with a discussion of the political languages of "freedom" in order to emphasize that the use of this term should not be taken for granted, as each claim of freedom, while it usually presumed a common understanding of what is meant by the idea, was, in fact, embedded in a set of assumptions, often unexamined. Freedom has always been a culturally constituted and, by extension, a culturally instituted political language. In the context of a slave society, ideas of freedom and liberty took on a particular understanding of the social reality: they exemplified the optimal status criteria of what it meant to be fully human in the society. These ideas represented the "ideology" of the society, but not in the sense of "false consciousness," an idea that alleges the existence of an absolute truth. Rather notions of freedom served to integrate Anglo-American societies on the basis of those who embodied this criterion of status over those who did not. In a systemic manner, the freedom of slaveholders and, secondarily, of White nonslaveholders, called for the enslavement of Blacks, as its ideological function (in the sense articulated by Ricoeur) remained the production of the society in a specific modality, and thus by producing cotton, tobacco, rice, and sugar, it was this modality of being in the world (its conception of freedom and of the common good implied therein) that was also being produced. Both the institutional apparatus and the conceptual framework were needed for the enactment of this social order, for its stabilization and replication.

Although it has been employed in multiple ways, and with diversified meanings, some common patterns of usage also emerged with the political language of freedom. When abolitionists, and in particular the slaves, called for freedom, they did so from a perspective that challenged the dominant understanding that perceived freedom to be possible only with enslavement, but they would often do so by assuming the validity of some concepts associated with the hegemonic conception of freedom. The political languages of independence and self-sufficiency provided a case in point. These ideas emerged with specific political connotations in the context of the 1776 revolution against the parliamentary monarchy of England, related to which were also familial and economic conceptions of independence and self-sufficiency. Abolitionists often adapted these concepts to their own purposes, reinterpreting slavery as being prohibitive for Blacks in achieving these political and philosophical ideals. However, some abolitionists, and here the former slaves in particular, would also attempt to move beyond these terms in their redefinition. Such claims, the demand for land being the most persistent, completely unsettled the social order, and indeed it was such sharply different, even conflictual, interpretations of freedom that remained responsible for the incomplete nature of the victory of abolition.

To sustain the dominant conception of freedom in the immediate postslavery context, as argued in the second chapter, the former slaveholders made political claims that constituted blatant attempts to replicate the order of things as they had existed under slavery. The insistence upon states' rights and local autonomy, the call for immigration, and the specious use of the vote served to indicate to the former slaves that although they were free, they should not expect too much change in the level of control over their lives. The Colonial Office and the U.S. federal government thwarted the most obvious efforts to resubordinate the freedpeople by nullifying and countermanding some legal acts. Despite this occurrence, however, the Black Codes in the South and the Abolition Acts in the British Caribbean should not be viewed as purely rhetorical and fictional. Rhetoric and fiction can be the most powerful motivators of human behaviors. Although there would be modifications, this understanding served in important ways for the basis of the official perspective on emancipation and consequently reemerged in other legal and extralegal acts. The special magistrates and agents of the Freedmen's Bureau adopted some of the same concepts in the postslavery era. For instance, the claim that the former slaves equated freedom with the license to abandon work and become vagrants was an idea utilized to legitimate slavery. Yet, after slavery, this understanding became a major preoccupation of these agents and their respective central governments. The way to secure stability in the postslavery era was imagined in similar terms as its antecedent, that is, with the disciplining and regulation of the behaviors of the former slaves.

The next two chapters amplified in more detail the perspectives of these officials as they interacted with the former slaves. It was argued that the orientation of their operations took two primary forms. One form, and this was more pronounced in South Carolina due to the then recent Civil War, involved handling the basic necessities of day-to-day survival. The other emphasis, and one not always separate from the first purpose, comprised the regulation of the lives of the former slaves. In fact, this dimension of their administration would often override the questions related to the material provisioning for the freedpeople. A clear example occurred when Commissioner Howard claimed that the suffering that originated from the emancipation process was "preferable to slavery, and is, to some degree the necessary consequence of events."[2] Greenville agent John William De Forest followed such a perspective to its most logical conclusion, insisting that distributing rations was demoralizing and encouraged idleness, and thus in principle he remained "merciless toward the few for the good of the many, refusing to feed the suffering lest [he] should encourage the lazy."[3]

At the heart of the issue lay the representation of slavery, one that implied in both societies a specific interpretation of the historic past. From the perspectives of the special magistrates and the agents of the Freedmen's Bureau, slavery was responsible for what later would be understood as the "damaged Black psyche,"[4] or what John Daughtrey understood as the "debasing effects" on the "negro mind." In both Jamaica and South Carolina, officials consistently made the claim that slavery contributed to the degradation of the slave by having encouraged certain habits. On this issue, there seemed to have been consensus among these "evangels of civilization." R. Standing Haly insisted that slavery "produced vices of idleness and theft" and thus the former slaves became morally corrupt. As a logical consequence, it became the responsibility of these "architects of freedom" to resocialize the former slaves, disabusing them of habits ostensibly developed under slavery as well as of beliefs and cultural forms derived from African symbolic systems such as John Canoe celebrations. As Orangeburg agent William Holton insisted, slavery "only released in a measure the colored people from the control of their masters," but not from "the superstitions, ignorance and vices engendered by long years of slavery." This understanding led many of these officials in both postslavery contexts to advocate the apprenticeship of children of former slaves in order to stave off what Edward Baynes referred to as the "contagion of example." Indeed, Baynes proposed the removal of children from Jamaican ex-slave families, suggesting they could be placed in asylums where they would learn habits appropriate to a situation of freedom.

The postslavery debate about the nature of slavery remained important because the understanding of the slave past determined in a significant manner the organization of the society in the postslavery context. From another perspective on the history of enslavement of Blacks, one could argue that these agents and their respective governments did not really "see" slavery at all—that is, certain aspects had to be excluded in order to effect emancipation in the terms in which it was being implemented. Or, yet, they did "see" slavery, but they saw it with a certain consciousness, one that remained unable to separate the institution of slavery from the slaves themselves. Simply because the institution attempted to degrade the slave should not have necessarily implied that the slave was, in fact, totally degraded. In this respect, a paradox arose. Antislavery activists had to represent slavery in degrading terms in order to legitimate its abolition; logically, this led to the complete representation of the system, including the slaves, within this conceptual frame.[5] One here is reminded of Frederick Douglass's statement made after his encounter with the "negro-breaker" overseer Edward Covey. Once Douglass had decided that he would no longer allow Covey to break his spirit, he concluded that "however long I might remain a slave in form, the day had passed forever when I could be a slave in fact."[6] Apparently the distinction between slavery as a political situation versus slavery as a mental condition was not evident to many of the officials involved with the process of emancipation.

As a possible counter to the official interpretation of the slavery past that was operative at the time, contemporary social history has provided the basis for an alternative understanding of the history of slavery, one that illustrates the centrality of slaves to the cultural formation of the societies in which they found themselves. Historians have analyzed in detail the independent production and related market activities of slaves throughout the Americas.[7] During the era of slavery in Jamaica, the slaves supplied most of the island's fresh produce, selling many of these provisions at weekly markets. The slaves grew these provisions under the most extraordinary of circumstances. The lands utilized were the less fertile scrublands and uplands not used for sugar cultivation. Often, these lands would be located miles from the plantations on which the slaves resided, sometimes being as much as five to seven miles from their homes.[8]

When coupled with the fact that slaves did not have much free time to work their provision grounds, what they were able to produce becomes all the more remarkable, exemplifying the sentiment articulated in the Negro spiritual "making a way out of no way." Moreover, given that after slavery the planters continued to push for cultivation of staple crops for export, this practice, whereby the former slaves cultivated produce for the island, continued into the postslavery context. This empirical reality could have been easily utilized to contradict several assertions that caused anxiety in the postslavery era: that the former slaves lacked independence and could not take care of themselves; that they had a negative interpretation of all physical labor; and that they lacked certain entrepreneurial abilities (which officials like John Daughtrey insisted needed to be taught to the former slaves). Moreover, given that the former slaves were producing an increasingly larger proportion of articles that were exported from the island, such a development could have easily been encouraged.[9] This position, of course, assumes that the economic motivations always determine political decisions. Yet gradually it became clear during the postslavery era that the primary constraints were not economic but, in fact, based upon the political languages employed to understand the social situation. These languages systematically ignored the labor and economic perspectives of the slaves and made claims of idleness, vagrancy, and dependence that in effect assigned to the emancipation process a disciplinary tenor.

In South Carolina, slaves who worked in the coastal and low-country rice regions as well as in the up-country cotton zone engaged in independent economic activities in a manner similar to the slaves in Jamaica. From the middle of the eighteenth century, when a law was passed that did not require slaves to work on Sundays, slaves living on coastal rice plantations utilized the "task system" to facilitate nonplantation economic endeavors. The organization of labor by tasks allowed the slaves to produce and sell a range of goods once they had finished their assigned jobs. Although it could be argued that up-country slaves working on cotton plantations had less time as they were confined for the most part to working all day, nonetheless, they too were able to engage in economic activities away from their specific plantations.[10]

Like their Jamaican counterparts, South Carolina slaves produced crops for subsistence as well as to be sold at markets. The slaves grew corn, potatoes, pumpkins, and melons, necessary provisions as the quantity of food provided by slaveholders could often be inadequate. Some slaves even utilized their time to grow tobacco that they could sell at markets. Again, like the former slaves in Jamaica, they sold items they manufactured, such as baskets and pottery. Given their constraints of time as well as of land made available to them, their productions take on the same impressive dimensions as those of Jamaican slaves. Moreover, in early nineteenth-century up country, some slaves worked for wages in order to supplement their income, giving further evidence of certain entrepreneurial inclinations.[11]

From Antigua to the Windward Islands, from Alabama to Virginia, the slaves demonstrated not only the ability but also a deep interest in laboring in order to secure a basic standard of living. When the questions arose in the postslavery context of whether the former slaves would or could labor without coercion or supervision, and, if indeed they could become self-sufficient, the deep-seated nature of the perception of the Blacks became ever more apparent. One could have responded as a former South Carolina slave did in a letter to the editor of a local Black newspaper: "We have enriched others, why can't we enrich ourselves[?] They say we can't take care of ourselves. It is strange that we took care of others and can't take care of ourselves."[12] Here the conflicting interpretations of the past emerged most clearly. Was slavery, as the actions of the respective central governments and many of their agents implied, a source of dependence, or was it, as the former slaves insisted, a source of wealth for White society?

In order for the perspective of the former slaves to have been minimized, certain aspects of the historical record needed to be expunged. Before 1838 in the British colonies, a head tax on slaves and apprentices provided the basic source of colonial revenue. This levy took the form of a poll tax of five to six shillings, and was assessed not only on slaves but on forms of personal property such as livestock and carriages.[13] From these measures, a system was instituted whereby slavery served to generate wealth for the planters in particular but, on a more general level, for the mother country as well. Conservative estimates have placed the level of profit of sugar plantations in the British Caribbean during the eighteenth century at an annual rate of 10 percent, although this figure could be much higher in certain cases. For instance, in mid-seventeenth-century Barbados profits mounted as high as 40 or 50 percent.[14] These profits, Eric Williams has argued, served as the basis of the capital utilized to finance the industrial revolution. To illustrate this relation, Williams pointed out that the rise of the banking industry in slave-trading centers provided evidence that the wealth generated by slavery became an important part of the process that made possible England's ascent to global economic dominance in the nineteenth century.[15]

Striking parallels emerge with the comparison of the structuring and systemic role of slavery in the United States. As occurred in the British colonies, a tax on slaves played a central role in generating revenue for the country. In 1798, during the second session of the Fifth Congress, military objectives involving France caused a need for funds that could not be met with existing sources. After a debate, Congress passed a bill that levied a direct tax on homes, slaves, and land, an approach that had already been instituted in South Carolina. As representative Robert Goodloe Harper, chairman of the House Committee on Ways and Means, noted, much of the state's revenue came directly from a tax on slaves.[16] In fact, from 1783, when the three-fifths ratio was adopted as a measure to determine the burden of taxation, slavery served as a source of wealth for the Southern planters as well as after the 1787 Constitutional Convention, a partial basis for political representation (although the slaveholders did not achieve the full extent of representation they desired).[17] Indeed, beginning as early as 1703, a colonial South Carolina act laid such a foundation for slavery's wealth-generating possibilities when the state received thousands of pounds in revenue from the importation of slaves. Acts such as these, as a 1716 statue stipulated, served to defray the public charges and expenses of the government. For instance, duties on the importation of slaves provided funds for poor White settlers in the colony. As well, fines and penalties imposed through slave codes were transferred to aid the poor.[18] Such a situation made clear that not only the slaveholders but Whites in general benefited from the institution of slavery.

Despite slaveholders' claims of slavery being an economic burden, the system generated profits for most planters, large and small, in most parts of the U.S. South. Like the owners of sugar estates in the British colonies, it has been claimed that the slaveholders' return on their investments hovered around 10 percent. The system also produced wealth for the nation in general. Exports of cotton, for instance, composed between 50 and 60 percent of the nation's exports. In this respect, aspects of the Williams thesis can be applied in the case of the United States, as the raw materials produced by slave labor remained indispensable for New England's textile mills and, indeed, became a central component of the industrialization process in the Northern states.[19] Besides the economic aspects, slavery took on a symbolic and signifying function as well, serving as the criterion of status that integrated the social system. A case in point occurred with the South Carolina cotton planter Peter Gaillard, who, like many of his counterparts, used slaves as marriage gifts to his sons and daughters. Once his estate was firmly established in the 1790s, Gaillard acquired slaves "primarily to give his sons their economic start."[20] Thus, again, slavery provided the basis for the realization of the well-being of Whites. As Edmund Morgan has aptly stated, "To a large degree it may be said that Americans bought their independence with slave labor."[21]

It is not being proposed here that all government officials should have been aware of the intricate details of slaveholding, such as the rate of return of the investment, although one would think that high-level government officials would have been aware of facts such as the margin of profit or a phenomenon like the independent production of the former slaves. It is, however, being suggested that herein lay the paradox of emancipation and the limits of abolitionist thought. For the representation of slavery as having degraded the slaves and rendered them dependent, as well as the political claim that the postslavery era was marked by a labor problem, contradicted the experience of the slaves and ex-slaves, exemplifying the incomplete victory of abolition.

The primary issue remained the representation of what constituted a socially significant ill, for such an understanding determined in a significant manner the way in which the emancipation process evolved. In other words, what could and could not be conceptualized as a problem held importance for the course of emancipation in the British Caribbean and the United States. The political language of there being a labor problem after slavery remained a case in point. As noted by Woodville Marshall in chapter 2: "This may be a loaded term. It suggests a particular perspective: a labour problem of a particular sort had to exist once the slaves were freed. This was evidently the view of the planters, of the Colonial Office, of the abolitionists: all of them said so, and in this regard their actions matched their words."[22] From the perspective of the former slaves, no labor problem existed; rather, what existed was a problem of *labor control* and the continued efforts to circumscribe their freedom.

At the same time, the economic burdens confronting the former slaves were not understood as a socially significant dilemma. In Jamaica, the transfer of the burden of taxation from its former dependence on slave heads to the freedpeople could not be seen as compromising what freedom must have meant to the ex-slaves. By shifting the weight of taxation in the post-slavery period from the planters to the former slaves, the relation whereby slaves served to generate wealth for the larger colonial society was replicated after abolition. The colonial government achieved this objective by imposing higher duties on imports into the country as well as the use of capitation taxes on all male heads. Not all officials, however, agreed with such a strategy. Colonial secretaries from Lord Glenelg to Edward Stanley as well as Permanent Under Secretary James Stephen objected to the levying of capitation taxes, which traditionally had been used to repair roads. However, Earl Grey's assumption of the office of colonial secretary in 1846 signaled a decisive change in imperial policy. Grey supported a system of taxation that raised the cost of basic necessities with high import duties, while at the same time he supported the reduction of the duties on staples produced for export. These policies were enabled by the belief that those who could not pay the taxes should be forced to work either on public roads or in gangs resembling the labor system of slavery. For this reason, officials such as Henry Taylor insisted that the former slaves enjoyed luxuries of which the English working classes were deprived, and therefore policies that shifted the burden of taxation were justified. These political languages, which echoed the ideas of Thomas Carlyle, remained inseparable from the chain of events that led to the Morant Bay rebellion, symbolizing the incomplete victory of abolition.[23]

This essentially laissez-faire conception of society (where all should be able to pay taxes regardless of historically accumulated disadvantages) articulated by the Colonial Office officials took a different form in the South Carolina example. The politics surrounding the 1871–72 Ku Klux Klan trials also showed the contradictions of emancipation and the limits of abolitionist thought. Of all the attempts to secure the political rights of ex-slaves, it has been argued that, aside from the Thirteenth Amendment, these trials represented "the most determined effort . . . to use constitutional amendments and federal statutes to change the political and social structure of the South." In the end, however, the Supreme Court interpreted most of the Reconstruction acts through such a narrow frame that not only were the former slaves not accorded the rights they must have expected, but many White South Carolinians could feel vindicated in their beliefs in home rule and states' rights. In this respect, South Carolina served as a compass indicating the direction of legal interpretation regarding the extent to which the federal government would go to enforce the civil rights of ex-slaves. In the infamous *United States v. Slaughter-House* (1873), which had little direct concern with the situation of ex-slaves, as well as in *United States v. Cruikshank* (1874) and *United States v. Reese* (1876), which involved an attempt to disenfranchise Blacks in Kentucky, the courts consistently ruled that the states retained the authority to enforce civil rights. When the courts considered the issues unfolding in the Ku Klux Klan trials, the narrow interpretation of the Fourteenth Amendment offered in the *Slaughter-House* case restricted the possibilities of expanding this law to enhance the rights of the former slaves in *Cruikshank* and *Reese*. The rulings argued that a distinction existed between rights associated with national citizenship and those which existed on the state level. In other words, "the Fourteenth Amendment did not nationalize the Bill of Rights." The implication remained that a state's failure to protect Blacks was not sufficient ground for federal intervention.[24] At this point, the emancipation process had come full circle, for one of the first impediments that the U.S. government had to overcome was the states' rights discourse of the Southern planters. It now seemed that the Supreme Court was willing to sanction legally in the post-slavery period the political language whose primary purpose remained the subordination of the Black population group.

In this vein, the sharply different perspectives on the nature of emancipation paved the way for the insurrection at Morant Bay as well as for Redemption in South Carolina and other states. When the 1842 Select Committee suggested that ex-slave wages were too high or when the queen's advice implied that the prosperity of the former slaves depended on their giving steady and continuous labor, it became evident that the Colonial Office had developed a perspective so widely at variance with those of the former slaves and their allies (such as the Baptist missionaries) that conflict was inevitable. Moreover, General Grant's contention that in the final analysis the Fifteenth Amendment had served neither Blacks nor Whites in the South represented a similar understanding. In both instances, what was being seen, or not seen, in order to make such arguments in the face of evidence that completely contradicted such an interpretation of the social reality? Why did the perspective on the history of enslavement that could have seen it as having resulted in habits of independent production as well as the source of societal wealth have to be so systematically ignored? Could these agents and government officials not "see" these aspects of slavery? Indeed, they actually saw the same system but interpreted the situation in vastly different terms from Blacks and their allies. In fact, each perspective was viewing the empirical reality with a different consciousness. Here the framework of political languages may assist in understanding the postslavery context. For these languages provided the basis on which the society was integrated, stabilized, and reproduced, and thus the public policies of emancipation were always conditioned by a specific understanding of the social situation. This understanding was one in the process of undergoing a transformation, remaining inseparable from the increasing industrialization of society and its related conception of freedom.

On the basis of the argument presented here, several implications emerge that may strike some readers as a departure from a traditional comparative study. Although some of the significant differences were discussed, the comparison delineated in this work emphasized the overwhelming similarities between the postslavery environments in Jamaica and South Carolina. The historical record validates why such a level of generality is merited as the institution of slavery was established and reproduced in precisely such a broad context, that is, one of a world system, and not that of a single nation. As their concern for the stability of slavery in other locations intimated, the proslavery interests understood well this dynamic, as well as the importance of slavery to an international economic system: "Slavery is no isolated system, but is so mingled with the business of the world, that it derives facilities from the most innocent transactions."[25] In the postslavery context, imperial Britain expressed this same attitude. After its abolition of the slave trade in 1808 and a declaration at the 1815 Treaty of Vienna, the English government made explicitly clear with its vigorous and elaborate attempts to suppress the trade in

Brazil and Cuba (efforts that completely disregarded the ostensible national sovereignty of these nations) that slavery functioned in a world system.[26]

For this reason, the approach in the present work did not deploy the nation as the "unit of analysis," but rather adapted to its purposes elements of Immanuel Wallerstein's proposed world systems approach.[27] Such an approach emphasizes the historical process in whose context the slave plantation system was established in the Caribbean from the earliest decades of the sixteenth century and in the United States a century and half before the formation of the nation in the late eighteenth century. Contrary to Frederick Jackson Turner's thesis that the frontier represented the major theme in U.S. history, Straughton Lynd has illustrated that it was the issue of slavery that, in the words of James Madison, formed the line of demarcation in the struggle to create the nation. Thus, rather than slavery coming out of the "imagined community of the nation," as it is often made to do in the traditional comparative history approach, in the present investigation it is the New World nations that emerge out of the context, as well as on the basis of, plantation slavery. As a result, although the argument centers on Jamaica and South Carolina so as not to deny the local specificity of each case, the unstated implication remains that slavery in the hemisphere of the Americas, and the effects to which abolition led, should be taken as the unit of analysis.[28]

This approach necessarily challenges the "American exceptionalism" thesis that has been implicit in the framework of comparative slavery and emancipation studies. This understanding has its own history, having emerged in the descriptions of the earliest European interpreters of the Americas after the 1492 encounter, and although it would later be contested, it has nevertheless remained a staple in the interpretation of the American social reality and, in particular, that of the United States. Intellectuals such as Hector St. John de Crèvecoeur, Alexis de Tocqueville, Adam Smith, Benjamin Franklin, and Thomas Paine extolled the widespread prosperity and political equality that existed among free Anglo-Americans. Some went as far as to advocate that the English colonies represented a utopia, "the most perfect society now existing in the world," insisting that until the creation of America "there had been no such thing as freedom left throughout the whole universe." From this standpoint, the "cause of America" became "the cause of all mankind." This representation necessarily implied that European culture constituted "the only truly significant culture"—that is, "the presumptive conceit" that European civilization represented the highest development of human existence.[29] Although appearing less imperial, more contemporary descriptions of the emancipation process in the United States as unique (which clearly in some ways it was, such as with the Fifteenth Amendment) speak only to one side of the issue.

One does not have to see the formation of the United States as a "miracle" to acknowledge its singularity,[30] for all historical contexts on one level have their own distinctiveness. For the purposes of the present argument, it should be simply noted that scholars working on the postslavery Americas seem particularly zealous to emphasize the uniqueness of the policies of Reconstruction in the United States vis-à-vis other postslavery contexts. This project has a different emphasis, illustrating for instance in the Jamaican context that a kind of postslavery Reconstruction did occur, and the special magistrates would be central to the initial stages of the process. Clearly, the terms differed, and it could be justifiably argued that the level of enfranchisement in the United States was not comparable anywhere in the Americas. Yet, by showing that despite the local differences, striking similarities emerged in the wake of the abolition of slavery in these two regions, the argument here makes clear that a *difference of strategy* should not be conflated with a *difference of situation*. When one considers that neither system of emancipation remained able to sustain a vision of freedom reflective of the perspective of the former slaves, local differences become secondary, and claims of exceptionalism and uniqueness can be made secondary to the ends (rather than the means) of emancipation. In both postslavery situations, the dominant society found a way to disempower (Jamaica) or disenfranchise (South Carolina) its respective Black majorities and still continue to see itself as being a nation that embodied free and democratic principles. It was this political language of freedom that, in the final analysis, the agents of emancipation could not reinterpret. As Du Bois so eloquently stated, such was the work that the Freedmen's Bureau did not do, because it could not. Nevertheless, as he intimated in his classic *The Souls of Black Folk*, Blacks held on to this ideal of freedom, despite the fact that "the horizon was ever dark, the mists were often cold, the Canaan was always dim and far away." This tenaciousness raises the issue as to whether the ideals of freedom and liberty, again in the words of Du Bois, sent Blacks "wooing false gods and invoking false means of salvation."[31] Were these notions, are these notions, "delusions of a false Canaan"?

Notes

Abbreviations

CO   Colonial Office Records, Series 137: Original Correspondence, Governors
of Jamaica, Public Record Office, Kew, England

FSSP   Freedmen and Southern Society Project, Department of History,
University of Maryland, College Park, Maryland

M 869 Office of the Assistant Commissioner for South Carolina, Microfilm, Series
869, Record Group 105: Records of the Bureau of Refugees, Freedmen,
and Abandoned Lands, National Archives, Washington, D.C.

PP   Great Britain, House of Commons, *Parliamentary Papers,* London

SFOR Subordinate Field Officers Records for South Carolina, Record Group 105:
Records of the Bureau of Refugees, Freedmen, and Abandoned Lands,
National Archives, Washington, D.C.

UWI   University of the West Indies, Mona, Kingston, Jamaica

Introduction

1. Woodward, "The Price of Freedom," 93; Fredrickson, "After Emancipation," 71. The classic pioneering work on comparative slavery is Tannenbaum's *Slave and Citizen: The Negro in the Americas.* Other examples of the impressive historiography include the work of David Brion Davis, *The Problem of Slavery in Western Culture* and *The Problem of Slavery in the Age of Revolution, 1770–1823.* See also Klein, *Slavery in the Americas;* Laura Foner and Genovese, *Slavery in the New World;* Duff and Greene, *Slavery;* Engerman and Genovese, *Race and Slavery in the Western Hemisphere;* McDonald, *The Economy and Material Culture of Slaves.* The question of the free Black presence in slave systems has also been treated in a comparative context. See Cohen and Greene, *Neither Slave nor Free.* A work that extends its focus beyond the New World is Weston, *Asian and African Systems of Slavery.*

2. A few examples include Azevedo, *Abolitionism in the United States and Brazil;* Cooper, Holt, and Scott, *Beyond Slavery;* Drescher, *From Slavery to Freedom;* Drescher and McGlynn, *The Meaning of Freedom;* Frey and Wood, *From Slavery to Emancipation in the Atlantic World;* Richardson, *Abolition and Its Aftermath;* Hayward, *Out of Slavery;* Rushford, "A Comparative Study of the Process and Policy of Emancipation." There also exists a plethora of articles, in particular by Drescher, Holt, and Scott, some of which are referenced in the present work.

3. In the debate on reparations, slavery has often been invoked as the causal fac-

tor of the current conditions of many Black Americans. Randall Robinson, however, has departed from this model of analysis in his recent book, ascribing the situation to "slavery and the century of legalized American racial hostility that followed it." See *The Debt*, 8.

4. See Toplin, *The Abolition of Slavery in Brazil*, viii. "Black" is capitalized in this work (as is "White") because instead of using it to refer to a color, I use it as a proper noun to refer to a population group as is normally the case when referring to a group on the basis of culture, descent, religion, or nationality. Had there been no Middle Passage, the question of naming would not be an issue. I prefer this term to "African American," which is generated from the immigrant analogy, because those of African descent did not voluntarily migrate to the Americas but were forced to come here as slaves. Paradoxically, this historical event led to Blacks becoming one of the founding civilizations in the Americas (along with indigenous peoples and European settlers-colonizers), serving a central role in instituting cultural forms. Thus, rather than considering African slaves as immigrants, it can be argued that they constituted an almost neo-indigenous population.

5. Knight, *Slave Society in Cuba during the Nineteenth Century*, 193–94.

6. Derrick Bell, *And We Are Not Saved*, 250.

7. See Eric Foner, *Nothing but Freedom*, 17. See also Rebecca Scott, "Exploring the Meaning of Freedom," 418, and *Slave Emancipation in Cuba*, 77.

8. Rushford's unpublished master's thesis is an exception.

9. Finley, *Ancient Slavery and Modern Ideology*, 92–110. Finley's interpretation of the treatment of slavery by historians of antiquity should provoke further exploration. He argued that the pre-eighteenth-century analytical tradition that examined ancient slavery (usually Roman, rather than Greek) was concerned primarily with questions of morality, usually within the framework of Christianity. He pointed, however, to a paradigm shift with the work of Johann Friedrick Reitemeier, who attempted to understand slavery as a labor system. Reitemeier, who analyzed Greek slavery (then rare), was later slighted by the German academic establishment. Nonetheless, he signaled a change in emphasis where slavery was discussed no longer in moral terms (although this influence lay in the background) but increasingly in terms of "stages of social evolution based on modes of subsistence" — that is, in terms of the new discipline of economics concerned with "property, production, and distribution." At this juncture, Finley noted that history was no longer conceived of as a source of paradigms but, indeed, as a discipline. Thus, the interpretation of slavery as a labor system seemed to be coterminous with the modern conception of history as a discipline. Michael Gillespie brilliantly elucidated this transformation in the conceptual foundations of the historical field in *Hegel, Heidegger, and the Ground of History*.

10. See Pagden, *The Fall of Natural Man*.

11. See Patterson, *Slavery and Social Death*, and Miers and Kopytoff, *Slavery in Africa*.

12. Goldsmith, "Mandeville and the Spirit of Capitalism," 65.

13. Baker, *Inventing the French Revolution*, 4–5.

14. See the "Ideas in Context" series editor's comments before the title page of Pagden, *The Languages of Political Theory in Early-Modern Europe,* and Pocock, "The Concept of Language," 19–38.

15. Anthony Pagden, introduction to *The Languages of Political Theory in Early-Modern Europe,* 1–2; Pocock, "1776: The Revolution against Parliament," in *Virtue, Commerce, and History,* 75.

16. Pocock, "Languages and Their Implications," in *Politics, Language, and Time,* 11–25. See also Kuhn, *The Structure of Scientific Revolutions,* especially the chapter "Crisis and the Emergence of Scientific Theories," 66–76. In both the United States and the British Caribbean, abolition came as a response to a crisis. The Civil War between the North and the South, despite claims to the contrary, testified that slavery had led to a crisis. In the West Indies, although there was no physical war, slavery polarized the British government, and the compromise of the 1832 Reform Bill, which led to its abolition, prevented the kind of revolution that occurred in France in the 1780s and again in July 1830. See Maehl, *The Reform Bill of 1832,* 1–7.

17. Pocock, "Languages and Their Implications," 11–15. See also Marx and Engels, *Capital: A Critique of Political Economy,* 25.

18. Marx and Engels, *The German Ideology,* 64–66.

19. Ricoeur, "Ideology and Utopia," 107–25. See Geertz, *The Interpretation of Cultures,* 193–233.

20. See Pocock, "Introduction: The State of the Art," in *Virtue, Commerce, and History,* 15, and "Languages and Their Implications," 17.

21. Pocock, "The Concept of Language," 36.

22. Ibid., 24, 36.

23. Ricoeur, "Ideology and Utopia," 119–20.

24. Ibid., 24.

25. Pocock, "*The Machiavellian Moment* Revisited," 49–72.

26. Brooks, *The Writings of Abraham Lincoln,* 6:123–24.

27. Current, "The Friend of Freedom," 38.

28. Gaspar, "With Rod of Iron," 343–66, and Watson, *Slave Law in the Americas,* 125.

29. Green, *British Slave Emancipation,* 129–30.

30. Lynd, "The Abolitionist Critique of the United States Constitution," 216–19; *Senate Executive Documents,* 38th Cong., 1st sess., Serial 1176, no. 53, p. 5.

31. Rose, *Rehearsal for Reconstruction;* Williamson, *After Slavery,* 10.

32. Watson, *Slave Law in the Americas* (emphasis in original).

33. Rose, *Rehearsal for Reconstruction,* 45, 217 (emphasis in original). See also Morris, *Reading, 'Riting, and Reconstruction,* ix. For Whittlesey's statement, see *House Executive Documents,* 39th Cong., 1st sess., Serial 1256, no. 70, p. 2.

34. Burn, *Emancipation and Apprenticeship,* 213; Eric Foner, *Politics and Ideology in the Age of the Civil War,* 101.

35. Marquis of Sligo, "To the Negro Population of the Island of Jamaica," enclosed in Sligo to Edward G. Stanley, 27 May 1834, CO 137/192, no. 18 (emphasis added).

36. Nott, "Climates of the South in Their Relations to White Labor," 168. Nott stated: "Without touching at all on the vexed question of original Unity or Diversity of Races, we may assert, without fear of contradiction, that the races of men, as we now see them, scattered over the face of the globe, if not so in the beginning, have become peculiarly adapted to certain climates."

37. However, as Stephen Jay Gould has noted, polygenesis, the "American school of ethnology," did not become the dominant understanding because it contradicted the biblical idea of the creation of a single human species derived from Adam and Eve. See *The Mismeasure of Man*, 62–104.

38. Lovejoy, *The Great Chain of Being;* Gould, *The Mismeasure of Man*, 43; Holt, "'An Empire over the Mind,'" 284.

39. Tocqueville, *Democracy in America*, 460–62.

40. Marshall, *The Colthurst Journal*, 52–53, 67.

41. Rooke, "Evangelical Missionaries, Apprentices, and Freedmen," 1–3. See also Bolt, *The Anti-Slavery Movement and Reconstruction*, 170, where she noted that the egalitarian philosophy of the abolitionists later legitimized the expansion of the British Empire. "The concept of Anglo-Saxon solidarity, which had once sustained humanitarian endeavour on both sides of the Atlantic now served only to encourage the prejudice and sense of mission which, though unpleasant features of the 1860s and 1870s, were to become most marked during the next great period of British imperialism towards the end of the century."

42. Fredrickson, *The Black Image in the White Mind*, 174.

43. See Eric Foner, *Free Soil, Free Labor, Free Men*, 265–66.

44. Pocock, "Languages and Their Implications," 19.

45. Horsman, *Race and Manifest Destiny*, 70. Disraeli's classification of Jews with Caucasians did present a problem for the rigid Anglo-Saxonists. Carlyle, "Occasional Discourse on the Nigger Question," 348–83; see also chapter 4, note 13.

46. Green, *British Slave Emancipation*, 187–244; Bakan, *Ideology and Class Conflict in Jamaica*, 71.

47. Woodward, *Reunion and Reaction*, 10, and *Origins of the New South*, 22.

Chapter One

1. Eric Foner, *The Story of American Freedom*, 5.

2. Blackstone's statement cited in Watson, *Slave Law in the Americas*, 122.

3. Isaiah Berlin, *Two Concepts of Liberty*, 13.

4. Miers and Kopytoff, *Slavery in Africa*, 17. Cooper, Holt, and Scott have noted that while Miers and Kopytoff's insights "rightly point to a real tension in the conceptual scheme" in the question of slavery, nevertheless, "in contrasting an essentially 'Western' concept of autonomy against an essentially 'African' concept of belonging, they miss the fact that such notions are contested in both contexts." While there may have been a need for more discussion of the contested meanings of freedom in the Western context and of belonging in the African, Cooper, Holt, and Scott "miss the

fact" that the oppositions of freedom-slavery and belonging–not belonging served as organizing principles of their respective cultural orders. Although contested, these oppositions reinforced the governing principles of the social orders as the challenges did not always move outside of the terms defining the political situation. See *Beyond Slavery*, 5.

5. Cambiano, "Aristotle and the Anonymous Opponents of Slavery," 21–41, and Veyne, *The Roman Empire*, 51–93.

6. Veyne does not see slavery in Rome as being a mode of production. Some contend, however, that slavery formed the basis of production for the Roman Empire; see Goody, "Slavery in Time and Space," 16–42.

7. [Walker], *David Walker's Appeal, in Four Articles*, 10.

8. Pagden, "The Legacy of Rome," 11–28.

9. Hartz, *The Liberal Tradition in America*, 6.

10. Pagden, "The Legacy of Rome," 18–24.

11. Pocock, "Civic Humanism and Its Role in Anglo-American Thought," in *Politics, Language, and Time*, 80.

12. Gordon Wood, *The Creation of the American Republic, 1776–1787*.

13. Shain, *The Myth of American Individualism*, 171–72.

14. See Pocock, "1776: The Revolution against Parliament," in *Virtue, Commerce, and History*, 86, 87–88, where he has insightfully pointed out that the Revolution of 1776, fought against forms of corruption, especially parliamentary patronage, preserved these very forms: "[W]e shall realize the paradox that the new republic, born of the revolt against empire, had a commitment to empire—and to empire of settlement—built into its structure in a way that the parent system never had. . . . Democratic federalism grew into the greatest empire of patronage and influence the world has known, and remains to this day dedicated to the principle that politics cannot work unless politicians do things for their friends and their friends know where to find them. New democrat is but old Whig writ large; and the Federal Constitution, that great triumph of the eighteenth-century political art, seems to have perpetuated the eighteenth-century world it was designed to deal with."

15. Gordon Wood, introduction to *The Rising Glory of America*, 10–11.

16. David Brion Davis has discussed the centrality of the discourse of progress on the part of the abolitionists. See *The Problem of Slavery in Western Culture*, 13–28, and *Slavery and Human Progress*.

17. Lincoln's statement cited in Hess, *Liberty, Virtue, and Progress*, 17; Calhoun, "Disquisition on Government," 10 (emphasis in original).

18. Statement cited by Horsman, *Race and Manifest Destiny*, 202.

19. Genovese, "The Slave South: An Interpretation," in *The Political Economy of Slavery*, 13–39, and *The World the Slaveholders Made*. See also Wyatt-Brown, *Honor and Violence*.

20. Fitzhugh, "Sociology for the South," 43, and "The Freedmen," 489–93.

21. Genovese, *The World the Slaveholders Made*, 135–36 (emphasis in original).

22. As William Darity Jr. has argued, the seeds of the Williams thesis can be found

in the writings of British economic historians during the late nineteenth and early twentieth centuries. Eric Williams, however, brought a fresh and more comprehensive interpretation to the question. Consequently, Darity has insisted that the dichotomy of conventional historiography that opposes Williams against the humanitarian school should be modified. See "The Williams Abolition Thesis before Williams," 29–41. In addition to these, as several scholars (including Williams himself) have noted, the Williams thesis also owes an intellectual debt to C. L. R. James (*The Black Jacobins*), Lowell Ragatz (*The Fall of the Planter Class*), and Franz Hockstetter (*Die wirtschaftslichen und politischen Motu für de Abochuffung des britishen Sklavenhandels*). See Minchinton, "Williams and Drescher," 81–105.

23. Eric Williams, *Capitalism and Slavery*. See Mathieson, *Great Britain and the Slave Trade*, 1, where he argued that when Great Britain "relinquished her slave trade in 1807, . . . her motives were disinterested." The primary target of Williams's critique was the argument of Sir Reginald Coupland. See his *The British Antislavery Movement*, 80. Although he emphasized the religious and humanitarian dimension of the struggle for the abolition of slavery, Coupland, under whose supervision Williams completed his thesis, acknowledged that he had neglected the economic aspect of the question. See Darity, "The Williams Abolition Thesis before Williams," 31.

24. Eric Williams, *Capitalism and Slavery*, 181.

25. Ibid., 136; Eltis, *Economic Growth and the Ending of the Transatlantic Slave Trade*, 4. The pamphlet referred to was Samuel Estwick, *Considerations on the Negro cause commonly so called* (London: J. Dosley, 1772).

26. See Davis, "Reflections on Abolitionism and Ideological Hegemony," 797, and Drescher, *Econocide*, 5–8.

27. Eric Williams, *Capitalism and Slavery*, 209–10. Woodson's review of *Capitalism and Slavery*, 93–95, made a similar point.

28. Du Bois, *Black Reconstruction*; James, *The Black Jacobins*. A very short list of Black intellectuals demonstrates the concurrence of this perspective across time and geography. The Négritude poet Aimé Césaire made this point in his extraordinary poem *Notebook of the Return to My Native Land*, originally written in 1939, during the same intellectual ferment as the rewriting of the historical framework: "And I say to myself Bordeaux and Nantes and Liverpool and New York and San Francisco / not an inch of this world devoid of my fingerprint." See *Notebook*, in *Aimé Césaire: The Collected Poetry*, 47. Frantz Fanon offered a similar analysis: "The well being and the progress of Europe have been built up with the sweat and the dead bodies of Negroes, Arabs, Indians, and the yellow races. . . . Europe is literally the creation of the Third World." See *The Wretched of the Earth*, 96, 102. The Reverend Martin Luther King Jr. argued that Blacks were "the creators of the wealth of the New World" and "the economies of several European nations owed their growth and prosperity to [Black slavery]." See *Where Do We Go from Here*, 71–72.

29. Rodney, *How Europe Underdeveloped Africa*. A refreshing exception has been William Darity Jr.'s general equilibrium model of the African slave trade. Darity subjected the thesis of the Caribbean school (James, Rodney, Williams) to this neoclassical

economic approach in order to "minimize the possibility of supporting the Caribbean School's position" as the "least-likely test," and it is intentionally chosen to resist providing support for a hypothesis. If support emerges from the approach, then the test provides overwhelming support for the postulate. Using this methodology in the most excruciating manner, Darity concluded that the Caribbean school's argument "reveals cases where those predictions hold under plausible parameterizations," which suggested that "the Williams-Rodney-James theory is quite robust as an explanation of the roots of European advance and African stagnation. Even a 'least-likely' test is unable to dismiss their central hypotheses." See Darity, "A General Equilibrium Model of the Eighteenth-Century Atlantic Slave Trade," 287–326.

30. For evidence of the dismissal of the argument that slavery constituted a central element in the formation of industrial capitalism, which appeared in the reexamination of *Capitalism and Slavery* that occurred as a result of its 1964 republication, see Antsey, "*Capitalism and Slavery:* A Critique," 307–20, where in his review of the work he unapologetically stated that he was making no pretense "to be comprehensive" and intentionally overlooked "the earlier part of the book where the role of the slave trade and slavery, and of mercantilism, in the British economy up to the closing years of the eighteenth century is considered." See also Drescher, *Econocide,* who has ardently attempted to refute the Williams thesis. This exclusion appears not only with the critics of Williams. In an otherwise extremely illuminating overview of the arguments of Williams and Seymour Drescher (which affirmed some of Williams's main contentions), Walter E. Minchinton acknowledged that his investigation was not concerned with the aspect of the Williams thesis where he argued that the "industrial revolution was financed out of the profits of the slave trade and plantation slavery." See Minchinton, "Williams and Drescher," 85.

31. Selwyn Carrington concluded that after the 1776 War of Independence in the United States the metropolis imposed mercantilist policies on the West Indian colonial possessions, causing shortages of goods that elevated the costs of certain plantation supplies, and thus there was an empirical basis to argue for declension: "What appeared to Drescher to be growth of the British West Indian economy during the French Revolutionary and Napoleonic Wars was a return to pre-1776 wartime conditions in the West Indies." See "The State of the Debate on the Role of Capitalism in the Ending of the Slave System," 20–41. As Walter E. Minchinton argued, "[i]f Drescher's case rests on the British West Indian share of total British trade, . . . then the case is non-proven." In a most interesting reversal, the criticism launched against Williams, that he selectively used his evidence to verify an unfounded argument, has now been applied to his major antagonist. Minchinton, who did not endorse the declension viewpoint, noted that Drescher chose his time frame "with care to support his argument," as the deluge of figures he employed did not refute the Williams thesis. Indeed, Michael Craton discerned that Drescher's analysis, "while overloaded with detail, is weakened by omissions and obscurities," and "his conception of the overall dynamics of abolition, though clouded with equivocation, verges on the simplistic." See Minchinton, "Williams and Drescher," 86, and Craton's review of *Econocide*.

32. Darity, "A General Equilibrium Model of the Eighteenth-Century Atlantic Slave Trade."

33. Haskell, "Capitalism and the Origins of the Humanitarian Sensibility," 339–42 (emphasis in original).

34. Davis, *The Problem of Slavery in the Age of Revolution,* 251, 466, and "Reflections on Abolitionism and Ideological Hegemony," 800.

35. Davis, *The Problem of Slavery in the Age of Revolution,* 349, and "Reflections on Abolitionism and Ideological Hegemony," 798–801.

36. Ashworth, "The Relationship between Capitalism and Humanitarianism," 813–15.

37. Statement cited in Eudell, "The Mind of Emancipation," 42.

38. Pocock, "Introduction: The State of the Art," in *Virtue, Commerce, and History,* 12.

39. For Ward's statement, see Turley, *The Culture of English Antislavery,* 115.

40. See Anthony Wood, *Nineteenth Century Britain,* 15.

41. Holland, *Letters and Diary of Laura M. Towne,* 187.

42. Davis, *The Problem of Slavery in the Age of Revolution,* 42, 467.

43. Pocock, "Languages and Their Implications," in *Politics, Language, and Time,* 17; Holt, *The Problem of Freedom,* 3–9, 21–41; Davis, *The Problem of Slavery in the Age of Revolution,* 251; Polanyi, *The Great Transformation,* 43–76 (emphasis added). In his cogently argued *From Mandeville to Marx,* Louis Dumont traced the emergence of the economics in its emancipation from politics and morality. Smith, *The Wealth of Nations,* 1:15.

44. Litwack, "The Emancipation of the Negro Abolitionist," 143, and Delany, *The Condition, Elevation, Emigration, and Destiny,* 28.

Chapter Two

1. Robert Peart to Sir Lionel Smith, 1 August 1838, enclosed in Smith to Glenelg, 13 August 1838, CO 137/231, no. 153. Peart's original preslavery name was Mahomod Cover.

2. John Clark to Smith, 3 August 1838, and Simon Martin, James Martin, William Bernard, and Francis Green to Smith, 2 August 1838, both enclosed in ibid. The pastor John Clark wrote the letter for Brown's Town Chapel, and Simon Martin et al. stated they were representing their "brethren" of Manchester.

3. James Reid and W. G. Barrett to Smith, 6 August 1838, enclosed in ibid.

4. Rufus Saxton to Oliver O. Howard, 13 October 1865, vol. 9, pp. 91–92, Letters Sent, ser. 2916, South Carolina, Assistant Commissioner, FSSP, [A-7152].

5. Howard Day, who spoke at one of the national meetings, stated that Blacks were "inspired by the noble sentiments they had heard enunciated in the glorious Declaration of Independence, viz: 'That all men were created free and equal, and with inalienable rights common to all.' . . . This is what we are here for to-day — to recognize

those principles." See "Celebration by the Colored People's Educational Monument Association in Memory of Abraham Lincoln, on the Fourth of July, 1865 in the Presidential Grounds, Washington, D.C.," in Philip Foner and Walker, *Proceedings of the Black National and State Conventions,* 1:12.

6. "Proceedings of the Colored People's Convention of the State of South Carolina Held in Zion Church, Charleston, November 1865. Together with the Declaration of Rights and Wrongs; An Address to the People; A Petition to the Legislature, and a Memorial to Congress," in Philip Foner and Walker, *Proceedings of the Black State Conventions,* 2:292 (emphasis in original).

7. John Clark to Smith, 7 August 1838, enclosed in CO 137/231, no. 153; Marshall, "'We Be Wise to Many More Tings,'" 12–20.

8. Cited by Eric Foner, *Reconstruction,* 160. See also Oubre, *Forty Acres and a Mule,* 53.

9. See Eric Foner, "Reconstruction and the Crisis of Free Labor," in *Politics and Ideology in the Age of the Civil War,* 107, where he argued that the claim by ex-slaves for land in order to be truly free was "actually very traditional in republican America."

10. Edward Stanley, "Circular Despatch to the Governors of His Majesty's Colonial Possessions," 13 June 1833, *PP* 1835, 50 (177): 6 (Despatch B).

11. Green, "The Creolization of Caribbean History," 30.

12. Potter, *The Impending Crisis,* 49.

13. Goveia, *Slave Society in the British Leeward Islands,* 329.

14. Ibid., vii. Goveia stated that she attempted "to identify the basic principles which held the white masters, coloured freedmen, and Negro slaves together as a community, and to trace the influence of these principles on the relations between the Negro slave and his white master, *which largely determined the form and content of the society*" (emphasis added).

15. Boyce, "The State of the Country," 133. Boyce made the statement in reference to President Johnson's polices during Reconstruction, but it is clearly appropriate for the ideology of Redemption, which, it could be argued, completed Johnson's objectives.

16. Goveia, "Amelioration and Emancipation," 11.

17. Frederick Douglass, "Reconstruction" (December 1866), in Philip Foner, *The Life and Writings,* 4:199.

18. Cited by Goveia, "Amelioration and Emancipation," 44.

19. See Le Goff, "Mentalities," 170.

20. See Long, *History of Jamaica,* and Edwards, *The History, Civil and Commercial, of the British Colonies in the West Indies.*

21. Earl of Belmore to Lord Goderich, 6 September 1831, CO 137/179, cited by Goveia, "Amelioration and Emancipation," 32; Assembly statement cited in Burn, *Emancipation and Apprenticeship,* 94.

22. Richard Barrett and Abraham Hodgson [on behalf of Committee] to Earl Grey and Viscount Goderich, 26 November 1832, CO 137/186.

23. Ibid.

24. Ibid. (emphasis added).

25. The power of the West India interest in Parliament was cut in half during the first general election held after the 1832 Reform Act: "Of the thirty-five West Indians sitting in the Commons at the end of 1832, sixteen lost their seats at the election: seven of the electorates were abolished, four lost one M.P. and Weymouth and Melcombe Regis, which was managed by a West Indian and returned two West Indians in 1832, was reduced from four to two M.P.s." The East Indian interest also suffered a significant decline in its parliamentary influence. See Higman, "The West India 'Interest' in Parliament," 1–19. See also Gross, "The Abolition of Negro Slavery and British Parliamentary Politics," 63–85.

26. 3 and 4 William IV cap. 73, Special Collections, UWI.

27. Eric Foner, *Nothing but Freedom*, 14.

28. Reckord, "The Jamaican Slave Rebellion of 1831," 108–25, and Turner, *Slaves and Missionaries*, 115.

29. See Wilmot, "Not 'Full Free,'" 2–10. Wilmot noted that by using militia force Governor Sligo quickly suppressed dissent on estates in the parishes of St. Ann and St. Thomas in the Vale in August 1834. In the Leeward Islands unrest also occurred. The military was called in Montserrat, riots occurred in St. Kitts, and martial law had to be declared in Antigua. See Douglas Hall, *Five of the Leewards*, 24.

30. Eric Foner, *Nothing but Freedom*, 14.

31. Burn, *Emancipation and Apprenticeship*, 120. In an often astute historical account, Burn frequently adopted the nineteenth-century discourse on race, suggesting at one point that some abolitionists refused "to appreciate the possible educational advantages of slavery," which with its "firm and rational discipline" would make Blacks "useful citizens." Ibid., 50.

32. Secretary Edward Stanley, "Circular Despatch to the Governors of His Majesty's Colonial Possessions," 20 May 1833, *PP* 1835, 50 (177): 4 (Despatch A).

33. Green, *British Slave Emancipation*, 99–105. See also Rushford, "A Comparative Study of the Process and Policy of Emancipation," 5–6.

34. Green, *British Slave Emancipation*, 104–5.

35. *Senate Reports*, 39th Cong., 1st sess., Serial 1273, no. 30, pp. x–xx.

36. Johannsen, *Lincoln, the South, and Slavery*, 30.

37. Douglas Hall, *Five of the Leewards*, 26–28.

38. Adamson, "The Reconstruction of Plantation Labour," 460–61.

39. Stanley to Marquis of Sligo, 20 February 1834, *PP* 1835, 50 (177): 33–36 (Despatch 8).

40. Ibid. Text of law in Lord Mulgrave to Stanley, 6 February 1834, CO 137/192, no. 54 (emphasis added).

41. Ibid. See also House of Commons Select Committee, *Negro Apprenticeship in the Colonies*, 6–7. For the statement of Parliament, see Governor Sligo's speech to the 1835 August session of the Assembly, enclosed in Sligo to Glenelg, 10 February 1836, CO 137/209, no. 316.

42. See Wharton, *The Negro in Mississippi*, 76.

43. Franklin, *Reconstruction*, 48; *Senate Executive Documents*, 39th Cong., 1st sess., Serial 1237, no. 2, pp. 16–17. For a general account, see Wilson, *The Black Codes of the South*.

44. Cash, *The Mind of the South*.

45. *Senate Executive Documents*, 39th Cong., 2d sess., Serial 1276, no. 6, pp. 170–230.

46. Ibid., 177, 185.

47. Ibid., 182, 213.

48. Ibid., 180, 209.

49. Ibid., 30, 90, 102, 180, 209. See Adamson, "The Reconstruction of Plantation Labor," 461, where he alluded to one of central elements constituting the ex-slave understanding of emancipation: "Throughout the West Indies, the parents of these children [those freed unconditionally on 1 August 1834] would not permit them to work on the estates, declaring that they were born free and that they would rather work 'their own fingers to the bone before they would [make] their children do the slightest work.'" These children were often called "Stanleys" after the colonial secretary Edward Stanley, who was a seminal figure in getting the Abolition Bill passed by the British Parliament.

50. Minnie Anderson vs. Albert Hamlin, SFOR, ser. 3028, box 47, Letters Received, Abbeville, 1866–68. In a rare situation, Minnie Anderson apprenticed her son, Sam, in August 1867, to Deborah Hamlin. Albert Hamlin, Deborah's husband, abducted sixteen-year-old Sam in November. After failing to release Sam to P. N. Wilson (charged with retrieving him), Albert Hamlin fled to a location near Albany, Georgia, and a rumor circulated that Hamlin would flee with young Anderson to Florida in the spring.

51. *Senate Executive Documents*, 39th Cong., 2d sess., Serial 1276, no. 6, pp. 170, 226.

52. Ibid., 192, 219. In South Carolina the definition was extended to dramatic actors and musicians.

53. *Senate Executive Documents*, 39th Cong., 1st sess., Serial 1237, no. 2, p. 21.

54. Green, *British Slave Emancipation*, 167. Text of vagrancy law in Lord Mulgrave to Stanley, 6 February 1834, CO 137/192, no. 54.

55. Sligo to Stanley, 29 May 1834, CO 137/192, no. 22.

56. Richard Barrett and Abraham Hodgson [on behalf of Committee] to Earl Grey and Viscount Goderich, 26 November 1832, CO 137/186.

57. 5 William IV cap. 42, "An Act to Establish Towns in This Island for the Reception of Emigrants." See "List of Laws Passed Session 1834," CO 137/197.

58. Sligo to Earl of Aberdeen, 22 February 1835, and William Ramsay to Sligo, 18 February 1835, both enclosed in CO 137/197, no. 26.

59. William Nunes to Herbert James (commissioner of accounts), 19 February 1835, enclosed in ibid.

60. A. A. Lindo, "Letter to the Proprietors & Mortgagees of Estates in the Island of

Jamaica of Promoting Immigration into That Country," 1 February 1836, CO 137/217; Arthur Welch, 30 December 1835, Sligo to Lord Glenelg, 1 January 1836, CO 137/209, no. 259.

61. Lindo, "To the Right Honorable the Earl of Aberdeen, Principal Secretary of State for the Colonies," 1 March 1835, CO 137/217.

62. Ibid.

63. "Memorial of Proprietors, Planters, and Others Concerned in the Management of Plantations in the Parish of Trelawney," enclosed in Sligo to Aberdeen, 20 May 1835, CO 137/198, no. 107. See also Douglas Hall, *Free Jamaica,* 21 (emphasis added).

64. Henry Barkly to the Duke of Newcastle, 26 May 1854; Lord Harris to Pakington, 7 August 1852; Minutes of Combined Court of British Guiana, 23 January 1850; Resolutions of House of Commons Committee on the West India Colonies; all in Kenneth Bell and Morrell, *Select Documents,* 422, 440, 443, 446.

65. Stewart, "A Slandered People," 192.

66. Green, *British Slave Emancipation,* 284. A small number of immigrants went to the other islands: "[I]n none of the Leeward Islands did planters call for large importations of indentured estate-labour such as were demanded in Trinidad, British Guiana, or Jamaica." Douglas Hall, *Five of the Leewards,* 32.

67. See Fleishman, "Opening of New Fields to Emigration," 87–91, and Cabell, "White Emigration to the South," 91–94. The author of the latter article stated: "To ensure not only the revival and prosperity of the Southern States, but the prosperity and greatness of the Republic, a large and intelligent *White population* must be introduced into the Southern country" (emphasis in original).

68. Berthoff, "Southern Attitudes toward Immigration," 337–38; Woody, "The Labor and Immigration Problem of South Carolina," 195; Wilson, *The Black Codes of the South,* 45.

69. The federal government also passed an "Act to encourage immigration" in April 1864, which resulted in many Europeans immigrating to the North. See Sanger, *The Statues at Large,* 385–87.

70. Pike, *The Prostrate State,* 56.

71. Rufus Saxton to James Black, 11 August 1865, M 869, vol. 9, Letters Sent, ser. 2916, r 1, 0039.

72. War Department, Circular No. 4, 21 May 1866, SFOR, ser. 3157, box 64, Miscellaneous Reports Received, Columbia, 1865–70.

73. Bancroft, *Speeches, Correspondence and Political Papers of Carl Schurz,* 1:361.

74. Woody, "The Labor and Immigration Problem of South Carolina," 195; Lowenberg, "Efforts of the South to Encourage Immigration," 384.

75. Herman Merivale, *Lectures on Colonization and Colonies,* 332, cited in Green, *British Slave Emancipation,* 266 (emphasis added).

76. Woody, "The Labor and Immigration Problem of South Carolina," 202; Green, *British Slave Emancipation,* 272–76; Douglas Hall, *Free Jamaica,* 107–11; Holt, *The Problem of Freedom,* 202, 209.

77. Eric Foner, *Nothing but Freedom*, 25; Williamson, *After Slavery*, 120.

78. Du Bois, *Black Reconstruction*, 6; Shklar, *American Citizenship*.

79. Borrowing the concept from W. E. B. Du Bois in *Black Reconstruction*, David Roediger has traced this phenomenon, whereby whiteness became the basis for civic entitlement for the White working class in his *The Wages of Whiteness*.

80. See Harding, "Political Liberty in the Middle Ages," 423–43. Harding argued that a new "vocabulary of freedom" emerged in the wake of the Franks conquering Gaul in the eleventh and twelfth centuries. "Chieftains and vassals within the warrior aristocracy of Franks all possessed a quality of freedom, a *franchisia*, which the conquered population lacked. A military vassal was necessarily a *liber homo* because he was a *franc homme*, and he expected to hold the land given him by his lord on conditions which were worthy of a freeman, *liberali potestate*. So, by another route, we arrive at land held free from certain obligations, and once again the word for it, *franchisia*, can mean the freedom itself and the land in which it is exercised." Ibid., 427.

81. Frederick Douglass, "What the Black Man Wants," in Philip Foner, *The Life and Writings*, 4:159–60.

82. See laws passed by Jamaica legislature for relief of Catholics, Jews, and free persons of color, *PP* 1831–32, 31 (59): 275–84.

83. "An Act to Remove Certain Disabilities from His Majesty's Subjects of the Roman Catholic Religion within This Island" (19 December 1829), in ibid. The terms of the oath, however, included more than simply swearing allegiance to the king. One of the conditions involved declaring "the Pope of Rome, or any other foreign prince, prelate, person, state or potentate hath or ought to have any temporal or civil jurisdiction, power, superiority or pre-eminence, directly or indirectly, within this realm" and therefore promising to never "exercise any privilege . . . *to disturb or weaken the Protestant religion or Protestant government* in the United Kingdom" (emphasis added).

84. "An Act to Remove Certain Disabilities of Persons of Free Condition" (13 February 1830), in ibid. See also Heuman, *Between Black and White*.

85. Sir Lionel Smith to Lord Glenelg, 30 December 1836, CO 137/213, no. 46.

86. Green, *British Slave Emancipation*, 176; Eric Foner, *Nothing but Freedom*, 23.

87. Marshall, "The Post-Slavery Labor Problem Revisited," 7–8 (emphasis added).

88. Lord John Russell to Sir Charles Metcalf, 17 September 1839, in Kenneth Bell and Morrell, *Select Documents*, 414.

Chapter Three

1. Lyman Abbott, "Southern Evangelization"; [Atkinson], "The Future Supply of Cotton," 485; Andrews, *The South since the War*, 4.

2. Eric Foner, *Reconstruction*, 155; Saville, *The Work of Reconstruction*, 2.

3. While protesting the power assigned to the special magistrates, a Jamaican planter and member of the House of Assembly alluded to the threat of physical retaliation, which lingered in the background if the planter class had not agreed to abolish

slavery: "Was it not enough that we surrendered our property at the command of an arbitrary government, *having the fear of bayonets before our eyes,* and that our surrender was declared acceptable by our British masters,—we must add to our degradation, by volunteering another leap into a lower depth of wretchedness and contempt?" *Kingston Chronicle,* 30 August 1834, reprinted in Madden, *A Twelvemonth's Residence in the West Indies,* 2:197–98 (emphasis added). Moreover, as argued earlier, the rebellions in the West Indies, Jamaica in particular, played a central role in the debates in the British Parliament.

4. Dookhan, *A Pre-Emancipation History of the West Indies,* 97; Burn, *Emancipation and Apprenticeship,* 196, 213.

5. See Sections XIV, XVII, and XVIII of *An Act for the Abolition of Slavery throughout the British Colonies,* 3 and 4 William IV cap. 73, passed 28 August 1833, Special Collections, UWI (emphasis added).

6. Text for *An Act to Establish a Bureau for the Relief of Freedmen and Refugees* in MacDonald, *Select Statutes,* 129–31 (emphasis added).

7. Sturge and Harvey, *The West Indies in 1837,* 209–10; Green, *British Slave Emancipation,* 137; Burn, *Emancipation and Apprenticeship,* 215–16; Lord Glenelg, "Circular Despatch Addressed to the Governors of the West India Colonies," 15 July 1836, *PP* 1833–35, 50 (278): 12 (Document K).

8. Richard Chamberlaine to Richard Hill, April 1837, enclosed in Sir Lionel Smith to Lord Glenelg, 12 June 1837, CO 137/220, no. 128; E. D. Baynes to C. H. Darling, 5 January 1837, enclosed in Smith to Glenelg, 4 April 1837, CO 137/219, no. 90; Sturge and Harvey, *The West Indies in 1837,* 210.

9. Bentley, *A History of the Freedmen's Bureau,* 76, 116.

10. Marquis de Sligo, "General Instructions to All Special Justices," enclosed in Sligo to Earl of Aberdeen, 5 March 1835, CO 137/198, no. 39.

11. Governor Sligo, "General Instructions to All Special Justices," in ibid. (emphasis added). See also Burn, *Emancipation and Apprenticeship,* 196.

12. Du Bois, "The Freedmen's Bureau," 355; Rufus Saxton, "To the Freedmen of South Carolina, Georgia and Florida," Headquarters Assistant Commissioner, Circular No. 2, 16 August 1865, and Oliver Howard, "Instructions to Assistant Commissioners and Other Officers," Circular No. 11, 12 July 1865, both in Chief Medical Officers Records, ser. 2992, box 46, SFOR. This box also contained records from the Inspector's Office, probably Series 2976, which could not be located and which may be the more accurate source of these circulars. For Howard's Circular, see also Select Series of Records Issued by the Commissioner of the Bureau, etc., M 742, 0042, National Archives, Washington, D.C.

13. Frederick Douglass, "What Shall Be Done with the Slaves If Emancipated?," in Philip Foner, *The Life and Writings,* 3:190.

14. [Atkinson], "The Future Supply of Cotton," 497; *House Executive Documents,* 39th Cong., 1st sess., Serial 1256, no. 70, pp. 230, 278.

15. Martin Abbott, *The Freedmen's Bureau in South Carolina,* 44.

16. "Proceedings of the Colored People's Convention of the State of South Carolina Held in Zion Church, Charleston, November 1865. Together with the Declaration of Rights and Wrongs; An Address to the People; A Petition to the Legislature, and a Memorial to Congress," in Philip Foner and Walker, *Proceedings of the Black State Conventions,* 2:297 (emphasis added).

17. The son of Prime Minister Earl Grey, Henry George Grey, was unique in his argument that the slaves were entitled to compensation as much as the slaveholders. See Holt, *The Problem of Freedom,* 29.

18. Paget, "The Free Village System in Jamaica," 37.

19. Marshall, "'We Be Wise to Many More Tings,'" 13.

20. Paget, "The Free Village System in Jamaica," 37; Lieutenant Frederick White to Colonel Doyle, 6 July 1834, in Sligo to Stanley, 20 July 1834, CO 137/192, no. 3. The complex position of the maroons during slavery can be understood from a petition submitted after abolition requesting compensation for their slaves who were not registered (the condition of compensation according to the terms of the 1833 Abolition Act). In making their argument as to why they should receive compensation for unregistered slaves, the Moore Town maroons stated: "Our well Known Services and devoted attachment to Government of this Island and its White Population in times of difficulty and of danger is well Known and Can be vouched for not only by the Gentlemen of our own Vicinity but like by every other respectable person in the Island." See "Petition of Moore Town Maroons to the King," enclosed in Sligo to Charles Grant, 6 June 1835, CO 137/199, no. 5.

21. John Daughtrey to Sligo, July 1836, enclosed in Sligo to Glenelg, 28 July 1836, CO 137/212, no. 551.

22. Douglas Hall, "The Flight from the Estates Reconsidered," 57; Marshall, "'We Be Wise to Many More Tings,'" 13; Pringle cited by Paget, "The Free Village System in Jamaica," 39.

23. Green, *British Slave Emancipation,* 192; Bolland, "Systems of Domination after Slavery," 107–23.

24. Lord Glenelg, "Circular Despatch Addressed to the Governors of the West Indian Colonies, &c," 30 January 1836, PP 1836, 48 (166): 10–12 (Document P) (emphasis added).

25. Ibid. (emphasis added).

26. Ibid.

27. John W. Alvord to Oliver Howard, 1 January 1866, *House Executive Documents,* 39th Cong., 1st sess., Serial 1256, no. 70, p. 347; Du Bois, *Black Reconstruction,* 123; Martin Abbott, *The Freedmen's Bureau in South Carolina,* 52; Rufus Saxton to James Beecher, 10 August 1865, and Saxton to E. A. Neide, 11 August 1865, both in M 869, vol. 9, Letters Sent, ser. 2916, r 1, 0091 and 0092.

28. Martin Abbott, *The Freedmen's Bureau in South Carolina,* 54–55. In an interview with President Johnson conducted by a delegation of Black leaders on 7 February 1866, Frederick Douglass pointed out that, by not granting Blacks the vote, "[y]ou

enfranchise your enemies and disenfranchise your friends." He had earlier expressed this idea at the April 1865 annual meeting of the Massachusetts Anti-Slavery Society. Then, Douglass asked what, after calling upon Blacks "to expose [themselves] to all the subtle machinations of [Southern] malignity" during the war, the federal government now proposed to do in times of peace. "To reward your enemies, and trample in the dust your friends? . . . Do you mean to give your enemies the right to vote, and take it away from your friends?" See Frederick Douglass, "What the Black Man Wants" and "Interview with President Andrew Johnson," both in Philip Foner, *The Life and Writings,* 4:163, 190.

29. Martin Abbott, *The Freedmen's Bureau in South Carolina,* 55–56; *House Executive Documents,* 39th Cong., 1st sess., Serial 1256, no. 70, pp. 16–18, 115–18.

30. Oubre, *Forty Acres and a Mule,* 86–89; Trachtenberg, *The Incorporation of America,* 21–22; Bentley, *A History of the Freedmen's Bureau,* 144–46.

31. Bleser, *The Promised Land,* 28–29, 144.

32. Douglass suggested that the public interest would be better served if the government gave land grants and loans to homesteaders rather than giving "millions upon millions of acres of public lands, to aid soulless railroad corporations to get rich." See Martin, *The Mind of Frederick Douglass,* 186.

33. Frederick Douglass, *Anti-Slavery Standard,* 29 May 1869, and "Plan to Buy Land to Be Sold to Freedmen," in Philip Foner, *The Life and Writings,* 4:31–32, and Philip Foner and Walker, *Proceedings of the Black National and State Conventions,* 1:xviii. Although one can assume that some ex-slaves may have felt entitled to being granted land without any conditions—as delegates at an Alabama convention contended, the property of the planters "was nearly all made by the sweat of our brow"— many Blacks nevertheless understood that the problem was not a simplistic issue of confiscation. Many of the plans for landownership resembled the proposal of Douglass, like the petition submitted to Congress as the result of a resolution passed at the December 1869 Colored National Labor Convention in Washington, D.C. The convention advocated for "every possible legitimate measure be taken . . . to overthrow the cruel barrier to our progress—the monstrous 'Land Monopoly' of the South." The emphasis, however, remained on public lands and not on confiscation. See Philip Foner and Walker, *Proceedings,* 1:xxii–xxiii.

34. Marquis of Sligo, "Letter and Instructions to Special Justices," 1 January 1836, enclosed in Sligo to Glenelg, 2 February 1836, CO 137/209, no. 298, and "To the Negro Population of the Island of Jamaica," enclosed in Sligo to Edward Stanley, 27 May 1834, CO 137/192, no. 18.

35. John Daughtrey to Sligo, 29 December 1835, enclosed in Sligo to Lord Glenelg, 1 January 1836, CO 137/209, no. 259.

36. Edward D. Baynes to Sligo, 1 July 1835, enclosed in Sligo to Glenelg, 7 July 1835, CO 137/200, no. 48; Richard Chamberlaine to Sligo, 30 March 1836, enclosed in Sligo to Glenelg, 2 April 1836, CO 137/210, no. 401; Baynes to Sligo, 30 June 1836, enclosed in Sligo to Glenelg, 9 July 1836, CO 137/212, no. 523; John Daughtrey to C. H. Dar-

ling, 4 October 1836, enclosed in Sir Lionel Smith to Glenelg, 12 November 1836, CO 137/213, no. 20.

37. See Rose, *Rehearsal for Reconstruction*, xiii, where she stated: "The Port Royal Experiment . . . was in effect a dress rehearsal for Reconstruction acted out on the stage neatly defined by the Sea Islands of South Carolina. It offers a rare opportunity to review the vast spectacle in miniature and see it in its germinal phase."

38. Sligo, "To the Negro Population," 27 May 1834; Samuel Pryce to Sligo, 29 December 1835, enclosed in Sligo to Glenelg, 1 January 1836, CO 137/209, no. 259; Richard Chamberlaine to Richard Hill, April 1837, enclosed in Sir Lionel Smith to Lord Glenelg, 12 June 1837, CO 137/220, no. 128.

39. William A. Green used the term "experiment" in the title of his book, *British Slave Emancipation: The Sugar Colonies and the Great Experiment, 1830–1865*. Thomas C. Holt entitled the first section of *The Problem of Freedom*, "The Mighty Experiment." This description has also emerged in U.S. emancipation historiography. In her very fine *Rehearsal for Reconstruction*, Willie Lee Rose also referred to the events on the Sea Islands during the Civil War as an "experiment." The question arises, From which perspective can freedom be described as an experiment? It can be argued that from the perspective of the ex-slaves abolition was not an experiment, a point emphasized by Frederick Douglass. Douglass exposed the presumption that underpinned the question, What shall be done with the slaves if emancipated? "It assumes that nature has erred: that the law of liberty is a mistake; . . . that slavery is the natural order of human relations, and that liberty is an experiment." See "What Shall Be Done with the Slaves If Emancipated?," 3:188.

40. House of Assembly Resolution passed 22 December 1834, enclosed in Sligo to Earl of Aberdeen, 1 January 1835, CO 137/197, no. 128; Chamberlaine to Sligo, 30 March 1836, enclosed in Sligo to Glenelg, 2 April 1836, CO 137/210, no. 401; Daughtrey to Sligo, 30 June 1835, enclosed in Sligo to Glenelg, 7 July 1835, CO 137/200, no. 48.

41. R. Standish Haly to Sligo, 25 June 1835, and Daughtrey to Sligo, 30 June 1835, both enclosed in Sligo to Glenelg, 7 July 1835, CO 137/200, no. 48; Richard Hill to Sligo, 4 July 1836, enclosed in Sligo to Glenelg, 9 July 1836, CO 137/212, no. 523; Thomas M. Oliver to Sligo, 30 September 1836, enclosed in Sir Lionel Smith to Glenelg, 12 November 1836, CO 137/213, no. 20.

42. Manderson-Jones, "Richard Hill of Jamaica," iii, 180, 498. See also "A List of the Names of All Persons Who Have Received Salaries as Special Magistrates in Jamaica," 31 March 1835, CO 137/198.

43. Burn, *Emancipation and Apprenticeship*, 179, 237; Sligo to Earl of Aberdeen, 5 March 1835, CO 137/198, no. 40; Richard Hill to Sligo, 4 July 1836, enclosed in Sligo to Glenelg, 9 July 1836, CO 137/212, no. 523.

44. R. C. Pennell to Sligo, 30 June 1835, enclosed in Sligo to Glenelg, 7 July 1835, CO 137/200, no. 48; Special Report of Arthur Welch, n.d., enclosed in Sligo to Glenelg, 4 November 1835, CO 137/204, no. 182; Daughtrey to Sligo, 29 December 1835, enclosed in Sligo to Glenelg, 1 January 1836, CO 137/209, no. 259.

45. Sligo to Aberdeen, 5 March 1835, CO 137/198, no. 40.

46. Daughtrey to Sligo, 27 October 1835, and T. Watkins Jones to Sligo, 1 November 1835, both enclosed in Sligo to Glenelg, 4 November 1835, CO 137/204, no. 182; Daughtrey to C. H. Darling, 11 April 1837, enclosed in Sligo to Glenelg, 12 June 1837, CO 137/220, no. 128.

47. T. Watkins Jones to Sligo, 1 November 1835; Richard Pennell to Sligo, 19 May 1835, enclosed in Sligo to Glenelg, 23 May 1835, CO 137/198, no. 116 (emphasis in original); Charles Hawkins to Sligo, 19 July 1836, enclosed in Sligo to Glenelg, 28 July 1836, CO 137/212, no. 551.

48. Sligo to Glenelg, 5 September 1835, CO 137/202, no. 101, and William G. Nunes (Secretary) to the Custodes, 25 August 1835, both enclosed in ibid.

49. John Gurly to Sligo, 29 December 1835, enclosed in Sligo to Glenelg, 1 January 1836, CO 137/209, no. 259; Daughtrey to Sligo, July 1836, enclosed in Sligo to Glenelg, 28 July 1836, CO 137/212, no. 551; Pryce to Sligo, 29 March 1836, enclosed in Sligo to Glenelg, 2 April 1836, CO 137/210, no. 401.

50. Bentley, *A History of the Freedmen's Bureau*, 77, 86.

51. Nordoff, *The Freedmen of South Carolina*, 18; Ware's letter of 28 December 1862 and Philbrick's letter of 20 March 1863, both in Pearson, *Letters from Port Royal*, 126, 180.

52. See Ira Berlin et al., *Freedom*, 3:92.

53. Edward Pierce to Salmon P. Chase, 3 February 1862, vol. 19, no. 72a, Port Royal Correspondence, 5th Agency, RG 366 [Q-8], in ibid., 127, 130, 141.

54. See, for example, Oliver Howard's autobiography, where he spoke of the "Anglo-Saxon courage" of the Confederate soldiers who returned home after their defeat, and who "did not succumb to the appalling difficulties" of the situation. *Autobiography of Oliver Otis Howard*, 2:163. For a comprehensive account of this ideology, see Horsman, *Race and Manifest Destiny*.

55. Pierce to Chase, 2 March 1862, vol. 19, no. 78, Port Royal Correspondence, 5th Agency, RG 366 [Q-9], and Edward S. Philbrick to Pierce, 27 March 1862, vol. 19, no. 106, Port Royal Correspondence, 5th Agency, RG 366 [Q-12], both in Ira Berlin et al., *Freedom*, 3:156, 175.

56. Sligo, "Letter and Instructions to Special Justices," 1 January 1836.

57. Sir Lionel Smith, "A Proclamation," 9 July 1838, enclosed in Smith to Glenelg, 27 July 1838, CO 137/231, no. 140.

58. Pierce to Chase, 3 February 1862, in Berlin et al., *Freedom*, 3:131–32.

59. Rose, *Rehearsal for Reconstruction*, 30, 48; [Pierce], "The Freedmen at Port Royal," 299; Pearson, *Letters from Port Royal*, 184; [Gannett and Hale], "Education of the Freedmen," 547.

60. [Gannett], "The Freedmen at Port Royal," 16, and letters of 26 January and 1 March 1863, in Pearson, *Letters from Port Royal*, 148, 166; Pease, "Three Years among the Freedmen," 106.

61. Philbrick, "Free Labor in South Carolina," 1, and Philbrick's letter to William C. Gannett of 8 July 1864, in Pearson, *Letters from Port Royal*, 276–77.

62. *Senate Executive Documents,* 38th Cong., 1st sess., Serial 1176, no. 53, pp. 20, 25, 99.

63. Ibid., 109–10.

64. Ibid., 4–7, 15, 21, 67.

65. As noted earlier, Scott's predecessor, Rufus Saxton, offered a proposal that the "elevation" of the ex-slaves could be achieved by making them landholders, demonstrating his tireless dedication, which probably led to his removal from the position of assistant commissioner at the end of 1865.

66. Robert K. Scott to Oliver O. Howard, 7 November 1867, Washington Headquarters, ser. 32 (Annual Reports), South Carolina, 1867, FSSP, [A-7364]; Williams's statement enclosed in R. K. Scott's report of 1 November 1866, reprinted in *Senate Executive Documents,* 39th Cong., 2d sess., Serial 1276, no. 6, p. 118; Philbrick quoted in Pearson, *Letters from Port Royal,* 317.

67. Samuel Place to E. L. Deane, 28 December 1867, and "Report of Officers of the Bureau R. F. and A. L. in the State of South Carolina Relative to the Necessity for Continuing the Freedmen's Bureau," both in M 869, Registered Letters Received, October 1867–January 1869, r 18, 0034–37, 0092–0114.

68. Place to Deane, 28 December 1867, and Erastus Everson to Horace Neide, 4 January 1868, in ibid., 0052–0055.

69. William H. H. Holton to Edward Deane, 20 December 1867, in ibid., 0075–0080.

70. Delany and De Forest's statements enclosed in "Report of Officers of the Bureau R. F. and A. L. in the State of South Carolina Relative to the Necessity for Continuing the Freedmen's Bureau"; William Stone to Edward Deane, 29 December 1867, in ibid., 0057–0063.

71. See Saville, *The Work of Reconstruction.*

Chapter Four

1. [Howard], *Autobiography of Oliver Otis Howard,* 2:244.

2. Nott, "Climates of the South in Their Relations to White Labor," 168; Wynter, "1492: A New World View," 34. Wynter argued that in the New World, a new ideology would take the place of caste, which had structured the social order of feudal Europe: "The new symbolic construct was that of 'race.' Its essentially Christian-heretical positing of the *nonhomogeneity of the human species* was to provide the basis for new metaphysical notions of order. Those notions provided the foundations of the post-1492 polities of the Caribbean and the Americas which, if in a new variant, continue to be legitimated by the nineteenth-century colonial systems of Western Europe, as well as the continuing hierarchies of our present global order."

3. Woodward, "White Racism and Black 'Emancipation,'" 5–11, and "Seeds of Failure in Radical Race Policy," 164; Frederick Douglass, "The Unholy Alliance of Negro Hate and Anti-Slavery," in Philip Foner, *The Life and Writings,* 2:387.

4. Botume, *First Days amongst the Contrabands,* 220, 228.

5. Ibid., 6, 225–28, 236. It is important to understand the context in which Botume made the statement "the negro mind had never been cultivated." Here, she spoke in the context of the fast rate at which the ex-slaves seemed to acquire certain academic skills. "The perceptions were quickened. . . . They memorized with wonderful ease and correctness." In light of this clarification, one can agree that, with respect to certain scholarly pursuits, the mind of the ex-slaves had not been "cultivated," but one does not have to agree that their minds were like "empty reservoirs, waiting to be filled." Hence, the insight coexisted with a certain blindness.

6. Rooke, "Evangelical Missionaries, Apprentices, and Freedmen," 1–14.

7. Stewart, "A Slandered People," 183–87, and *Religion and Society in Post-Emancipation Jamaica,* 37.

8. Furley, "Protestant Missionaries in the West Indies," 232–42.

9. James Phillippo to Sligo, 24 October 1835, CO 137/203.

10. Ibid. Thomas Burchell, parson in Montego Bay, made a similar assertion in 1836 that Blacks were unprepared to be trained as pastors for the Baptist Missionary Society. See Stewart, "A Slandered People," 186.

11. John Daughtrey to C. H. Darling, 4 October 1836, enclosed in Sir Lionel Smith to Lord Glenelg, 12 November 1836, CO 137/213, no. 20.

12. Holt, *The Problem of Freedom,* xviii–xix.

13. Carlyle, "Occasional Discourse on the Nigger Question," 352.

14. T. Watkins Jones to Sligo, 13 July 1836, enclosed in Sligo to Glenelg, 9 July 1836, CO 137/212, no. 523.

15. Edward D. Baynes to C. H. Darling, 5 January 1837, enclosed in Smith to Glenelg, 4 April 1837, CO 137/219, no. 90; Henry Walsh to Sir Lionel Smith, enclosed in Smith to Glenelg, 12 November 1836, CO 137/213, no. 20.

16. William Ramsay, Richard Hill, G. Ouseley Higgins to Sir Lionel Smith, 20 October 1836, enclosed in Smith to Glenelg, 12 November 1836, CO 137/213, no. 20.

17. Sligo to Lord Glenelg, 4 June 1836, CO 137/211, no. 476.

18. Sligo to Glenelg, 15 May 1836, CO 137/211; William Marlton to Sligo, 22 December 1835, enclosed in Sligo to Glenelg, 1 January 1836, CO 137/209, no. 259.

19. J. Kennet Dawson to Sligo, 17 March 1835, enclosed in Sligo to Earl of Aberdeen, 27 March 1835, CO 137/198, no. 58.

20. R. Sydney Lambert to C. H. Darling, 30 September 1836, enclosed in Smith to Glenelg, 12 November 1836, CO 137/213, no. 20; James Harris to C. H. Darling, 1 January 1837, enclosed in Smith to Glenelg, 4 April 1837, CO 137/219, no. 90.

21. Edward D. Baynes, 30 December 1835, enclosed in Sligo to Glenelg, 1 January 1836, CO 137/209, no. 259, and Baynes to C. H. Darling, 5 January 1837, enclosed in Smith to Glenelg, 4 April 1837, CO 137/219, no. 90 (emphasis added).

22. "Report of Special Justice John Daughtrey," 27 October 1835, enclosed in Sligo to Glenelg, 4 November 1835, CO 137/204, no. 182.

23. Arthur Welch to Sir Lionel Smith, 1 October 1836, enclosed in Sir Lionel Smith to Lord Glenelg, 12 November 1836, CO 137/213, no. 20.

24. William Carnaby to Sir Lionel Smith, 4 August 1836, and William F. Marlton to Smith, 31 October 1836, both enclosed in ibid.

25. Richard Chamberlaine to Sligo, 6 July 1836, enclosed in Sligo to Glenelg, 9 July 1836, CO 137/212, no. 523; S. R. Ricketts to Sir Lionel Smith, 1 July 1837, enclosed in Smith to Glenelg, 8 September 1837, CO 137/220, no. 172.

26. Ricketts to Smith, 1 July 1837.

27. John Daughtrey to C. H. Darling, 11 April 1837, enclosed in Sir Lionel Smith to Lord Glenelg, 12 June 1837, CO 137/220, no. 128; James Harris to C. H. Darling, 1 January 1837, enclosed in Sir Lionel Smith to Glenelg, 4 April 1837, CO 137/219, no. 90; Patrick Dunne to Sligo, 29 June 1836, enclosed in Sligo to Glenelg, 9 July 1836, CO 137/212, no. 523.

28. Sligo to Glenelg, 1 January 1836, CO 137/209, no. 259; Sir Lionel Smith to Lord Glenelg, 17 January 1838, CO 137/226, no. 13.

29. Report of T. Watkins Jones, 1 November 1835, enclosed in Sligo to Lord Glenelg, 4 November 1835, CO 137/204, no. 182.

30. R. C. Pennell to Sligo, 19 May 1835, enclosed in Sligo to Aberdeen, 23 May 1835, CO 137/198, no. 116.

31. For examples, see Stanley Rowlinson to Sligo, 2 July 1836, enclosed in Sligo to Glenelg, 9 July 1836, CO 137/212, no. 523; R. Cocking's Response to Circular No. 63, 15 July 1836, enclosed in Sir Lionel Smith to Glenelg, 12 November 1836, CO 137/213, no. 20; and W. H. Bell to C. H. Darling, 1 April 1837, where he states the ex-slaves "do not work as cheerfully as I would wish." Bell's report enclosed in Sir Lionel Smith to Glenelg, 12 June 1837, CO 137/220, no. 128.

32. Hall Pringle to S. R. Warren (governor's secretary), 25 July 1837, enclosed in Sir Lionel Smith to Glenelg, 8 September 1837, CO 137/220, no. 172; R. C. Pennell to Sligo, 30 June 1835, enclosed in Sligo to Glenelg, 7 July 1835, CO 137/200, no. 48.

33. Arthur Welch to Sligo, 30 December 1835, enclosed in Sligo to Glenelg, 1 January 1836, CO 137/209, no. 259.

34. John Daughtrey to Sligo, 25 August 1835, enclosed in Sligo to Glenelg, 6 September 1835, CO 137/202, no. 105; R. L. Cooper to Sligo, 29 December 1835, and Daughtrey to Sligo, 29 December 1835, both in Sligo to Glenelg, 1 January 1836, CO 137/209, no. 259; Daughtrey to Sligo, July 1836, enclosed in Sligo to Glenelg, 28 July 1836, CO 137/212, no. 551.

35. Alexander N. MacLeod, "Special Report," 1 July 1836, enclosed in Sligo to Glenelg, 9 July 1836, CO 137/212, no. 523; Thomas Davies to C. H. Darling, 1 October 1836, enclosed in Sir Lionel Smith to Glenelg, 12 November 1836, CO 137/213, no. 20.

36. A. G. Fyfe to Sligo, 25 August 1835, enclosed in Sligo to Glenelg, 6 September 1835, CO 137/202, no. 105.

37. Ibid.

38. R. S. Cooper to Sligo, 11 August 1835, enclosed in ibid. (emphasis in original).

39. Edward D. Baynes to C. H. Darling, 14 April 1837, enclosed in Sir Lionel Smith to Glenelg, 12 June 1837, CO 137/220, no. 128; Thomas Davies to C. H. Darling, 1 Octo-

ber 1836, enclosed in Sir Lionel Smith to Glenelg, 12 November 1836, CO 137/213, no. 20; Edward Baynes to Sligo, 1 July 1835, enclosed in Sligo to Glenelg, 7 July 1835, CO 137/200, no. 48. See Joseph Rawlins Thomas to Sligo, 30 June 1835, enclosed in ibid., where he stated: "I consider continued and unflinching discipline as necessary to preserve the present order of things and regulation among the negro population, whose weak minds are prone to take advantage of the magistrate's relaxation and lenity." Samuel Lloyd made the statement of the "natural idle disposition" of the ex-slaves in his 16 March 1835 letter to Sligo, enclosed in Sligo to Earl of Aberdeen, 27 March 1835, CO 137/198, no. 58.

40. *Senate Executive Documents,* 38th Cong., 1st sess., Serial 1176, no. 53, pp. 22–23.

41. Ibid., 20, 23 (emphasis in original).

42. Ibid., 106; Frederick Douglass, "West India Emancipation," in Philip Foner, *The Life and Writings,* 2:436.

43. *Senate Executive Documents,* 38th Cong., 1st sess., Serial 1176, no. 53, pp. 22–23, 25, 64–65.

44. *House Executive Documents,* 39th Cong., 1st sess., Serial 1256, no. 70, pp. 366–70.

45. Ibid. As George Bentley suggested, it was precisely this kind of thinking that led to Saxton's dismissal from the position of assistant commissioner: "The Bureau was beginning to appear to [President Andrew Johnson] to be an opponent of his kind of Reconstruction and a threat to states' rights. He already was rid of [Thomas] Conway [of Louisiana], one of the two most Radicals original assistant commissioners, and in January 1866 he ousted the other — Saxton." See *A History of the Freedmen's Bureau,* 107.

46. C. H. Howard to R. Saxton, 29 November 1865, M 869, r 36, Miscellaneous Reports, 0218–0228; D. T. Corbin's statement cited in R. K. Scott to O. O. Howard, 21 May 1866, M 869, r 1, Letters Sent, 0229–0234. Corbin stated (as many bureau agents had) that he remained concerned about scarce provisions. While the humanitarian dimension was genuine, he felt that he knew what was best for the ex-slaves: "[The ex-slaves] have been required to contract where they persist in staying, and have gone to work clearing land and planting, but a season's experience, however well they may labor, will demonstrate to them their folly."

47. J. M. Johnston to H. W. Smith, 31 May 1867, M 869, r 35, Reports of Conditions and Operations, January 1867–May 1868, 0135–0142; R. K. Scott, Circular Letter, 26 December 1866, M 869, r 36, General Orders and Circulars Issued, 0259–0260.

48. R. K. Scott, Circular Letter, 26 December 1866.

49. George E. Pingree to Edward L. Deane, 16 March 1867, M 869, r 35, 0068–0073. For examples of planters' actions and bureau officials' lack of power, see W. E. Seighton to R. K. Scott, 5 March 1866, M 869, r 10, Letters Received, 0510–0514, where he stated: "With very few exceptions the Freedmen were turned from the plantations with no compensation whatever for their services in the year 1865. And but for the presence of US Troops would have received nothing to help them in the ensuing year."

50. A. E. Niles to H. W. Smith, 2 May 1866, M 869, r 10, Letters Received, 0698–0699.

51. Ralph Ely to J. A. Clark, 9 January 1866, M 869, r 34, Reports of Conditions and Operations, July 1865–December 1866, 0394–0396; D. T. Corbin to H. W. Smith, 28 February, 1866, M 869, r 24, Unregistered Letters Received, 1868–May 1869, 0440–0442.

52. H. W. Smith, Circular Letter, 2 December 1865, M 869, r 11, Letters Received, October 1865–December 1866, 0331–0333; A. J. Willard to George Hooker, 7 November 1865, M 869, r 8, Letters Received, May–December 1865, 0636–0640.

53. F. W. Liedtke to H. W. Smith, 15 May 1866, M 869, r 10, Letters Received, October 1865–December 1866, 0547–0552.

54. W. P. Richardson to H. W. Smith, 22 November 1865, M 869, r 8, 0083–0085.

55. Chartock, "A History and Analysis of Freedmen's Bureau Contracts," 44, 111, 143, 151, 159.

56. Edward O'Brien to A. M. Crawford, 1 October 1866, and J. S. Power to H. W. Smith, 14 July 1866, both in M 869, r 34, 0785–0787, 0620–0622; George Pingree to E. L. Deane, 30 November 1867, M 869, r 35, 0532–0534. The idea of the "thrifty accumulator," J. G. A. Pocock has noted, was invoked as a new model of citizenship that would allow the trading bourgeoisie to meet the classical republican requirement, whereby the private interests are subordinated to the public good. By the time the industrial revolution was in full force, the securing of one's private interest had become synonymous with the public good, as the political discourse of the Freedmen's Bureau agents reflects. See Pocock's essay, "Civic Humanism and Its Role in Anglo-American Thought," in *Politics, Language, and Time*, 80–103.

57. W. F. Young to Rufus Saxton, 10 July 1865, M 869, r 8, 0688–0691 (emphasis added). Young made his comment in the context of the behaviors of the soldiers, and the kind of example he thought they should embody for the ex-slaves. He noted, however, that these attitudes ("prejudice, apparent among subordinate commands to what is derisively termed 'negro equality'") were not limited to the White soldiers; some of the Black troops also adhered to such notions. J. E. Cornelius to H. W. Smith, 23 October 1866, and William Stone's report enclosed in L. Walker to H. W. Smith, October 1866, both in M 869, r 34, 0809–0817, 0889–0894. See also Chartock, "A History and Analysis of Freedmen's Bureau Contracts," 114.

58. De Forest, *A Union Officer in the Reconstruction,* 117; Fredrickson, *The Black Image in the White Mind,* 314. Fredrickson also noted that this discourse was central to the "White Man's burden" mission in the colonial enterprise.

59. Hijiya, *J. W. De Forest and the Rise of American Gentility,* 67; Douglass, "The Unholy Alliance of Negro Hate and Anti-Slavery," 2:387. Three Newberry ex-slaves described in August 1866 what was happening to Blacks in the area as a "reign of terror." See J. Franklin, Parris Simpkins, and P. L. Cot to Major General Sickles, 8 August 1866, M 869, r 10, 0201–0202.

Chapter Five

1. Sir Lionel Smith, "A Proclamation," 9 July 1838, enclosed in Smith to Lord Glenelg, 27 July 1838, CO 137/231, no. 140 (emphasis in original).

2. Edward D. Baynes, "To the Labouring Population of Jamaica," *West Indian and Jamaica Gazette*, 23 August 1838, in CO 137/229.

3. Ibid. (emphasis added).

4. Ibid. See also [Howard], *Autobiography of Oliver Otis Howard*, 2:186 (emphasis in original).

5. "Report of Captain J. W. Pringle on Prisons in the West Indies," 17 July 1838, *PP* 1837–38, 40 (596): 1–14.

6. Green, *British Slave Emancipation*, 187. Taylor reprinted the memorandum, originally written 19 January 1839, in his autobiography. See *Autobiography of Henry Taylor*, 1:211.

7. [Taylor], *Autobiography of Henry Taylor*, 1:210.

8. Ibid., 208, 213.

9. Ibid., 208, 211–12.

10. Ibid., 205, 216–18.

11. "The persuasory and recommendatory process may appear to be the more conciliatory at first; but I am convinced that the appearance is fallacious. The West Indian legislatures have neither the will nor the skill to make such laws as you want made; and they cannot be converted on the point of willingness, and they will not be instructed." Ibid., 205–6.

12. James Stephen to G. W. Hope, 15 September 1841, CO 137/256, in Kenneth Bell and Morrell, *Select Documents*, 419–21.

13. Sir Charles Metcalf to Marquess of Normanby, 16 October 1839, CO 137/240, cited in Douglas Hall, "Sir Charles Metcalf," 90–100.

14. Ibid.

15. Ibid.

16. Sir Charles Metcalf to Lord John Russell, 30 March 1840, CO 137/248, no. 50.

17. Ibid.

18. Thomas F. Abbott to Marquess of Normanby, 11 June 1839, enclosed in Sir Lionel Smith to Normanby, 24 June 1839, CO 137/239, no. 123.

19. Ibid., and Metcalf to Russell, 30 March 1840.

20. Ibid.

21. Ibid.

22. Metcalf to Russell, 30 March 1840.

23. Douglas Hall, *Free Jamaica*, 7; Green, *British Slave Emancipation*, 165–68.

24. Green, *British Slave Emancipation*, 85.

25. "Report from the Select Committee on West India Colonies," *PP* 1842, 13 (479): iii–xv.

26. Ibid.

27. Ibid.

28. Ibid.

29. Q. 4511 and Q. 5964, both in ibid.

30. Q. 5975, 5981, 5982, all in ibid. See also Eisner, *Jamaica,* 192.

31. "Report from the Select Committee on West India Colonies," Q. 4474, 4509.

32. Green, *British Slave Emancipation,* 176.

33. "Third Report from the Select Committee on Sugar and Coffee Planting," *PP* 1847–48, 23 (167); Earl Grey to Walker, 30 June 1848, in Kenneth Bell and Morrell, *Select Documents,* 439.

34. Metcalf to Normanby, 16 October 1839; "Report from the Select Committee on West India Colonies," Q. 5322–23.

35. Metcalf to Normanby, 16 October 1839. Metcalf was not totally displeased with the ex-slaves exerting themselves, stating that while difficulties would come as result of this situation, "we cannot but rejoice at so much good." See also Eisner, *Jamaica,* 212.

36. See Brereton, "Post-Emancipation Protest in the Caribbean," 110–23; Chan, "The Riots of 1856 in British Guiana," 39–50; Craton, "Continuity Not Change," 144–70; Marshall, "Vox Populi," 84–115.

37. Underhill, *The Tragedy of Morant Bay,* ix–xix.

38. Semmel, *The Governor Eyre Controversy,* 43.

39. Ibid., 43–44.

40. Underhill, *The Tragedy of Morant Bay,* 58.

41. Ibid., 59–61; "Report of the Jamaica Royal Commission," *PP* 1866, 30 (3683 – pt. 1): 14.

42. Underhill's original analysis has stood the test of time as a lucid and comprehensive account of events surrounding the uprising. See *The Tragedy of Morant Bay* as well as Green, *British Slave Emancipation,* 381–405, and Semmel, *The Governor Eyre Controversy.* See also Bakan, *Ideology and Class Conflict in Jamaica,* 68–93, and Heuman, *The Killing Time.*

43. Underhill, *The Tragedy of Morant Bay,* 61. The Royal Commission certainly did not agree with Underhill's account. It found the letter to be evidence of a political ploy: "It seemed to be relied upon as showing the peaceable intentions of the writers. We confess we cannot look upon it in that light. Its language is that of a scarcely concealed defiance, and looking at its terms, at the time at which it was written, and the acts by which it was accompanied and followed, it seems to us to partake rather of the character of a manifesto preparatory to and attempting to justify a recourse to violence." See "Report of the Jamaica Royal Commission," 14.

44. "Report of the Jamaica Royal Commission," 25, 39–41.

45. Ibid., 18, 40.

46. Bakan, *Ideology and Class Conflict in Jamaica,* 78.

47. Semmel, *The Governor Eyre Controversy,* 55; Bakan, *Ideology and Class Conflict in Jamaica,* 90–91.

48. Helg, *Our Rightful Share,* 194. See also Butler, *Freedoms Given, Freedoms Won.*

49. Lord Elgin to Edward Stanley, 5 August 1845, CO 137/284, in Kenneth Bell and Morrell, *Select Documents*, 424–28.

50. Oliver O. Howard, War Department, Bureau of Refugees, Freedmen, and Abandoned Lands, 19 May 1865, Circular No. 2, Select Series of Records Issued by the Commissioner of the Bureau, etc., M 742, r 7, Circulars and Special Orders Issued, 0037, National Archives, Washington, D.C.

51. Lt. Walker to H. W. Smith, 6 October 1866, M 869, r 34, Reports of Conditions and Operations, July 1865–December 1866, 0770–0774; Geo[rge] E. Pingree to Edw[ard] L. Deane, 31 July 1867, M 869, r 35, Reports of Conditions and Operations, January 1867–May 1868, 0247–0249.

52. J. E. Lewis to Captain Geo[rge] E. Pingree, 1 August 1867, M 869, r 35, Reports of Conditions and Operations, January 1867–May 1868, 0250–0252.

53. De Forest, *A Union Officer in the Reconstruction*, 60–61, 69–89.

54. Ibid., 88n; O[liver] O. Howard, War Department, Bureau of Refugees, Freedmen, and Abandoned Lands, 22 August 1866, SFOR, ser. 3097, box 57, Letters Received, October 1865–June 1969, and Orders Received and Issued, July 1863 and October 1865–June 1868, Beaufort. See also Select Series of Records Issued by the Commissioner of the Bureau, etc., M 742, r 7, Circulars and Special Orders Issued, 0052, 0059.

55. Katz, *The Undeserving Poor*, 5. See also his work focusing specifically on the nineteenth century, *In the Shadow of the Poorhouse*. De Forest contended that the poorhouse "was a shadow which blighted self-respect and tortured the sensibilities of the meanest white and the most shiftless Negro." See *A Union Officer in the Reconstruction*, 59. See also W. H. Danilson to H[orace] Neide, 28 December 1868, SFOR, ser. 3123, vol. 152, Letters Sent, 1868, Charleston, Subdistrict of Charleston.

56. Oliver Howard, War Department, Bureau of Refugees, Freedmen, and Abandoned Lands, 30 May 1865, Circular No. 5, "Rules and Regulations for Assistant Commissioners."

57. G. P. McDougall to Captain E. R. Chase, 31 October 1866, and McDougall to [William] Stone, 31 January 1867, both in SFOR, ser. 3065, vol. 105, Letters Sent, 1866, Anderson Court House.

58. Captain E. R. Chase to Benjamin Runkle, 17 October 1866, SFOR, ser. 3077, vol. 90, Letters Sent, 4 June–6 December 1866, Aiken.

59. [William J.] Harkisheimer to E. L. Deane, 28 December 1867, SFOR, ser. 3153, vol. 133, Letters Sent, 2 January 1867–12 November 1868, Columbia, Subdistrict of Columbia, RG 105; [William] Nerland to [William] Stone, 1 January 1868, SC, SFOR, ser. 3077, vol. 126, Letters Sent, Barnwell Court House, 27 March 1867–24 April 1868, RG 105; J. E. Lewis to George E. Pingree, 31 October 1867, SFOR, ser. 3186, box 65, Darlington, 1866–68, RG 105.

60. Flora Murphy to D. T. Corbin, 23 May 1866, SFOR, ser. 3278, box 81, Letters Received Relating to Rations, June 1866–July 1867, Moncks Corner, 1866–68/Mount Pleasant, 1866–68 (emphasis in original).

61. Gillette, *Retreat from Reconstruction*, 6.

62. Simkins, "The Ku Klux Klan in South Carolina," 606; Eric Foner, *Reconstruction*, 425–30. The Regulators, who constituted only one of such groups, others being Jayhawkers and Bushwhackers, were also mentioned in the records related to Georgia. See N. M. Reeve to [Davis] Tillson, 27 November 1865, and Davis Tillson to Oliver O. Howard, 28 November 1865, both in M 869, r 8, Registered Letters Received, May–December 1865, 0448–0450, 0452–0453. After the 1760-61 Cherokee War, a vigilante group emerged in the South Carolina backcountry known as the Regulators. The transition from the displacement and expropriation of the lands inhabited by the Cherokee led to disorder and lawlessness. As a consequence a group of property holders in the backcountry formed the Regulators to "end lawlessness, to discipline the lower people, and to establish an orderly society." In effect, the Regulators became "the prototype of American vigilante movements," and in fact may have served as the inspiration for the group of the same name which appeared in South Carolina during Reconstruction. See Brown, *The South Carolina Regulators*, 135.

63. Lou Williams, *The Great South Carolina Ku Klux Klan Trials*, 19–20; N. M. Reeve to [Davis] Tillson, 27 November 1865, and Davis Tillson to Oliver O. Howard, 28 November 1865; Eric Foner, *Reconstruction*, 431–32.

64. Simkins, "The Ku Klux Klan in South Carolina," 610–11, 647. See also the copious testimony from the Ku Klux Klan trials in *House Reports*, 42d Cong., 2d sess., Serial 1529, no. 22, and Serial 1531-33 (Testimony for South Carolina).

65. See MacDonald, *Select Statutes*, 227–35, 262–68.

66. Eric Foner, *Reconstruction*, 454–55.

67. Pingree to R. K. Scott, 3 August 1866, and Pingree to Geo[rge] W. Gile, 19 June 1866, both in M 869, r 11, Registered Letters Received, October 1865–December 1866, 0072–0074, 0076–0078.

68. Simkins, "The Ku Klux Klan in South Carolina," 608; Trelease, *White Terror*, 352–53; Williamson, *After Slavery*, 259.

69. Williamson, *After Slavery*, 259.

70. W. E. Towne to Rufus Saxton, 17 August 1865, M 869, r 8, Registered Letters Received P–Y, May–December 1865, 0331–0338; Saville, *The Work of Reconstruction*, 143–95.

71. Trelease, *White Terror*, 349–65; Williamson, *After Slavery*, 259–61.

72. Trelease, *White Terror*, 366–80.

73. Ibid., 387–88, 411.

74. Ibid., 406; Kermit Hall, "Political Power and Constitutional Legitimacy," 941n.

75. Kermit Hall, "Political Power and Constitutional Legitimacy," 926–29; Williamson, *After Slavery*, 364.

76. Kermit Hall, "Political Power and Constitutional Legitimacy," 930–31, 941.

77. Ibid., 942–44.

78. Trelease, *White Terror*, xv; Gillette, *Retreat from Reconstruction*, 46.

79. Eric Foner, *Reconstruction*, 510, 527.

80. Kermit Hall, "Political Power and Constitutional Legitimacy," 94ln; Trelease, *White Terror*, 415–17.

81. See Eric Foner, *Reconstruction*, 530–31, 544, and Lou Williams, *The Great South Carolina Ku Klux Klan Trials*, 134.

82. Eric Foner, *Reconstruction*, 573–74; "Report of the Jamaica Royal Commission," 14.

83. Eric Foner, *Reconstruction*, 577, 587. See also William Stone to Edw[ard] L. Deane, 29 December 1867, M 869, r 18, 0057–0063. Writing from Edgefield, an area notorious for its outrages, Stone suggested that "now that colored men have been endowed with the same civil and political rights as the whites, it is a question whether they ought to be the *subjects of special legislation*" (emphasis added).

Conclusion

1. Pocock, *"Machiavellian Moment,"* 6; Goveia, *Historiography*, 176–77.

2. Oliver Howard, "Instructions to Assistant Commissioners and Other Officers," Circular No. 11, 12 July 1865, Chief Medical Records, ser. 2992, box 46, SFOR.

3. De Forest, *A Union Officer in the Reconstruction*, 60–61, 69–89.

4. See Daryl Scott, *Contempt and Pity.*

5. Blacks (free and formerly enslaved) were not immune from this line of reasoning. Yet there does seem to have been a difference in that it did not become the raison d'être of their antislavery argument. Nineteenth- and twentieth-century Black intellectuals, including Frederick Douglass, Anna Julia Cooper, Alexander Crummel, and Ida B. Wells, to name just a few, also saw slavery as having somehow damaged Blacks. Yet this understanding was always coupled with a systemic critique of American society and its continued brutality toward Blacks.

6. Douglass, *Narrative of the Life of Frederick Douglass, an American Slave*, 113.

7. See the essays in Ira Berlin and Morgan, *Cultivation and Culture.*

8. McDonald, *The Economy and Material Culture of Slaves*, 23–31.

9. In his history of Jamaica, William Gardner, a missionary who worked in Jamaica for twenty-five years, noted that while a minority of the former slaves have not "greatly improved in their habits and conditions," many have obtained land and "are producing an annually augmenting proportion of the articles exported from the colony." See Gardner, *A History of Jamaica*, 459.

10. John Campbell, "As 'a Kind of Freeman'?," in Ira Berlin and Morgan, *Cultivation and Culture*, 243–74.

11. Ibid. See also Philip Morgan, "Work and Culture," 563–99.

12. *South Carolina Leader* 1, no. 12 (23 December 1865).

13. Green, *British Slave Emancipation*, 184; Holt, *The Problem of Freedom*, 202.

14. Ward, "The Profitability of Sugar Planting in the British West Indies," 81–93.

15. Eric Williams, *Capitalism and Slavery.*

16. Donald Robinson, *Slavery in the Structure of American Politics*, 257–63.

17. Ibid., 157, 198–201. See also Lynd, "The Abolitionist Critique of the United States Constitution," 209–39.

18. Higginbotham, *In the Matter of Color,* 190–92.

19. See Fogel and Engerman, *Time on the Cross,* 59–106; Stampp, *The Peculiar Institution,* 383–418; Wright, *The Political Economy of the Cotton South,* 139–44.

20. Cody, "Naming, Kinship, and Estate Dispersal," 192–93.

21. Edmund Morgan, *American Slavery, American Freedom,* 5.

22. Marshall, "The Post-Slavery Labor Problem Revisited," 7–8 (emphasis added).

23. Green, *British Slave Emancipation,* 184–87.

24. Lou Williams, *The Great South Carolina Ku Klux Klan Trials,* 2, 134–41.

25. Eudell, "The Mind of Emancipation," 35–42. The quotation is from David Christy's *Cotton Is King* (1856).

26. Leslie Bethell has excellently detailed the campaign in Brazil extending over several decades, which included a series of compromises, unenforced treaties, and economic trade threats, such as excluding Brazilian exports from the world market as well as a reduction in loans sought for economic development. See *The Abolition of the Brazilian Slave Trade.* For the Cuban example, where similar diplomatic strategies were employed, see Corwin, *Spain and the Abolition of Slavery in Cuba,* 17–128.

27. See Wallerstein, *The Modern World System,* 15–16, where he argued that it is a world system, "not because it encompasses the whole world, but because it is larger than any juridically-defined political unit." For Wallerstein, "it is an economic but not a political entity, unlike empires, city-states and nation-states." My argument, however, is that from the sixteenth century, Western culture expanded, and thus, this world system can as well be understood in intellectual and cultural terms.

28. Lynd, "The Abolitionist Critique of the United States Constitution," 209–39; Bowen, *Miracle at Philadelphia,* 201. See also Anderson, *Imagined Communities.*

29. Greene, *The Intellectual Construction of America,* 95–161. See also O'Gorman, *The Invention of America,* 137, cited by Greene, 125.

30. Bowen, *Miracle at Philadelphia.*

31. Du Bois, *The Souls of Black Folk,* 47, 49.

Bibliography

Primary Sources

Freedmen and Southern Society Project, Department of History, University of Maryland, College Park, Maryland
    Records related to South Carolina
Howard University, Washington, D.C.
    Moorland Spingarn Collection, Negro Newspapers
Library of Congress, Washington, D.C.
    Rare Book Reading Room, Miscellaneous Documents
National Archives, Washington, D.C.
    Record Group 105: Records of the Bureau of Refugees, Freedmen, and Abandoned Lands
    Office of the Assistant Commissioner for South Carolina (M 869)
    Selected Series of Records Issued by the Commissioner of the Bureau of Refugees, etc., M 742, roll 7, Circulars and Special Orders Issued
    Subordinate Field Officers Records for South Carolina
Public Record Office, Kew, England
    Colonial Office Records
        Series 137: Original Correspondence, Governors of Jamaica
Special Collections, University of the West Indies, Mona, Kingston, Jamaica
    Miscellaneous Documents

Government Documents

Great Britain

House of Commons. *Parliamentary Papers.* London.
    1831–32, 31 (59): "Laws Passed by Jamaica Legislature for Relief of Catholics, Jews, and Free Persons of Colour."
    1835, 50 (177): "Papers in Explanation of Measures to Give Effect to Act for Abolition of Slavery." Part 1, Jamaica, 1833–35. Part 2, 1835, 50 (278).
    1836, 48 (166): "Papers Relating to the Abolition of Slavery."
    1837–38, 40 (596): "Report of Captain J. W. Pringle on Prisons in the West Indies."
    1842, 13 (479): "Report from the Select Committee on West India Colonies."
    1847–48, 23 (167): "Third Report from the Select Committee on Sugar and Coffee Planting."

1866, 30 (3683—pt. 1): "Report of the Jamaica Royal Commission."

House of Commons. Select Committee. *Negro Apprenticeship in the Colonies: A Review of the Report of the Select Committee of the House of Commons.* London: John Hatchard and Son, 1837.

United States

Congressional Record. Washington, D.C., various years.

House Executive Documents, 39th Cong., 1st sess., Serial 1256, no. 70: Circulars and General Orders Issued by the Freedmen's Bureau.

House Reports, 39th Cong., 1st sess., Serial 1272, no. 33: Report on the Committee on the Judiciary.

House Reports, 42d Cong., 2d sess., Serial 1529, no. 22: Report of Joint Select Committee on the Affairs in Late Insurrectionary States. Also Serials 1531–33: Testimony in South Carolina.

Senate Executive Documents, 38th Cong., 1st sess., Serial 1176, no. 53: Preliminary and Final Reports of American Freedmen's Inquiry Commission.

Senate Executive Documents, 39th Cong., 1st sess., Serial 1237, no. 2: Reports of Carl Schurz and Lieutenant General Grant.

Senate Executive Documents, 39th Cong., 2d sess., Serial 1276, no. 6: Reports of Assistant Commissioners and Laws Respecting Persons of Color.

Senate Reports, 39th Cong., 1st sess., Serial 1273, no. 30: Report of the Joint Committee on Reconstruction.

Published Primary Sources

Abbott, Lyman. "Southern Evangelization." *New Englander* 23 (October 1864): 699–708.

Andrews, Sidney. *The South since the War: As Shown by Fourteen Weeks of Travel and Observation in Georgia and the Carolinas.* Boston: Ticknor and Fields, 1866.

[Atkinson, Edward.] "The Future Supply of Cotton." *North American Review* 98 (April 1864): 477–97.

Bancroft, Frederic, ed. *Speeches, Correspondence and Political Papers of Carl Schurz.* Vol. 1. New York: G. P. Putnam's Sons, 1913.

Bell, Kenneth, and W. P. Morrell, eds. *Select Documents on British Colonial Policy, 1830–1860.* Oxford: Clarendon Press, 1928.

Berlin, Ira, Barbara J. Fields, Thavolia Glymph, Joseph P. Reidy, and Leslie S. Rowland, eds. *Freedom: A Documentary History of Emancipation, 1861–1867.* Series 1. Vol. 2: *The Destruction of Slavery.* New York: Cambridge University Press, 1985.

Berlin, Ira, Thavolia Glymph, Stephen F. Miller, Joseph P. Reidy, Leslie S. Rowland, and Julie Saville, eds. *Freedom: A Documentary History of Emancipation, 1861–1867.* Series 1. Vol. 3: *The Wartime Genesis of Free Labor: The Lower South.* New York: Cambridge University Press, 1990.

Botume, Elizabeth Hyde Botume. *First Days amongst the Contrabands.* Boston: Lee and Shepard Publishers, 1893.

Boyce, W. W. "The State of the Country." *De Bow's Review* 1, no. 2 (February 1866): 132–46.

Brooks, Arthur, ed. *The Writings of Abraham Lincoln.* Vol. 6: *1862–1863.* New York: G. P. Putnam's Sons [Knickerbocker Press], 1906.

Cabell, E. C. "White Emigration to the South." *De Bow's Review* 1, no. 1 (January 1866): 91–94.

Calhoun, John C. "Disquisition on Government" (1854). In *Slavery Defended: The Views of the Old South,* edited by Eric L. McKitrick, 6–11. Englewood Cliffs, N.J.: Prentice-Hall, 1963.

De Forest, John William. *A Union Officer in the Reconstruction.* New Haven, Conn.: Yale University Press, 1948.

Delany, Martin Robinson. *The Condition, Elevation, Emigration, and Destiny of the Colored People of the United States.* 1852. Reprint, New York: Arno Press, 1968.

[De Large, Robert C.] "Whither Are We Drifting." *South Carolina Leader* 1, no. 3 (21 October 1865): 2.

Douglass, Frederick. *Narrative of the Life of Frederick Douglass, an American Slave.* 1845. Reprint, New York: Penguin Books, 1982.

Edwards, Bryan. *The History, Civil and Commercial, of the British Colonies in the West Indies.* 4 vols. London, 1801.

Fitzhugh, George. "The Freedmen." *De Bow's Review* 2 (November 1866): 489–93.

———. "Sociology for the South" (1854). In *Slavery Defended: The Views of the Old South,* edited by Eric L. McKitrick, 34–56. Englewood Cliffs, N.J.: Prentice-Hall, 1963.

Fleishman, C. L. "Opening of New Fields to Immigration." *De Bow's Review* 1, no. 1 (January 1866): 87–91.

Foner, Philip S., ed. *The Life and Writings of Frederick Douglass.* 5 vols. New York: International Publishers, 1950.

Foner, Philip S., and George Walker, eds. *Proceedings of the Black National and State Conventions, 1865–1900.* Vol. 1. Philadelphia: Temple University Press, 1986.

———. *Proceedings of the Black State Conventions, 1840–1865.* Vol. 2. Philadelphia: Temple University Press, 1980.

[Gannett, William C.] "The Freedmen at Port Royal." *North American Review* 101, no. 208 (July 1865): 1–28.

[Gannett, William C., and Everett E. Hale.] "Education of the Freedmen." *North American Review* 101 (October 1865): 528–49.

Gardner, William. *A History of Jamaica: From Its Discovery by Christopher Columbus to the Year 1872.* 1873. Reprint, London: Frank Cass, 1971.

Holland, Rupert Sargent, ed. *Letters and Diary of Laura M. Towne.* 1912. Reprint, New York: Negro Universities Press, 1969.

[Howard, Oliver Otis.] *Autobiography of Oliver Otis Howard.* Vol. 2. New York: Baker and Taylor, 1907.

Long, Edward. *History of Jamaica.* 3 vols. London, 1774.

MacDonald, William, ed. *Select Statutes and Other Documents Illustrative of the History of the United States, 1861–1898.* New York: Macmillan, 1903.

Madden, Robert R. *A Twelvemonth's Residence in the West Indies, during the Transition from Slavery to Apprenticeship: With Incidental Notices of the State of Society, Prospects, and Natural Resources of Jamaica and Other Islands.* Vol. 2. 1835. Reprint, Westport, Conn.: Negro Universities Press, 1970.

Marshall, Woodville K., ed. *The Colthurst Journal: Journal of a Special Magistrate in the Islands of Barbados and St. Vincent, July 1835–September 1838.* Millwood, N.Y.: KTO Press, 1977.

Nordoff, Charles. *The Freedmen of South Carolina: Some Account of Their Appearance, Character, Condition, and Peculiar Customs.* New York: Charles T. Evans, 1863.

Nott, Josiah C. "Climates of the South in Their Relations to White Labor." *De Bow's Review* 1, no. 2 (February 1866): 166–73.

Pearson, Elizabeth Ware, ed. *Letters from Port Royal, 1862–1868: Written at the Time of the Civil War.* Boston: W. B. Clark, 1906.

Philbrick, Edward. "Free Labor in South Carolina: Results of Practical Experiments." *New York Evening Post* (3 March 1864): 1.

[Pierce, Edward L.] "The Freedmen at Port Royal." *Atlantic Monthly* 12 (September 1863): 291–315.

Pike, James S. *The Prostrate State: South Carolina under Negro Government.* New York: D. Appleton, 1874.

Sanger, George P. *The Statutes at Large, Treaties and Proclamations of the United States from December 1863, to December 1865.* Boston: Little, Brown, 1866.

Smith, Adam. *An Inquiry into the Nature and Causes of the Wealth of Nations.* Vol. 1. 1776. 5th ed. Reprint, London: Methuen, 1930.

Straker, David August. *New South Investigated.* Detroit: Ferguson Printing, 1888.

Sturge, Joseph, and Thomas Harvey. *The West Indies in 1837; Being the Journal of a Visit to Antigua, Montserrat, Dominica, St. Lucia, Barbadoes, and Jamaica; Undertaken for the Purpose of Ascertaining the Actual Condition of the Negro Population of Those Islands.* 2d ed. London: Hamilton, Adams, 1838.

[Taylor, Henry.] *Autobiography of Henry Taylor, 1800–1875.* Vol. 1. New York: Harper and Brothers, 1885.

Tocqueville, Alexis de. *Democracy in America.* Cambridge: Welch, Bigelow, 1863.

Underhill, Edward Bean. *The Tragedy of Morant Bay: A Narrative of the Disturbances in the Island of Jamaica in 1865.* London: Alexander and Shepherd, 1895.

[Walker, David.] *David Walker's Appeal in Four Articles to the Colored Citizens of the World, But in Particular, and Very Expressly, to Those of the United States of America.* 1829. Reprint, New York: Hill and Wang, 1991.

Secondary Sources

Abbott, Martin. *The Freedmen's Bureau in South Carolina, 1865–1872.* Chapel Hill: University of North Carolina Press, 1967.

Adamson, Alan H. "The Reconstruction of Plantation Labour after Emancipation: The Case of British Guiana." In *Race and Slavery in the Western Hemisphere: Quantitative Studies,* edited by Stanley Engerman and Eugene D. Genovese, 457–73. Princeton, N.J.: Princeton University Press, 1975.

Anderson, Benedict. *Imagined Communities: Reflections on the Origins and Spread of Nationalism.* New York: Verso, 1983.

Antsey, Roger. "*Capitalism and Slavery:* A Critique." *Economic History Review,* 2d ser., 21, no. 2 (August 1968): 307–20.

Ashworth, John. "The Relationship between Capitalism and Humanitarianism." *American Historical Review* 92, no. 4 (October 1987): 813–28.

Azevedo, Celia M. *Abolitionism in the United States and Brazil: A Comparative Perspective.* New York: Garland, 1995.

Bakan, Abigail B. *Ideology and Class Conflict in Jamaica: The Politics of Rebellion.* Montreal: McGill-Queen's University Press, 1990.

Baker, Keith Michael. *Inventing the French Revolution: Essays on French Political Culture in the Eighteenth Century.* Cambridge: Cambridge University Press, 1990.

Beckles, Hilary, and Verene Shepherd, eds. *Caribbean Freedom: Economy and Society from Emancipation to the Present.* Kingston, Jamaica: Ian Randle Publishers, 1993.

Bell, Derrick. *And We Are Not Saved: The Elusive Quest for Racial Justice.* New York: Basic Books, 1987.

Bentley, George R. *A History of the Freedmen's Bureau.* Philadelphia: University of Pennsylvania Press, 1955.

Berlin, Ira, and Philip D. Morgan, eds. *Cultivation and Culture: Labor and the Shaping of Slave Life in the Americas.* Charlottesville: University Press of Virginia, 1993.

Berlin, Isaiah. *Two Concepts of Liberty.* Oxford: Oxford University Press, 1958.

Berthoff, Rowland T. "Southern Attitudes toward Immigration, 1865–1914." *Journal of Southern History* 27, no. 3 (August 1951): 328–60.

Bethell, Leslie. *The Abolition of the Brazilian Slave Trade: Britain, Brazil, and the Slave Trade Question, 1807–1869.* Cambridge: Cambridge University Press, 1970.

Bleser, Carol K. Rothberg. *The Promised Land: The History of the South Carolina Land Commission, 1869–1890.* Columbia: University of South Carolina Press, 1969.

Bolland, O. Nigel. "Systems of Domination after Slavery: The Control of Land and Labour in the British West Indies after 1838." In *Caribbean Freedom: Economy and Society from Emancipation to the Present,* edited by Hilary Beckles and Verene Shepherd, 107–23. Kingston, Jamaica: Ian Randle Publishers, 1993.

Bolt, Christine. *The Anti-Slavery Movement and Reconstruction: A Study of Anglo-American Co-operation, 1833–1877.* London: Oxford University Press/Institute of Race Relations, 1969.

Bowen, Catherine Drinker. *Miracle at Philadelphia: The Story of the Constitutional Convention, May to September 1787.* Boston: Little, Brown, 1966.

Brereton, Bridget. "Post-Emancipation Protest in the Caribbean: The 'Belmanna Riots' in Tobago, 1876." *Caribbean Quarterly* 30, nos. 3–4 (September–December 1984): 110–23.

Brown, Richard Maxwell. *The South Carolina Regulators.* Cambridge, Mass.: Harvard University Press, 1963.

Burn, William L. *Emancipation and Apprenticeship in the British West Indies.* London: Jonathan Cape, 1937.

Butler, Kim D. *Freedoms Given, Freedoms Won: Afro-Brazilians in Post-Abolition, São Paulo and Salvador.* New Brunswick, N.J.: Rutgers University Press, 1998.

Cambiano, Giuseppe. "Aristotle and the Anonymous Opponents of Slavery." *Slavery and Abolition* 8, no. 1 (May 1987): 22–41.

Carlyle, Thomas. "Occasional Discourse on the Nigger Question." In *Critical and Miscellaneous Essays,* 4:348–83. London: Chapman and Hall, 1899.

Carrington, Selwyn. "The State of the Debate on the Role of Capitalism in the Ending of the Slave System." *Journal of Caribbean History* 22, nos. 1–2, Special Issue to Commemorate the 150th Anniversary of Slave Emancipation in the British Caribbean (1988): 20–41.

Cash, Wilbur J. *The Mind of the South.* New York: Alfred A. Knopf, 1941.

Césaire, Aimé. *Discourse and Colonialism.* New York: Monthly Review Press, 1972.

———. *Notebook of the Return to My Native Land* (1939). In *Aimé Césaire: The Collected Poetry,* translated by Clayton Eshleman and Annette Smith. Berkeley: University of California Press, 1983.

Chan, V. O. "The Riots of 1856 in British Guiana." *Caribbean Quarterly* 16, no. 1 (March 1970): 39–51.

Cody, Cheryl Ann. "Naming, Kinship, and Estate Dispersal: Notes on Slave Family Life on a South Carolina Plantation, 1786 to 1833." *William and Mary Quarterly,* 3d ser., 39 (January 1982): 192–211.

Cohen, David W., and Jack P. Greene, eds. *Neither Slave nor Free: The Freedmen of African Descent in the Slave Societies of the New World.* Baltimore: Johns Hopkins University Press, 1972.

Cooper, Frederick, Thomas C. Holt, and Rebecca J. Scott. *Beyond Slavery: Explorations of Race, Labor, and Citizenship in Postemancipation Societies.* Chapel Hill: University of North Carolina Press, 2000.

Corwin, Arthur F. *Spain and the Abolition of Slavery in Cuba, 1817–1886.* Austin: University of Texas Press, 1967.

Coupland, Reginald. *The British Antislavery Movement.* 1933. Reprint, London: Frank Cass, 1969.

Craton, Michael. "Continuity Not Change: The Incidence of Unrest among Ex-Slaves in the British West Indies, 1838–1876." *Slavery and Abolition* 9, no. 2 (September 1988): 144–70.

————. Review of *Econocide* by Seymour Drescher. *Canadian Journal of History* 13, no. 2 (August 1978): 295–97.

Current, Richard N. "The Friend of Freedom." In *Reconstruction: An Anthology of Revisionist Writings*, edited by Kenneth M. Stampp and Leon F. Litwack, 25–47. Baton Rouge: Louisiana State University Press, 1969.

Curtin, Philip D. *The Atlantic Slave Trade: A Census*. Madison: University of Wisconsin Press, 1969.

Darity, William, Jr. "A General Equilibrium Model of the Eighteenth-Century Atlantic Slave Trade: A Least-Likely Test for the Caribbean School." *Research in Economic History* 7 (1982): 287–326.

————. "The Williams Abolition Thesis before Williams." *Slavery and Abolition* 9, no. 1 (May 1988): 29–41.

Davis, David Brion. *The Problem of Slavery in the Age of Revolution, 1770–1823*. Ithaca: Cornell University Press, 1975.

————. *The Problem of Slavery in Western Culture*. Ithaca: Cornell University Press, 1966.

————. "Reflections on Abolitionism and Ideological Hegemony." *American Historical Review* 92, no. 4 (October 1987): 797–812.

————. *Slavery and Human Progress*. New York: Oxford University Press, 1984.

Dookhan, Isaac. *A Pre-Emancipation History of the West Indies*. Essex, England: Longman Caribbean, 1971.

Drescher, Seymour. *Econocide: British Slavery in the Era of Abolition*. Pittsburgh: University of Pittsburgh Press, 1977.

————. *From Slavery to Freedom: Comparative Studies in the Rise and Fall of Atlantic Slavery*. New York: New York University Press, 1999.

————. "The Historical Context of British Abolition." In *Abolition and Its Aftermath: The Historical Context, 1790–1916*, edited by David Richardson, 3–24. London: Frank Cass, 1985.

Drescher, Seymour, and Frank McGlynn, eds. *The Meaning of Freedom: Economics, Politics, and Culture after Slavery*. Pittsburgh: University of Pittsburgh Press, 1992.

Du Bois, W. E. B. *Black Reconstruction in America: An Essay toward a History of the Part Which Black Folk Played in the Attempt to Reconstruct Democracy in America, 1860–1880*. 1935. Reprint, New York: Atheneum, 1983.

————. "The Freedmen's Bureau." *Atlantic Monthly* 87 (March 1901): 354–65.

————. *The Souls of Black Folk*. 1903. Reprint, New York: Signet/Penguin, 1982.

Duff, John B., and Larry A. Greene, eds. *Slavery: Its Origin and Legacy*. New York: Thomas Y. Crowell, 1975.

Dumont, Louis. *From Mandeville to Marx: The Genesis and Triumph of Economic Ideology*. Chicago: University of Chicago Press, 1977.

Eisner, Gisela. *Jamaica, 1830–1930: A Study in Economic Growth*. Manchester: Manchester University Press, 1961.

Eltis, David. *Economic Growth and the Ending of the Transatlantic Slave Trade.* New York: Oxford University Press, 1987.

Engerman, Stanley L., and Eugene D. Genovese, eds. *Race and Slavery in the Western Hemisphere: Quantitative Studies.* Princeton, N.J.: Princeton University Press, 1975.

Fanon, Frantz. *The Wretched of the Earth.* Translation of *Les damnés de la terre* by Constance Farrington. New York: Grove Press, 1963.

Finley, Moses I. *Ancient Slavery and Modern Ideology.* 1980. Reprint, Princeton, N.J.: Markus Wiener Publishers, 1998.

Fogel, Robert William, and Stanley L. Engerman. *Time on the Cross: The Economics of American Negro Slavery.* Boston: Little, Brown, 1974.

Foner, Eric. *Free Soil, Free Labor, Free Men: The Ideology of the Republican Party before the Civil War.* New York: Oxford University Press, 1970.

———. *Nothing but Freedom: Emancipation and Its Legacy.* Baton Rouge: Louisiana State University Press, 1983.

———. *Politics and Ideology in the Age of the Civil War.* New York: Oxford University Press, 1980.

———. *Reconstruction: America's Unfinished Revolution, 1863–1877.* New York: Harper and Row, 1988.

———. *The Story of American Freedom.* New York: W. W. Norton, 1998.

Foner, Laura, and Eugene D. Genovese, eds. *Slavery in the New World: A Reader in Comparative History.* Englewood Cliffs, N.J.: Prentice Hall, 1969.

Franklin, John Hope. *Reconstruction: After the Civil War.* Chicago: University of Chicago Press, 1961.

Fredrickson, George. "After Emancipation: A Comparative Study of the White Responses to the New Order of Race Relations in the American South, Jamaica, and the Cape Colony of South Africa." In *What Was Freedom's Price?,* edited by David G. Sansing, 71–92. Jackson: University Press of Mississippi, 1978.

———. *The Black Image in the White Mind: The Debate on Afro-American Character and Destiny, 1871–1914.* New York: Harper and Row, 1971.

Frey, Sylvia R., and Betty Wood, eds. *From Slavery to Emancipation in the Atlantic World.* London: Frank Cass, 1999.

Furley, O. W. "Protestant Missionaries in the West Indies: Pioneers of a Non-Racial Society." *Race: The Journal of the Institute of Race Relations* 6, no. 3 (January 1965): 232–42.

Gaspar, David Barry. "With Rod of Iron: Barbados Slave Laws as a Model for Jamaica, South Carolina, and Antigua, 1661–1697." In *Crossing Boundaries: Comparative History of Black People in Diaspora,* edited by Darlene Clark Hine and Jacqueline McLeod, 343–66. Bloomington: Indiana University Press, 1999.

Geertz, Clifford. *The Interpretation of Cultures.* New York: Basic Books, 1973.

Genovese, Eugene D. *The Political Economy of Slavery: Studies in the Economy and Society of the Slave South.* New York: Vintage, 1967.

———. *The World the Slaveholders Made.* New York: Pantheon Books, 1969.

Gillespie, Michael Allen. *Hegel, Heidegger, and the Ground of History*. Chicago: University of Chicago Press, 1984.

Gillette, William. *Retreat from Reconstruction, 1869–1879*. Baton Rouge: Louisiana State University Press, 1979.

Goldsmith, M. M. "Mandeville and the Spirit of Capitalism." *Journal of British Studies* 17, no. 1 (Fall 1977): 63–81.

Goody, Jack. "Slavery in Time and Space." In *Asian and African Systems of Slavery*, edited by James L. Watson, 16–42. Berkeley: University of California Press, 1980.

Gould, Stephen Jay. *The Mismeasure of Man*. New York: W. W. Norton, 1981.

Goveia, Elsa. *Slave Society in the British Leeward Islands at the End of the Eighteenth Century*. New Haven: Yale University Press, 1965.

———. *A Study of the Historiography of the British West Indies to the End of the Nineteenth Century*. 1956. Reprint, Washington, D.C.: Howard University Press, 1980.

Green, William A. *British Slave Emancipation: The Sugar Colonies and the Great Experiment, 1830–1865*. Oxford: Clarendon Press, 1976.

———. "The Creolization of Caribbean History: The Emancipation Era and a Critique of Dialectical Analysis." In *Caribbean Freedom: Economy and Society from Emancipation to the Present*, edited by Hilary Beckles and Verene Shepherd, 28–40. Kingston, Jamaica: Ian Randle Publishers, 1993.

Greene, Jack P. *The Intellectual Construction of America: Exceptionalism and Identity from 1492 to 1800*. Chapel Hill: University of North Carolina Press, 1993.

Gross, Izhak. "The Abolition of Negro Slavery and British Parliamentary Politics, 1832–3." *Historical Journal* 23, no. 1 (1980): 63–85.

Hall, Douglas. *Five of the Leewards, 1834–1870: The Major Problems of the Post-Emancipation Period in Antigua, Barbuda, Montserrat, Nevis and St. Kitts*. Aylesbury, Bucks: Caribbean University Press/Ginn, 1971.

———. "The Flight from the Estates Reconsidered: The British West Indies, 1838–1842." In *Caribbean Freedom: Economy and Society from Emancipation to the Present*, edited by Hilary Beckles and Verene Shepherd, 55–63. Kingston, Jamaica: Ian Randle Publishers, 1993.

———. *Free Jamaica, 1838–1865: An Economic History*. New Haven: Yale University Press, 1959.

———. "Sir Charles Metcalf." *Caribbean Quarterly* 3 (1953): 90–100.

Hall, Kermit L. "Political Power and Constitutional Legitimacy: The South Carolina Ku Klux Klan Trials, 1871–1872." *Emory Law Journal* 33 (Fall 1984): 921–51.

Harding, Alan. "Political Liberty in the Middle Ages." *Speculum* 55, no. 3 (July 1980): 423–43.

Hartz, Louis. *The Liberal Tradition in America: An Interpretation of American Political Thought since the Revolution*. New York: Harcourt, Brace, and World, 1955.

Haskell, Thomas L. "Capitalism and the Origins of the Humanitarian Sensibility." Parts 1 and 2. *American Historical Review* 90, nos. 3–4 (April–June 1985): 339–61, 547–66.

———. "Convention and Hegemonic Interest in the Debate over Antislavery: A Reply to Davis and Ashworth." *American Historical Review* 92, no. 4 (October 1987): 829–78.

Hayward, Jack, ed. *Out of Slavery: Abolition and After.* London: Frank Cass, 1985.

Helg, Aline. *Our Rightful Share: The Afro-Cuban Struggle for Equality, 1886–1912.* Chapel Hill: University of North Carolina Press, 1995.

Hess, Earl J. *Liberty, Virtue, and Progress: Northerners and Their War for the Union.* New York: New York University Press, 1988.

Heuman, Gad J. *Between Black and White: Race, Politics, and the Free Coloreds in Jamaica, 1792–1865.* Westport, Conn.: Greenwood Press, 1981.

———. *The Killing Time: The Morant Bay Rebellion in Jamaica.* Knoxville: University of Tennessee Press, 1994.

Higginbotham, A. Leon. *In the Matter of Color: Race and the American Legal Process: The Colonial Period.* New York: Oxford University Press, 1978.

Higman, Barry W. "The West India 'Interest' in Parliament, 1807–1833." *Historical Studies* 13, no. 49 (October 1967): 1–19.

Hijiya, James A. *J. W. De Forest and the Rise of American Gentility.* Hanover, N.H.: Brown University Press/University Press of New England, 1988.

Hirschman, Albert O. *The Passions and the Interests: Political Arguments for Capitalism before Its Triumph.* Princeton, N.J.: Princeton University Press, 1977.

Holt, Thomas C. *Black over White: Negro Political Leadership in South Carolina during Reconstruction.* Urbana: University of Illinois Press, 1977.

———. "'An Empire over the Mind': Emancipation, Race, and Ideology in the British West Indies and the American South." In *Race, Region, and Reconstruction: Essays in Honor of C. Vann Woodward,* edited by J. Morgan Kousser and James M. McPherson, 283–313. New York: Oxford University Press, 1982.

———. *The Problem of Freedom: Race, Labor, and Politics in Jamaica and Britain, 1832–1938.* Baltimore: Johns Hopkins University Press, 1992.

Horsman, Reginald. *Race and Manifest Destiny: The Origins of American Racial Anglo-Saxonism.* Cambridge, Mass.: Harvard University Press, 1981.

James, C. L. R. *The Black Jacobins: Toussaint L'Ouverture and the San Domingo Revolution.* 1938. Reprint, New York: Vintage Books, 1963.

———. *A History of Negro Revolt.* 1938. Reprint, New York: Haskell House Publishers, 1969.

Johannsen, Robert W. *Lincoln, the South, and Slavery: The Political Dimension.* Baton Rouge: Louisiana State University Press, 1991.

Katz, Michael B. *In the Shadow of the Poorhouse: A Social History of Welfare in America.* New York: Basic Books, 1986.

———. *The Undeserving Poor: From the War on Poverty to the War on Welfare.* New York: Pantheon Books, 1989.

King, Rev. Martin Luther. *Where Do We Go from Here: Chaos or Community?* New York: Harper and Row, 1967.

Klein, Herbert S. *Slavery in the Americas: A Comparative Study of Virginia and Cuba.* Chicago: University of Chicago Press, 1967.

Knight, Franklin W. *Slave Society in Cuba during the Nineteenth Century.* Madison: University of Wisconsin Press, 1970.

Kuhn, Thomas. *The Structure of Scientific Revolutions.* 1962. Reprint, Chicago: University of Chicago Press, 1970.

Le Goff, Jacques. "Mentalities: A History of Ambiguities." In *Constructing the Past: Essays in Historical Methodology,* edited by Jacques Le Goff and Pierre Nora, 166–80. Cambridge: Cambridge University Press, 1985.

Litwack, Leon F. "The Emancipation of the Negro Abolitionist." In *The Antislavery Vanguard: New Essays on the Abolitionists,* edited by Martin Duberman, 137–55. Princeton, N.J.: Princeton University Press, 1965.

Lovejoy, Arthur. *The Great Chain of Being: A Study of the History of an Idea.* Cambridge, Mass.: Harvard University Press, 1936.

Lowenberg, Bert James. "Efforts of the South to Encourage Immigration, 1865–1900." *South Atlantic Quarterly* 33 (1934): 363–85.

Lynd, Straughton. "The Abolitionist Critique of the United States Constitution." In *The Anti-Slavery Vanguard: New Essays on the Abolitionists,* edited by Martin Duberman, 209–39. Princeton, N.J.: Princeton University Press, 1965.

Maehl, William Henry, Jr., ed. *The Reform Bill of 1832: Why Not Revolution?* New York: Holt, Rinehart and Winston, 1967.

Marshall, Woodville. "The Post-Slavery Labor Problem Revisited." Elsa Goveia Memorial Lecture, 15 March 1990. Mona, Jamaica: Department of History, University of West Indies, 1991.

———. "Vox Populi: The St. Vincent Riots and Disturbances of 1862." In *Trade Government and Society in Caribbean History, 1700–1920,* edited by Barry Higman, 85–115. Kingston: Heinemann Educational Books Caribbean, 1983.

———. "We Be Wise to Many More Tings: Blacks' Hopes and Expectations of Emancipation." In *Caribbean Freedom: Economy and Society from Emancipation to the Present,* edited by Hilary Beckles and Verene Shepherd, 12–20. Kingston, Jamaica: Ian Randle Publishers, 1993.

Martin, Waldo E. *The Mind of Frederick Douglass.* Chapel Hill: University of North Carolina Press, 1984.

Marx, Karl, and Frederick Engels. *Capital: A Critique of Political Economy.* Edited by Ernest Untermann. New York: Modern Library, 1906.

———. *The German Ideology.* Edited by C. J. Arthur. New York: International Publishers, 1970.

Mathieson, William Law. *Great Britain and the Slave Trade, 1839–1865.* London: Longman, Green, 1929.

McDonald, Roderick A. *The Economy and Material Culture of Slaves: Goods and Chattels on the Sugar Plantations of Jamaica and Louisiana.* Baton Rouge: Louisiana State University Press, 1993.

Miers, Suzanne, and Igor Kopytoff, eds. *Slavery in Africa: Historical and Anthropological Perspectives.* Madison: University of Wisconsin Press, 1977.

Minchinton, Walter E. "Williams and Drescher: Abolition and Emancipation." *Slavery and Abolition* 4, no. 2 (September 1983): 81–105.

Morgan, Edmund S. *American Slavery, American Freedom: The Ordeal of Colonial Virginia.* New York: W. W. Norton, 1975.

Morgan, Philip D. "Work and Culture: The Task System and the World of Lowcountry Blacks, 1700 to 1880." *William and Mary Quarterly,* 3d ser., 39, no. 4 (October 1982): 563–99.

Morris, Robert C. *Reading, 'Riting, and Reconstruction: The Education of Freedmen in the South, 1861–1870.* 1976. Reprint, Chicago: University of Chicago Press, 1981.

Moynihan, Daniel Patrick. *The Negro Family: The Case for National Action.* Washington, D.C.: Office of Policy Planning and Research, U.S. Department of Labor, 1965.

O'Gorman, Edmundo. *The Invention of America: An Inquiry into the Historical Nature of the New World and the Meaning of Its History.* Bloomington: Indiana University Press, 1961.

Oubre, Claude F. *Forty Acres and a Mule: The Freedmen's Bureau and Black Land Ownership.* Baton Rouge: Louisiana State University Press, 1978.

Pagden, Anthony. *The Fall of Natural Man: The American Indian and the Origins of Comparative Ethnology.* Cambridge: Cambridge University Press, 1982.

———. "The Legacy of Rome." In *Lords of All the World: Ideologies of Empire in Spain, Britain and France c. 1500–c. 1800,* 11–28. New Haven: Yale University Press, 1995.

———, ed. *The Languages of Political Theory in Early-Modern Europe.* Cambridge: Cambridge University Press, 1987.

Paget, Hugh. "The Free Village System in Jamaica." *Jamaica Historical Review* 1, no. 1 (1945): 31–48.

Patterson, Orlando. *Slavery and Social Death: A Comparative Study.* Cambridge, Mass.: Harvard University Press, 1982.

Pease, William H. "Three Years among the Freedmen: William C. Gannett and the Port Royal Experiment." *Journal of Negro History* 42 (1957): 98–117.

Pocock, J. G. A. "The Concept of Language and the *Métier d'Historien:* Some Consideration on Practice." In *The Languages of Political Theory in Early-Modern Europe,* edited by Anthony Pagden, 19–38. Cambridge: Cambridge University Press, 1987.

———. "*The Machiavellian Moment* Revisited: A Study in the History and Ideology." *Journal of Modern History* 53, no. 1 (March 1981): 49–72.

———. *Politics, Language, and Time: Essays on Political Thought and History.* 1971. Reprint, Chicago: University of Chicago Press, 1989.

———. *Virtue, Commerce, and History: Essays on Political Thought and History, Chiefly in the Eighteenth Century.* 1985. Reprint, Cambridge: Cambridge University Press, 1991.

Polanyi, Karl. *The Great Transformation: The Political and Economic Origins of Our Time.* Boston: Beacon Press, 1944.

Potter, David M. *The Impending Crisis, 1848–1861.* New York: Harper Torchbooks, 1976.

Reckord, Mary. "The Jamaican Slave Rebellion of 1831." *Past and Present: A Journal of Historical Studies* no. 40 (July 1968): 108–25.

Richardson, David, ed. *Abolition and Its Aftermath: The Historical Context, 1790–1916.* London: Frank Cass, 1985.

Ricoeur, Paul. "Ideology and Utopia as Cultural Imagination." In *Being Human in a Technological Age,* edited by Donald M. Borchert and David Stewart, 107–25. Athens: Ohio University Press, 1979.

Robinson, Donald. *Slavery in the Structure of American Politics, 1765–1820.* 1971. Reprint, New York: W. W. Norton, 1979.

Robinson, Randall. *The Debt: What America Owes to Blacks.* New York: Dutton, 2000.

Rodney, Walter. *How Europe Underdeveloped Africa.* Washington, D.C.: Howard University Press, 1974.

Roediger, David R. *The Wages of Whiteness: Race and the Making of the American Working Class.* New York: Verso, 1990.

Rooke, Patricia T. "Evangelical Missionaries, Apprentices, and Freedmen: The Psycho-Sociological Shifts of Racial Attitudes in the British West Indies." *Caribbean Quarterly* 25, nos. 1–2 (March–June 1979): 1–14.

Rose, Willie Lee. *Rehearsal for Reconstruction: The Port Royal Experiment.* New York: Vintage, 1965.

Saville, Julie. *The Work of Reconstruction: From Slave to Wage Laborer in South Carolina, 1860–1870.* New York: Cambridge University Press, 1996.

Scott, Daryl Michael. *Contempt and Pity: Social Policy and the Image of the Damaged Black Psyche, 1880–1996.* Chapel Hill: University of North Carolina Press, 1997.

Scott, Rebecca J. "Exploring the Meaning of Freedom: Postemancipation Societies in Comparative Perspective." *Hispanic American Historical Review* 68, no. 3 (August 1988): 407–28.

―――. *Slave Emancipation in Cuba: The Transition to Free Labor, 1860–1899.* Princeton, N.J.: Princeton University Press, 1985.

Semmel, Bernard. *The Governor Eyre Controversy.* London: MacGibbon and Kee, 1962.

Shain, Barry Alan. *The Myth of American Individualism: The Protestant Origins of American Political Thought.* Princeton, N.J.: Princeton University Press, 1994.

Shklar, Judith. *American Citizenship.* Cambridge, Mass.: Harvard University Press, 1991.

Simkins, Francis B. "The Ku Klux Klan in South Carolina, 1868–1871." *Journal of Negro History* 12, no. 4 (October 1927): 606–47.

Stampp, Kenneth M. *The Peculiar Institution: Slavery in the Ante-Bellum South.* New York: Vintage, 1956.

Stewart, Robert. *Religion and Society in Post-Emancipation Jamaica.* Knoxville: University of Tennessee Press, 1992.

―――. "A Slandered People: Views on 'Negro Character' in the Mainstream Christian Churches in Post-Emancipation Jamaica." In *Crossing Boundaries: Comparative History of Black People in the Diaspora,* edited by Darlene Clark Hine and Jacqueline McLeod, 179–201. Bloomington: Indiana University Press, 1999.

Tannebaum, Frank. *Slave and Citizen: The Negro in the Americas.* New York: Vintage, 1946.

Toplin, Robert Brent. *The Abolition of Slavery in Brazil.* New York: Atheneum, 1972.

Trachtenberg, Alan. *The Incorporation of America: Culture and Society in the Gilded Age.* New York: Hill and Wang, 1982.

Trelease, Allen W. *White Terror: The Ku Klux Klan Conspiracy and Southern Reconstruction.* New York: Harper and Row, 1971.

Turley, David. *The Culture of English Antislavery, 1780–1860.* London: Routledge, 1991.

Turner, Mary. *Slaves and Missionaries: The Disintegration of Jamaican Slave Society, 1781–1834.* Urbana: University of Illinois Press, 1982.

Ullman, Victor. *Martin R. Delany: The Beginnings of Black Nationalism.* Boston: Beacon Press, 1971.

Veyne, Paul. *The Roman Empire.* Translated by Arthur Goldhammer. Cambridge, Mass.: Harvard University Press, 1997.

Wallerstein, Immanuel. *The Modern World System: Capitalist Agriculture and the Origins of the European World-Economy in the Sixteenth Century.* New York: Academic Press, 1974.

Ward, J. R. "The Profitability of Sugar Planting in the British West Indies, 1650–1834." In *Caribbean Slave Society and Economy: A Student Reader,* edited by Hilary Beckles and Verene Shepherd, 81–93. Kingston, Jamaica: Ian Randle Publishers, 1991.

Watson, Alan. *Slave Law in the Americas.* Athens: University of Georgia Press, 1989.

Weston, James L., ed. *Asian and African Systems of Slavery.* Berkeley: University of California Press, 1980.

Wharton, Vernon Lane. *The Negro in Mississippi, 1865–1890.* 1947. Reprint, New York: Harper and Row, 1965.

Williams, Eric. *Capitalism and Slavery.* 1944. Reprint, London: Andre Deutsch, 1964.

Williams, Lou Falkner. *The Great South Carolina Ku Klux Klan Trials, 1871–1872.* Athens: University of Georgia Press, 1996.

Williamson, Joel. *After Slavery: The Negro in South Carolina during Reconstruction, 1861–1877.* 1965. Reprint, Hanover, N.H.: University Press of New England, 1990.

Wilmot, Swithin. "Not 'Full Free': The Ex-Slaves and the Apprenticeship System in Jamaica, 1834–1838." *Jamaica Journal* 17, no. 3 (August–October 1984): 2–10.

———. "The Politics of Protest in Free Jamaica—The Kingston John Canoe Christmas Riots, 1840–1841." *Caribbean Quarterly* 36, nos. 3–4 (December 1990): 65–75.

Wilson, Theodore. *The Black Codes of the South.* University: University of Alabama Press, 1965.

Wood, Anthony. *Nineteenth Century Britain, 1815–1914.* London: Longman, 1960.

Wood, Gordon S. *The Creation of the American Republic, 1776–1787.* 1969. Reprint, New York: W. W. Norton, 1972.

———. Introduction to *The Rising Glory of America, 1760–1820*. New York: George Braziller, 1971.

Woodson, Carter G. Review of *Capitalism and Slavery* by Eric Williams. *Journal of Negro History* 30, no. 1 (January 1945): 93–95.

Woodward, C. Vann. *Origins of the New South, 1877–1913*. Baton Rouge: Louisiana State University Press, 1951.

———. "The Price of Freedom." In *What Was Freedom's Price?*, edited by David G. Sansing, 93–113. Jackson: University of Mississippi Press, 1978.

———. *Reunion and Reaction: The Compromise of 1877 and the End of Reconstruction.* Garden City, N.Y.: Doubleday, 1956.

———. "Seeds of Failure in Radical Race Policy." In *American Counterpoint: Slavery and Racism in the North/South Dialogue*, 163–83. New York: Oxford University Press, 1982.

———. "White Racism and Black 'Emancipation.'" *New York Review of Books* 12, no. 4 (27 February 1969): 5–11.

———, ed. *The Comparative Approach to American History*. New York: Basic Books, 1968.

Woody, Robert H. "The Labor and Immigration Problem of South Carolina during Reconstruction." *Mississippi Valley Historical Review* 28 (June 1931–March 1932): 195–212.

Wright, Gavin. *The Political Economy of the Cotton South: Households, Markets, and Wealth in the Nineteenth Century*. New York: W. W. Norton, 1978.

Wyatt-Brown, Bertram. *Honor and Violence in the Old South*. New York: Oxford University Press, 1986.

Wynter, Sylvia. "1492: A New World View." In *Race, Discourse and the Origin of the Americas*, edited by Vera Hyatt and Rex Nettleford, 5–57. Washington, D.C.: Smithsonian Institution Press, 1995.

Unpublished Manuscripts

Chartock, Lewis. "A History and Analysis of Freedmen's Bureau Contracts in South Carolina." Ph.D. dissertation, Bryn Mawr College, 1973.

Eudell, Demetrius. "The Mind of Emancipation: Toward a Comparative History of Post-Slavery Thought in the Anglo-Americas." Ph.D. dissertation, Stanford University, 1997.

Goveia, Elsa. "Amelioration and Emancipation in the British Caribbean." Seminar paper, Department of History, University of the West Indies, March 1977. Pamphlet A, Special Collections, University of the West Indies, Mona, Jamaica.

Manderson-Jones, Marlene. "Richard Hill of Jamaica, His Life and Times, 1795–1872." Ph.D. dissertation, University of the West Indies, 1973.

Rushford, Claire. "A Comparative Study of the Process and Policy of Emancipation in the British West Indies and Southern States of America." Master's thesis, University of Kent, 1992.

Index